D0398036

A Treasury of
WHITE HOUSE COOKING

A TREASURY
OF WHITE HOUSE
COOKING

by *former White House Chef*
FRANÇOIS RYSAVY
as told to
FRANCES SPATZ LEIGHTON

G. P. Putnam's Sons
New York

Copyright © 1957, 1962, 1972 by
François Rysavy and Frances Spatz Leighton

*All rights reserved. This book, or parts thereof,
must not be reproduced in any form without
permission. Published on the same day in Canada
by Longmans Canada Limited, Toronto.*

Portions of this book, in different form, appeared in *White House Chef,* copyright © 1957 by François Rysavy and Frances Spatz Leighton, and *White House Menus and Recipes,* copyright © 1962 by François Rysavy and Frances Spatz Leighton.

SBN: 399-10939-0

Library of Congress Catalog Card Number: 79-175273

PRINTED IN THE UNITED STATES OF AMERICA

Contents

I

⇒⇒⇒⇒⇒⇐⇐⇐⇐

JACKIE KENNEDY ONASSIS
RETURNS TO THE WHITE HOUSE—
AND OTHER NOSTALGIC MOMENTS

It was the best-kept secret in Washington. Jackie—Jacqueline Kennedy Onassis—was coming to dinner at the Nixons'. It would be her first visit to the White House since she left it in 1963, after the assassination of her husband, President Kennedy.

Nobody knew until she left that she had been there, let alone that the former First Lady had dined sumptuously.

I am pleased to have the menu of that historic meal and the recipes from Chef Henri Haller himself for each of the dishes:

PRESIDENT NIXON'S FAMILY DINNER AT THE WHITE HOUSE
FOR JACQUELINE KENNEDY ONASSIS

February 3, 1971

Timbale of Seafood Américaine
Fleurons
Filet of Beef Rôti
Marchand de Vin
Artichokes St. Germain
Mushrooms Provençale
Hearts of Palms Vinaigrette
Soufflé au Grand Marnier
Sauce Sabayon

It seems just yesterday that I was the Eisenhowers' chef at the White House. But even though I have left the scene, I still feel very much a part of the White House kitchens and keep returning to Washington, where my daughter still lives.

There is something about working at the White House that gets into one's blood and makes one a bit of a historian forever after. While I was in the White House, I collected all the historic First Family recipes I could lay my hands on. My interest now is greater, if anything.

Since leaving the White House, I have collected more Jefferson recipes and lore than I did at the White House. And even now when people learn that I once was a White House chef, they dig deep into their family records to share with me something pertaining to the White House cookery or something that was served to a First Family fifty years ago by an ancestor.

Not long ago, for example, I learned from Lillian Rogers Parks, who was a maid and seamstress at the White House when I was there, about the Lace Wafers that Mrs. Herbert Hoover served daily at the White House at her four o'clock teas. The recipe was given to Mrs. Parks by a former White House cook, and you will come upon it later in the book.

When I left the White House in June, 1957, I was bursting with White House kitchen lore going back to Abigail Adams and Dolley Madison and even to George Washington and the favorite dishes he served at the Presidential residences in Philadelphia and New York and at Mount Vernon, since he never lived at the White House.

I wrote a book, *White House Chef* (G. P. Putnam's Sons, 1956), relating my experiences at the White House. But so much has happened at the White House since and I have collected so many "new" recipes, menus, and exciting bits of information about the food interests of the Presidents and their families that I could not resist writing a new book.

But to return to that hush-hush dinner at the White House. The occasion was the unveiling of the Aaron Shikler portraits of John F. and Jacqueline Kennedy. Jacqueline had come for the preview before the two portraits would be shown to the press.

Only the immediate families were there: the President and Mrs. Nixon, daughters Tricia and Julie, the former First Lady and her children, Caroline and John, now thirteen and ten respectively.

Little John was seated at the right of Mrs. Nixon in the family dining room, and I am told he kept her amused with his account of the battery-run automobile he got for Christmas.

A little later after 8 p.m. the Kennedys left as they had come, on a small military Jetstar plane which the President had sent for them. The next day, word came back to the White House that ten-year-old John had been so excited over his trip to the White House that he had had a hard time going to sleep.

And now for the recipes, so that you can serve the exact meal to your guests.

TIMBALE OF SEAFOOD AMÉRICAINE

3-3/4 cups sifted flour

1/2 pound butter

3/4 to 1 cup water

1-1/2 teaspoons salt

Spread the flour in a circle on the board, make a well in the middle, and put in butter, water, and salt. First mix the butter, water, and salt together; then, little by little, incorporate the flour.

Knead twice, roll the paste in a ball, and wrap in a cloth.

Keep in a cold place until ready for use (lining paste should always be made several hours before it is needed, and the less this paste is handled, the better, as it quickly becomes tough).

TIMBALE CASE

Butter the interior of a large charlotte mold, and decorate the sides with little decorative shapes of the pastry dough.

Roll some of the pastry dough into a ball. Roll out the ball into a round 8 inches in diameter. Sprinkle the round of pastry lightly with flour, and fold in half. Take the points of this half-circle, and draw them together. Roll it out once to make an even thickness of about 1/3 inch. Put it in the bottom of the mold. Press the bottom and around the sides to make the paste adhere to the mold, and raise gently up the sides, without disturbing the decorations already in place.

Line the bottom and the sides of the paste with a buttered fine paper, and fill it with dried raw beans or uncooked rice, as for a flan case or tart. Put a dome-shaped piece of paper on top of the dry filling, and put a thin sheet of pastry on top of this, joining the edges together with the pastry lining, by gently pressing with the fingers. Make the rim of the pie by pinching this border with pastry pincers. Lightly moisten the part forming the lid with water, and decorate with details—leaves, roses, etc., cut from a thin sheet of pastry, with a special pastry cutter or with a knife.

After the case is baked, remove the lid. Take out the paper and dried beans or rice, gild the inside with egg, and let it dry in the oven for a few minutes.

SEAFOOD AMÉRICAINE

1 tablespoon butter	1 cup blanched Long Island
1 tablespoon finely chopped	scallops
shallots	2 ounces brandy
1 cup cooked tiny shrimp	2 cups Sauce Americaine
2 cups coarsely diced lobster	1 tablespoon chopped parsley

First prepare Sauce Américaine (see below) and let simmer while you are preparing the rest of the ingredients.

Melt butter in sauté pan; add shallots, and simmer until golden brown. Add shrimp, lobster, and scallops. Add brandy, and cover sauté pan. When all the brandy is reduced, remove from heat, and add Sauce Américaine. Adjust seafood mixture with salt if necessary. Serve in timbale case. Garnish with parsley. Serves 6.

SAUCE AMÉRICAINE

1 cup chopped onions	2 tablespoons tomato puree
1/2 cup chopped celery	1 tablespoon flour
1/2 cup chopped leeks	2 large tomatoes, peeled and
2 tablespoons corn oil	chopped
6 lobster carcasses	2 cups dry white wine
12 peppercorns	2 cups fish stock or water
Pinch of thyme, marjoram, and	Sprig of parsley
oregano	Salt to taste
1/4 cup brandy	

Sauté onions, celery, and leeks in corn oil for 5 minutes. Add lobster carcasses. Add peppercorns, thyme, marjoram, and oregano, and simmer on very hot flame for 5 minutes, stirring constantly. Add brandy; then turn flame to low, and add tomato puree and flour. Mix well with lobster carcasses. Add tomatoes, wine, and fish stock. Add parsley and salt.

Bring sauce to a boil, stirring well during that time; then cover saucepan. Simmer sauce for 45 minutes (this will reduce the sauce by a third). Test for flavor, and strain through a very fine sieve. Makes approximately 2 cups.

PORTLAND COMMUNITY
COLLEGE LIBRARY

FILET OF BEEF RÔTI

7 pounds filet of beef, tied and
  oven-ready
Seasoning salt
1 pound vegetable mirepoix (2
  onions, coarsely chopped; 1
  cup red wine (Burgundy) 1

carrot, coarsely chopped; 2
cups beef stock; 2 pieces of
celery; 1 bay leaf; 1
tablespoon whole black
pepper; pinch each of thyme
and marjoram)

Season beef with seasoning salt; then roast in a 425° oven for 30 minutes. Add mirepoix, and roast for 15 minutes more, or until the meat is medium rare. Remove filet from roasting pan, and add red wine and beef stock to mirepoix. Simmer for 15 minutes, and strain juice through cheesecloth.

Let beef rest for 15 minutes; then slice into 1/4 inch slices, and arrange on a platter.

Arrange Artichokes St. Germain alongside the slices of beef on the platter, and garnish with watercress. Serve pan juices separately.

ARTICHOKES ST. GERMAIN

1 pound green split peas
4 cups water
1/4 pound butter
1 cup heavy cream

1 teaspoon salt
Pinch of white pepper
Pinch of nutmeg
8 fresh artichoke bottoms

Soak split peas in water for 2 hours; then cook in a covered saucepan until tender. Puree in blender. Remove from blender. Place in a bowl with butter and mix; then add cream, and mix again. Adjust seasoning. Put puree of peas into a dressing bag. With a #8 star tube, decorate artichokes with puree (rosette design). Bake in a 375° oven until the artichokes are lightly browned. Serves 6 to 8.

MUSHROOMS PROVENÇALE

1 tablespoon butter
1 tablespoon chopped shallots
1 clove garlic, chopped very fine
1-1/2 pounds tiny fresh
  mushrooms
1 tablespoon lemon juice

Salt and white pepper to taste
2 large tomatoes, peeled, seeded,
  and sliced julienne
2 tablespoons olive oil
1/2 tablespoon chopped parsley

Put butter into sauté pan; add shallots, and sauté until golden brown. Add garlic to shallots; then add mushrooms, which have been washed in cold water, and lemon juice. Add salt and white pepper. Cover mushrooms, and cook them swiftly until all juice is absorbed. To serve, put mushrooms into a flat vegetable dish, and top with tomatoes, which have been sautéed in olive oil and seasoned with salt and pepper. Sprinkle tomatoes and mushrooms with chopped parsley. Serves 6 to 8.

VINAIGRETTE DRESSING FOR HEARTS OF PALMS

4 shallots, chopped
1 clove garlic, very finely
   chopped
1 bunch fresh tarragon, chopped
Pinch of white pepper
Juice of 1 lemon
1/2 teaspoon English mustard

2 egg yolks
1/2 juice glass red wine vinegar
1-1/2 cups olive oil
Salt to taste
1/2 teaspoon monosodium
   glutamate

Put shallots, garlic, tarragon, pepper, lemon juice, English mustard, egg yolks, and vinegar in stainless steel bowl. Mix thoroughly with a steel whip. Blend olive oil slowly into mixture. Add salt and monosodium glutamate to taste.

(Can also be used for Bibb lettuce.)

CHEF HALLER'S SOUFFLÉ AU GRAND MARNIER

1/4 pound butter
1 cup flour
3/4 cup sugar
1 pint milk, scalded

8 egg yolks
2 teaspoons vanilla
4 tablespoons Grand Marnier
12 egg whites

Melt butter, add flour, and mix well. Add half of sugar to scalded milk; then add to butter and flour. Stir vigorously with plastic spatula over moderate fire. Add the egg yolks to mixture one at a time, stirring constantly. Add vanilla and Grand Marnier. Whip the egg whites with the rest of the sugar until stiff; then fold egg whites into the mixture.

Fill into soufflé form, which has been coated with butter and dusted with sugar. Fill form four-fifths full. Cook in 375° oven for 45 minutes. Serves 6 to 8.

SAUCE SABAYON À LA HALLER

1 cup sugar
6 egg yolks

1-1/4 cups white wine (dry Chablis preferably)

Mix sugar with egg yolks in a stainless-steel bowl. Add wine. Set into a pan of hot water. Stir mixture vigorously with wire whip until mixture is stiff.

I wonder if Jackie Kennedy Onassis was remembering another evening at the White House, when she herself was entertaining another ex-Presidential family?

It was an important occasion when the Kennedys invited the Trumans and their daughter, Margaret, with her husband, Clifton Daniel, Jr., to the White House and entertained them at a formal dinner with about forty other friends of President Truman.

President Truman, in turn, entertained the party by playing Paderewski's Minuet in G on the piano which he had bought for the White House.

But what most interested me was to see what one President—John F. Kennedy—served another.

DINNER
IN HONOR OF PRESIDENT AND MRS. TRUMAN

November 1, 1961

Crab Mousse

Roast Grouse with Wild Rice
Green Beans
Braised Celery

Salad Mimosa

Pineapple in Half-Pineapple Shell
Petits Fours

Demitasse

But such occasions are not what they used to be. When President-elect Rutherford B. Hayes and his wife were being dined at the White House by the outgoing First Family, the Ulysses S. Grants, it was a dazzling affair. In fact, a huge nine-foot azalea was placed behind Mrs. Hayes' chair, making her appear almost part of a huge bouquet:

PRESIDENT GRANT'S FORMAL DINNER
FOR PRESIDENT ELECT AND MRS. RUTHERFORD B. HAYES

March 3, 1877

Consommé Impérial
Bisque de Grevisse
Sherry

Woodcock Patties   Salmon
White Wine

Roast of Beef
Breast of Pheasant
Crawfish Pudding
Goose Livers
Roman Punch

Turkey
Artichokes
Canvasback Duck
Champagne

Sweet Warm Dish
Red Wine

I have a copy of the menu that was served on another occasion when yet another First Family returned to the White House. That was in 1929, when the Coolidges came to the Presidential mansion to dine with President and Mrs. Hoover.

FORMAL DINNER IN HONOR OF FORMER PRESIDENT AND MRS. COOLIDGE

Consommé
Curled Celery
Rolled Toast   Salted Almonds

Brook Trout
Potato Curls   Cucumber Aspic

Chicken Supreme
Sweet Potato Croquettes
Julienne String Beans   Clarified Apples
Hearts of Lettuce

Assorted Cheeses
Vanilla Ice Cream
Pound Cake
Crystallized Pears
Candies   Fruits

Coffee

You can see that there were many more courses in the old days. It was Jacqueline Kennedy who cut the number of courses of a formal meal to four so that the guests would have more time to wander around and enjoy themselves.

One of the most notable gastronomic occasions on which a First Lady returned to the White House occurred during the Lyndon B. Johnson administration when Mrs. Dwight D. Eisenhower was guest of honor at a luncheon that featured favorite recipes of early Presidents. It was the Senate ladies' luncheon which Mamie Eisenhower had once presided over as First Lady and it brought happy tears to her eyes as she looked at the State Dining Room. Each table was set with china from previous administrations.

The table at which Mrs. Eisenhower sat, at the right of Lady Bird Johnson, was set with President Cleveland's china, delicately edged in blue. Also on the table was a Chinese porcelain tureen of Jefferson's holding a lovely bouquet of bright spring blossoms.

The menu was indeed memorable:

LADY BIRD JOHNSON'S LUNCHEON
HONORING MAMIE EISENHOWER

May 12, 1967

Monroe's Quaking Jelly
(Jellied Madrilene)
LBJ's Minced Ham Turnovers
Jefferson's Filled Pannequaiques
Bouquet of Garden Vegetables à la John Adams
Andrew Jackson's Burnt Cream
(Créme Brûlée Hermitage)

Here are the recipes for making these dishes as Mrs. Johnson had them made from actual recipes used by the various Presidents:

MONROE'S QUAKING JELLY

2 tablespoons unflavored gelatin	1 teaspoon chopped onion
1/2 cup cold water	2 tablespoons dry sherry
2 cups tomato juice	1 tablespoon lemon juice
2 cups chicken stock	Salt and pepper to taste
Rind of 1/4 lemon	Garnishings of sour cream and
2 teaspoons chopped parsley	chopped chives

Soak gelatin in cold water while preparing other ingredients. Put tomato juice in saucepan with chicken stock, lemon rind, parsley, and onion and bring to a boil. Now take out a little of the liquid, and combine with the gelatin mixture, before adding the gelatin to the balance of hot liquid.

Let stand, and when cool, add sherry, lemon juice, and seasonings to taste. Pour into mold. Refrigerate. Serve garnished with sour cream and chives. Serves 6 to 8.

Lady Bird's husband's favorite Minced Ham Turnovers go very well, served with the Quaking Jelly, or Jellied Madrilene, as it is now called. This is Mrs. Johnson's own recipe for the Minced Ham Turnovers:

LBJ'S MINCED HAM TURNOVERS

1 rounded tablespoon butter	1/4 onion, chopped
1 pound cooked ham, diced	Pinch of thyme
1 tablespoon chopped parsley	1/2 cup Cream Sauce (below)

Melt butter in heavy skillet, and add ham, parsley, onion, and thyme. Mix with the Cream Sauce.

Prepare enough of a rich pastry dough required for a two-crust pie. Cut dough in 2-inch rounds after rolling very thin, and place a heaping teaspoon of the ham mixture on top of each round. Fold top over, and press edges together with fork. Brush top with melted butter, and bake at 350° until lightly browned. Makes 30.

CREAM SAUCE FOR LBJ'S MINCED HAM TURNOVERS

1-1/2 teaspoons butter	2 tablespoons heavy cream
1 tablespoon flour	1/8 teaspoon nutmeg
1/2 cup milk, plus 1 tablespoon, scalded	Salt and pepper to taste

Melt butter in small saucepan; add flour over low heat stirring constantly to work a roux. Do not let it brown. Gradually add scalded milk to the roux, beating all the while with a whisk. Let sauce come to a boil, stirring it constantly; then lower heat, and simmer for a few minutes until it thickens. Add cream and seasonings and bring to a boil for another instant before using immediately in the Ham Turnovers.

The main course, with the quaint name of Filled Pannequaiques, was just Jefferson's way of saying filled pancakes or crêpes. Jefferson's favorite crêpes were filled with chicken and mushrooms:

JEFFERSON'S FILLED PANNEQUAIQUES

1/4 to 1/2 cup chopped onion	1 egg yolk, beaten
1/4 pound butter	12 five-inch crêpes
3/4 cup sliced mushrooms	1/2 cup hollandaise sauce
1-3/4 cups cooked chicken, diced	1/2 cup cream sauce
2 tablespoons dry sherry	1-1/2 cups whipped cream
1/2 cup milk	Parmesan cheese

Sauté onion in butter, add mushrooms, and continue cooking on low flame for a few minutes, being careful not to let the onion get brown. Now add chicken, cook a minute longer, and cool.

When cool enough, add the sherry, milk, and egg yolk.

Place 2 tablespoons of the mixture in the center of each crêpe, and roll, placing side by side on a platter. Top with a sauce made by combining the hollandaise sauce and cream sauce and folding in the whipped cream.

When the crêpes are nicely covered, sprinkle generously with Parmesan cheese and pop under the broiler for a few moments until the sauce starts to brown. Serve immediately, 2 or 3 to a person.

BOUQUET OF GARDEN VEGETABLES À LA JOHN ADAMS

Butter	2 cups green peas
1 teaspoon grated onion	1/2 cup water
2 cups shredded lettuce	Salt

In saucepan melt butter; then lightly sauté onion and lettuce. Add peas and water; cook rapidly for about 25 minutes. Drain off excess water, add 1 tablespoon butter, salt to taste, and toss over heat until the butter evenly coats vegetables and excess moisture is gone. Serves 6 to 8.

As I look at the recipe for Crème Brûlée as President Andrew Jackson liked it, with almond flavor, I cannot help comparing it with the equally exciting Burnt Creams or Crème Brûlées served by Thomas Jefferson, who added the flavors of lemon and orange, and the Brûlée of Jacqueline Kennedy, who served it to her husband with real vanilla beans, as you can see by the recipes later in this book.

ANDREW JACKSON'S BURNT CREAM
(CRÊME BRÛLÉE HERMITAGE)

6 egg yolks	5/8 cup granulated sugar
10 tablespoons powdered sugar	Garnish of marmalade or
2 teaspoons almond extract	preserved fruit, preferably
2 cups heavy cream	raspberries
6 egg whites	

Preheat oven to 300°.

Beat egg yolks with half the powdered sugar, and continue to beat until creamy. Add almond extract to cream, and bring almost to a boil. Now gradually add the egg mixture, beating all the while.

Bake in an earthen dish, which should be placed in a metal pan partially filled with water. Bake for about 1 hour, or until the custard is set. Remove from oven, and set aside to cool.

While brûlée cools, beat the egg whites until they make peaks, and then gradually add the granulated sugar, continuing to beat until all is absorbed and peaks are fluffy. Pile the meringue on the surface, and then carefully sprinkle the rest of the powdered sugar all across the top.

Place dish back in oven, which has been preset and raised to 325°, and let bake for 10 or 12 minutes. Serve immediately while still hot, garnished with marmalade or raspberry preserves (or other fruits or berries). Serves 6.

Martha Washington never lived in the White House, but her influence was there all right. I prepared some of the dishes I served as she might have served them to guests. Of course, in Martha's day recipes were written in a very quaint way, and Chicken Fricassee might come out "Chicken Frykasie," pancakes could be "Pannequaiques," and pie might come out "pye." I enjoyed researching her recipes at Mount Vernon with the curator, a fine Washington historian Christine Meadows.

It amused me to learn that the cookbook Martha Washington swore by and took with her wherever she lived was a British cookbook written by a man who used the pen name Hannah Glass.

Martha Washington's most famous recipe is her Great Cake, but she served other goodies as well, including chess cakes and oil cakes, the latter being a sort of doughnut—sweetened yeast dough made into small balls, stuffed with chopped fruits such as raisins, and oiled in lard and boiled in deep lard. They were served rolled in powdered sugar.

What amuses me most is to see Martha Washington's old recipe for frying tripe, the stomach of a cow. The recipe is still used in the South. As carefully preserved by the Mount Vernon Ladies Association, the recipe reads:

TO FRY TRIPE

"Cut your tripe into piecef about three inchef long, dip them in the yolk of an egg and a few crumf of bread, fry them of a fine brown, and then take them out of the pan and lay them in a difh to drain. Have ready a warm diſh to put them in, and fend them to table, with butter and muſtard in a cup."

It was Abigail Adams who gave the first party at the White House, but it was a fiasco. The John Adamses had moved into the White House just in time for New Year's Day celebration 1801.

The place was so cold that guests left early. The celebration, incidentally, was held in the second-floor Oval Room, which today is not used for public entertainment but as a private sitting room for the First Family. When Abigail sat receiving guests that day so long ago, the dominant color was red, but today it is a light and airy yellow and gold.

Historic grandeur and an aura of mystery surround the White House kitchens. For those who combine a love of history and fine foods, what greater thrill can there be than carrying on tradition by making say, Martha Washington's Crab Bisque, Dolley Madison's Gingerbread, or Jacqueline Kennedy's Boula-Boula Soup?

The link with the past is a strong one, and I, a chef in the French tradition, who became an American through choice, feel it even more strongly, perhaps, than the persons born in America.

I confess that I always look for a link between the present and the past. And I am thrilled when I find it. I am looking now at the menu for the formal dinner which the Kennedys served the First Lady's sister, Princess Radziwill, and I see Poulet à l'Estragon, which I sometimes prepared for Mrs. Eisenhower when she entertained. You can find the recipe in the Index.

And then I turn to the menu of the luncheon which President and Mrs. Kennedy served Princess Grace and Prince Rainier of Monaco, and I see a dessert of Strawberries Romanoff. Again, I feel a thrill as I recall that this was the favorite dessert of President Franklin D. Roosevelt. You will find that recipe here, too.

How I cherish the knowledge of the food habits of Presidents—the fact that President Kennedy loved whipped cream, that Mr. Nixon likes buttermilk, and LBJ loved deermeat sausage. Teddy Roosevelt demanded Indian pudding. Thomas Jefferson gloried in serving baked Alaska, which he had brought back from France and introduced into the American diet.

How nice it was to have a First Lady at the White House who was so well grounded in the French tradition of food, who appreciated French cooking and savored the sauces. When I heard that Mrs. Kennedy had been saving recipes since she became engaged, I was touched, and I added the fact to my collection of White House lore, along with the fact that President Eisenhower liked to read cookbooks and that President Nixon rewards himself now and then with a piece of Key lime pie.

As I watch from a distance the new influx of foreign dignitaries arriving to dine at the White House, I remember vividly the last formal dinner which I served there.

I recalled the dazzling display of all-pink flowers against the sea of white and gold in the State Dining Room of the White House. Pink snapdragons and pink carnations stood proudly in gold vases as if they had read the place cards of the sixty-three world-famous persons who would eat at the executive mansion that night.

I glanced at some of those place cards—Vice President and Mrs. Richard M. Nixon; Secretary of State and Mrs. John Foster Dulles; Senate Majority Leader and Mrs. Lyndon B. Johnson; House Minority Leader Joseph W. Martin; J. Edgar Hoover, director of the FBI; and two couples representing the business world—Mr. and Mrs. Bernard F. Gimbel and Mr. and Mrs. William S. Paley.

The menu, as always, had been planned by Charles, the head butler, and me, with the advice of the State Department's Division of Protocol, which makes certain that no item on the menu is contrary to the religious practices of the guests. Mrs. Eisenhower herself had approved the menu. The color pink, we had learned, was the favorite color of the guest of honor.

The first course was Mousse de Foie Gras in port wine jelly. It fluffed perfectly. How carefully I had blended the goose liver, truffles, and butter with port wine and then with heavy cream before molding it into individual forms.

Soup, of course, followed—Cream of Green Pea Soup with Croutons fried in butter to a golden brown. As always, I started with the fresh green peas. As I mixed this soup to a rich, mellow consistency, I marveled again at the inventiveness of America. I have found the electric blender an indispensable aid in the proper mixing of soups.

We progressed through the hearts of celery and queen ripe olives to a fish course—Crab Meat Mornay, which is flaked crab meat gently folded into a white sauce made with chicken stock and sherry.

Sliced tomatoes and cucumbers, marinated, and bread-and-butter sandwiches made with Boston brown bread accompanied this, and a white wine, Château Climens 1942.

The main course was Roast Long Island Duckling with my own dressing (unusual only in that I use no sage). Apple rings, gravy, wild rice with mushrooms, buttered asparagus, and a second wine, this time red Burgundy, Beaune-Grèves 1952.

On the asparagus, incidentally, the Eisenhowers preferred the simplicity of lemon butter to the richer hollandaise and cheese sauces, and that is what I served. It is only the work of a moment to make. The butter is melted, a lemon squeezed. *Voila!* Lemon butter.

The salad was simple, too. A spring salad of Bibb lettuce served with a dramatic Green Goddess dressing. This most distinguished dressing is made with sour cream and mayonnaise. Its personality comes from the anchovy paste which is added, and its color from onion greens which have been chopped and whirled through the blender.

To complement the salad I served Cheese Crescents. These are made with a flaky dough—similar to pie dough—gently folded over a heart of cheese and shaped into the half-moon crescents from which they get their name.

Mrs. Eisenhower had chosen the dessert herself—Frosted Mint Delight. It seemed just the right note on which to close the meal as it is a foamy blend of crushed pineapple, mint jelly, gelatin, and whipped cream. It was sparkling cool and as green as an emerald. Petits fours were served with it and a champagne, Pol Roger 1945.

Assorted nuts, candies, and coffee completed the meal, and my duties were over for the day.

In the years to come I know how I will treasure the memory this menu will bring back. I have other souvenirs, too, of the years I spent in the White House.

Little David Eisenhower's thank-you letter—yes, the same David who is now the son-in-law of President Nixon—is a treasured one. The President's grandson was an energetic penman. His writing was big and slanted, and a few words cover a full page in bold, confident characters. He sent me his delightful note after his eighth birthday party in April, 1956. David said that everything was "very, very, very, very good."

He added, "It was the best party I every [here, he had attempted to cross out the extra *y*] had. Thank you! love [with a small *l*] David Eisenhower."

Yes, I was the White House chef. I worked with pride and apprehension in the great stainless-steel kitchens of the White House. It was my pride that I, above all other chefs of the world, had been chosen. I knew apprehension because upon that stomach, to put it indelicately, rode the health of the economy of the nation. Early in June, 1957, when the papers recorded that President Eisenhower had eaten too much blueberry pie, the stomach upset he suffered had caused a "sympathy pain" on Wall Street that sent the stock market dashing down millions of dollars.

"Rysavy," my friends kidded me, "what have you done to the President?"

Though I felt very sorry to hear of the stomach upset of the President, I was also vastly relieved that I had not been the chef. I had a clean record on that score and can safely say that the President never suffered a stomach reversal on my account. The ileitis attack which rocked the nation a year before the pie episode happened after a dinner at a Washington hotel.

I cooked for the President in the White House only. I did not travel with the President. My duty was to keep the home fires burning in the kitchens of the White House and to have always ready on time his favorite dishes, as well as to satisfy the tastes of his many guests whether they were Americans, European heads of state, or Oriental potentates.

I had cooked on three continents. Therefore, I was, you might say, qualified to cater to the varied tastes of the procession of the world's great who visited President Eisenhower and sat in the State Dining Room of the White House dipping a gold fork or gold spoon into a dish I had prepared.

My nostalgia is strong each time I visit the White House. Since we are talking of Jackie Kennedy's return to the White House, let me tell you what comes to mind.

I had just arrived at the White House and had made my recipe for Chicken Tetrazzini for the Sunday dinner. It was the recipe I had brought with me from a resort hotel on the Adriatic which had gotten wonderful compliments every time I served it.

Though Mrs. Eisenhower preferred Southern-style cooking to Italian, she was enchanted with the Tetrazzini and told me I must make it for her upcoming luncheon for the Senate wives on April 26, 1955.

Jacqueline Kennedy, then the wife of a freshman Senator, was of course invited, but little did I dream, as I cooked, that I was preparing food not only for the current First Lady but also for a future First Lady.

For the Senate ladies I used twelve large Pyrex dishes, but let me give you the recipe as I made it for the First Family with just four servings:

CHICKEN TETRAZZINI

1/3 cup truffles, sliced julienne
3/4 cup cooked spaghetti
   broken into 1/2-inch
   lengths before cooking
1 teaspoon butter
Salt to taste
1-2/3 cup White Sauce (below)
1-1/2 cups cooked chicken,
   sliced julienne

3/4 cup sliced sautéed
   mushrooms
1/3 cup finely chopped hearts of
   celery
White pepper to taste
1/2 cup grated Parmesan cheese
1 tablespoon chopped chives

Reserve 1 teaspoon of the truffles for topping.

Drain the spaghetti, butter it so it will not stick, and salt to taste. Put the spaghetti in a greased casserole, making a hollow place in the center for the chicken mixture. Make sure to leave a thin coating of spaghetti over the bottom center of the pan.

In a mixing bowl combine all the other ingredients—White Sauce, chicken, mushrooms, truffles and celery, seasoning to taste with salt and white pepper. Then pile this in the hole which has been made in the center of the spaghetti. Sprinkle the top—spaghetti and all—with the leftover truffles, Parmesan cheese, and chives. Serves 4.

WHITE SAUCE FOR TETRAZZINI

2-1/2 tablespoons butter
2 tablespoons flour
3/4 cup milk

3/4 cup chicken stock or
   consommé
Salt and white pepper to taste

Melt the butter in a pan, blend in the flour, chicken stock or consommé and milk, salt and pepper. Cook until it thickens.

2

➤➤➤-➤➤)〈〈〈-〈〈〈

THE MAKING OF A WHITE HOUSE CHEF

Nothing is wasted that one learns about cookery. As I study the menus President Nixon serves to his guests at white tie functions, I realize that these are things I learned to make many years ago in the four corners of the world. Gourmet cooking is the same wherever one goes.

For example, a dish I served many times in Hollywood later turned up at the White House. In fact, I am looking at it now in the menu which President Richard Nixon served the Chief Justice of the United States in 1969 and which I also served at the White House.

I knew it as Tournedos Rossini, its French name, but the Nixon White House has Anglicized the name to Filet Mignon Rossini.

We'll get to that Nixon menu later in this chapter, but first let me continue with the story of the making of a White House chef—at least this one—and how everything seemed to prepare me for the White House kitchens.

I say that I worked in Hollywood. I did indeed. I worked there before and after I worked at the White House. Most recently I cooked for steel magnate Earl Jorgensen, in Bel Air, where Governor Ronald Reagan and his wife, Nancy, were frequently guests. As a matter of fact, I took a leave of absence from my job there to finish this book.

The last time I saw the Reagans I made Breast of Chicken Paprikas, Hungarian style. It is a dish I had made at the White House for the Eisenhowers and which Jackie Kennedy also liked:

BREAST OF CHICKEN PAPRIKAŠ

4 tablespoons butter
2 medium onions, sliced thin
3 teaspoons good Hungarian
    paprika (such as you get in a
    gourmet shop)
1 teaspoon pepper
3/4 teaspoon salt

4 large chicken breasts, split in
    half
3 cups chicken stock
2 tablespoons flour
1 tablespoon butter
1 cup sour cream

Melt 4 tablespoons butter in a heavy skillet, and sauté the onions. Simmer until onions are light brown. Add paprika, pepper, salt, and chicken, and braise the chicken on top of the onions. When the skin is slightly golden, add the chicken stock, cover, and let simmer until chicken breasts are tender.

Now remove the chicken breasts, and make a roux with the flour, the butter, and all the liquid in which the chicken was cooked, as follows: melt the butter; add the flour to it, stirring constantly until the flour starts to brown; then gradually add all the liquid from the chicken, blending all of it in your blender until all the onions have disappeared and the sauce is smooth.

Just before serving, pour the sauce from the blender, and lightly stir in the sour cream. Put the chicken back in the sauce to heat for just a moment. Serves 8—one-half chicken breast per person.

Serve with Oriental Rice:

ORIENTAL RICE

2 cups long-grain rice
4 cups boiling chicken bouillon
2 tablespoons butter
1/2 pound fresh mushrooms,
    diced

Salt, pepper, and minced garlic to
    taste
1 medium onion, finely chopped
1 large green pepper, diced

Cook the rice in the usual way with all the other ingredients added to it. Make sure to cook the rice so it is done a few minutes before the Chicken Paprikaš is ready. Serves 6 to 8.

Looking back, I can safely say that thirty years went into my preparation for cooking at the White House. Even as a child in

Czechoslavakia, I think I knew somehow that my life would be involved with cooking and baking. One of my earliest memories is of standing spellbound in front of a pastry shop window one wintry day watching a man with a tall white hat fill pieces of dough with jelly and pop them in the oven. I stood there so long the owners finally became annoyed at the steam my nose was making on the window.

My foster mother, whom I called Teta—Aunt—recognized my special interest and taught me to make many things at an early age. Both my parents had died when I was a baby.

Strangely enough one of the first things she taught me to make was something I served almost exactly the same way at the White House. But in my childhood, it was the Sunday treat, served after church. We called it *Teleci Hrudi Nadivane,* meaning stuffed veal breast. For the Eisenhowers, who ordered it often, I had to serve it without the stuffing.

You can try it both ways. But let me tell you how Teta made it:

ROAST STUFFED BREAST OF VEAL

1 5-pound breast of veal	2 egg yolks
1/2 loaf stale white bread, soaked in milk	1 teaspoon chopped parsley
	1 clove garlic, crushed
1/4 pound butter	3 tablespoons green peas
1 medium onion, chopped	Salt and pepper to taste
1/2 pound raw chicken livers, chopped	Pinch of nutmeg

Teta asked the butcher to make a pocket inside the veal breast. She prepared her stuffing Sunday morning before church. She soaked the bread in milk, and when it was soft, she squeezed the milk from it. She melted the butter and sautéed the onion to a light brown. In a large wooden bowl she mixed the bread with the onion and butter, the chicken livers, egg yolks, parsley, garlic, green peas, salt, pepper, and nutmeg.

If the stuffing was not moist enough, she added a little milk. She stuffed the pocket, sewing the stuffing in with thread so that it would not run out, and rubbed the outside with 2 teaspoons salt. Teta had her oven hot—about 350°—and she kept the roast in about 1-1/2 hours. She basted the roast with water, but I recommend that you use chicken consommé instead of water, as I did when I basted my veal at the White House years later. The chicken consommé improves the flavor of the meat and makes a better gravy. When the meat was tender, Teta took out the roast and added a tablespoon of flour and a little water to make her gravy. Serves 10 to 12.

At the White House the Eisenhowers liked the roast veal with rice and spinach.

Another favorite food of mine was the Czechoslovakian danish pastry called *Kolace,* which was served on Fridays, the meatless days. The meal would consist of cabbage or vegetable soup and the special treat of *Kolace* washed down with water.

Little did I know, as I watched Teta push her fingers into the hearts of the little rolls and insert the filling, that some forty years later I would be making this same pastry in the White House. I made *Kolace*—a mountain of them—for the Christmas party for the White House staff.

KOLACE

1-1/2 cakes fresh yeast	1/2 teaspoon salt
1/3 cup lukewarm milk	1 teaspoon grated lemon rind
Pinch of sugar	3 eggs
1/4 pound butter, melted	2 cups flour
3 tablespoons sugar	

Dissolve the yeast in the milk with the pinch of sugar. As soon as the yeast rises to the top of the milk, it is ready for use. In a separate mixing bowl combine the butter, sugar, salt, lemon rind, and eggs. The moist ingredients are then stirred into the flour. Beat the dough vigorously. Let it rest in a warm place for about a half hour, covering it so that it won't dry too much.

Cut dough into small pieces, making them into round shapes with your hands. Put them about 2 inches apart on a greased baking sheet. Let them stand in a warm place for about 20 minutes, and when they have raised, press them down in the center with the first two fingers of both hands.

The pressure of your four fingers makes a round hollow which you fill with a plum or cottage cheese filling:

CHEESE FILLING FOR KOLACE

1 pound cottage cheese	1/2 cup seedless raisins
2 egg yolks	1 teaspoon vanilla
2/3 cup sugar	1/4 cup butter, melted

Mix the ingredients, and fill in the round hollow you have made in the dough.

For plum filling use fresh plums pitted and covered with cinnamon and sugar. Let the dough rise a little bit more. Brush the border with egg yolk diluted with 1 teaspoon water to make a shiny crust when baked. After it has risen for about 10 minutes, bake the Kolace in a 400° oven for 20 minutes. Makes 30 to 36 small Kolace.

When I made Kolace for the White House Christmas party, I used dried prunes because I did not have fresh plums available. I cooked and pitted the prunes, chopped them fine, added sugar and a bit of cinnamon. My ratio was 1 cup prune mixture to 1/3 cup sugar.

When I was nine, Teta died, and I was again an orphan. This time I was sent to stay with a couple who lived above a pastry shop. When I was through with grammar school, an uncle came to take me to his farm in a nearby town, Orechov, Czechoslovakia, where many of my relatives lived.

But even then, I could not see myself as a farmer, and I pleaded with him until he apprenticed me to the pastry shop downstairs.

Eventually, after four years I earned my diploma at a pastry school, which I managed to attend in spite of my working hours at the shop, which started at 4:30 a.m every day.

The moment I had the certificate in my hands, I left the little town to seek my fortune, becoming from that moment on a rolling stone.

Ambition drove me to Prague, the capital, and I went from store to store with my certificate until I was hired finally as a helper in one of the best pastry shops in Prague: Antoine Vosatka.

One day I read a newspaper ad for a master pastryman to go to Italy to work in a hotel and pastry shop. They would pay transportation. Italy! I thought. Adventure, travel! A chance to see the world!

I accepted the job and was on my way. As I saw Italy for the first time, I felt moments of complete panic. Did I know enough to be a pastryman? But then I remembered the compliments I had received on my French puff paste. This was the hardest lesson I had learned and the single most important pastry in French baking. "François," I had been told, "if you can make puff paste like that, you will never be without a job again." Puff paste became my lifesaver. I soon found myself making it 25 pounds at a time and filling it in various ways. As a youth, folding and rolling that puff paste, I little dreamed that one day I would be doing the same thing in the White House.

Every hostess who enjoys pastrymaking should learn to make good puff paste.

French puff paste is the base for so many things—desserts, main dishes, and appetizers—that I make a large amount and always keep it on hand in the freezer. I take a square of puff paste out of the freezer the night before I am going to use it, wrap it in a moist cloth, and leave it in the refrigerator overnight. The next day it is ready for rolling.

I always made at least 4 or 5 pounds at a time at the White House, but I will give you my recipe based on 1 pound of butter:

PUFF PASTE

1 pound butter	1/2 teaspoon salt
4 cups flour	Ice water

I use a marble table because it is the coolest surface, but formica will do. Make a heap of two-thirds of the flour in the center of your working area. Put the butter, cold from the refrigerator, into the center of the flour and work it with your hands until all the flour has been absorbed. Then flatten it into a square about 1/2-inch thick. Make the square perfect by cutting little pieces off the sides where necessary with a knife. That gives you trimmings which equal about the size of 1 stick butter. Put the square into floured waxed paper, and keep it cool in the refrigerator.

Take the trimmings and the rest of the flour—about 1-1/3 cups—and place them in the center of the work area and add the salt. Add enough ice water to make a stiff dough—stiffer than pie dough. Now knead the dough for some time until it no longer sticks to table surface. Let it rest for 15 minutes in a small ball on work surface covered with a dry cloth. Roll the dough into a square, leaving the center portion a little thicker than the edges. Now take the chilled square from the refrigerator and place it like a diamond on the larger square which is on the worktable.

Fold the larger square over the chilled "diamond" like an envelope so that the chilled square is completely covered. Lift the "envelope" slightly, and flour under it. Then sprinkle flour on the top, and roll the dough with a rolling pin into a large rectangle a little more than twice the size of the "envelope." Fold the ends of the rectangle to the center so that you have two thicknesses, and then fold it right down the center so that you have four thicknesses. Wrap in a cloth, and place in the refrigerator for a half hour.

Now roll it again into another rectangle about 1/2 inch thick, and fold it as before from the outer edges to the center and down the middle to make four thicknesses. Again rest it for a half hour in the refrigerator, wrapped. Roll it a third time exactly the same way. The rollings are necessary in order to make little flaky layers. When you bake puff paste, the fat between the countless layers causes it to have amazing flakiness, far superior to piecrust. Three times is enough to roll the dough and fold it, but four or five times will make it still lighter when you bake it.

You are now ready to use the puff paste. You can make little sections of the unused portion, wrap them in plastic wrap, and store them in the freezer. It will keep as long as a year.

PUFF PASTE APPETIZERS

Roll the puff paste to a quarter-inch thickness. Cut the dough into 1-1/2-inch squares. Moisten each corner of each square with egg yolk diluted with a few drops of water, and fold into the center to make a little envelope, pressing each corner down. The egg yolk will keep the puff from bursting open while baking.

Place on an ungreased baking sheet, and bake in a 400° oven until they are brown and have formed little puff balls—about 15 minutes. While they are still warm, puncture them with the handle of a knife or any small instrument, in order to make a hole for stuffing the appetizer shell.

You will see all through this book how puff paste dough is used for pastries and appetizers at White House receptions and teas and for such seafood courses as Lobster Victoria at formal dinners.

But back to the making of a White House chef. After working in several places in Italy and a sumptuous resort hotel in Trieste, I was offered a chance to be a pastry chef in a fine hotel in that mecca for gamblers, Monte Carlo.

At Monte Carlo, I learned how to get rid of a week's pay in two hours. Finally, one payday I decided I had had enough, and I took the blue train to Paris, where I went to work at the luxurious pastry shop-restaurant

Rumpelmayer's. There, at four o'clock each day, the ladies would pause in their shopping along the fashionable rue de Rivoli and stop in for tea or ice cream. The Peach Melba I learned there I later served at the White House:

PÊCHE MELBA

1 scoop vanilla ice cream   Melba sauce
1 fresh peach half   Browned almond slices
Whipped cream

In an individual glass compote dish place the ice cream. Place the peach half on top of this with the rounded side of the peach up. Decorate around the peach with whipped cream, leaving the top clear. Top with Melba sauce (a combination of raspberries and sugar syrup you can buy at a specialty store or make with raspberry jam). Finally, sprinkle the almond slices over the sauce. Serves 1.

In Paris I continued studying pastrymaking, and I also studied French cooking under the finest chefs. I learned how to use wine to improve the flavor of meats and fish. I learned to poach fish in a delicious court bouillon, which you will find, if you check the Index, to be vegetables cooked in a bag in water to which you have added almost one cup dry white wine to each quart water. I served fish many times at the White House this way, poached and garnished with chopped parsley and lemon butter.

I learned the importance of fresh spices—ground pepper from a pepper mill and real garlic cloves instead of powdered dry garlic.

In Paris, too, I developed my own recipe for salad dressing that became a standard at the White House. So that you can make it up in your electric blender to keep on hand in your refrigerator, here is the recipe:

FRENCH DRESSING RYSAVY

2 cups vegetable oil   1 tablespoon horse-radish
1/3 cup wine vinegar   mustard
1 medium onion, chopped   1 teaspoon salt
2 cloves garlic, chopped   1/3 teaspoon white pepper

Mix the ingredients, put in blender, and blend for 2 minutes, starting the blender speed at low for a few seconds, then increasing to high speed. Makes a little more than a pint.

This dressing is wonderful on any kind of raw or cooked vegetable salad and shrimp or any other seafood salad.

From Paris I rolled from city to city. Antwerp, Belgium, then back to Paris, then on to the French Riviera, then to a lake resort hotel, Grand Hotel du Parc on the Swiss border.

Then on to Casablanca, where I cooked in a plush hotel, but soon rolled on to Marrakesh, Morocco, then back to France to Bagnoles de l'Orne, a Normandy spa, then back to Nice and then again to Morocco—all within a year.

So greatly did I enjoy the footloose life of a rolling chef that I even, for a time, cooked on the famous Orient Express, between Paris and Bucharest. I left the Orient Express to help open a new Austrian restaurant in Paris, Au Danube Bleu.

One of the things I served there was Boeuf Braisé, which I later served at the White House as Pot Roast of Beef. It was a twice-a-month favorite of the Eisenhowers. If you like, you can leave out the garlic, as I did for the Eisenhowers, but let me give you the complete recipe:

POT ROAST OF BEEF
(BOEUF BRAISÉ)

Pot roast of beef
1 teaspoon salt per pound of
    meat
Pepper to taste
Flour
Fat

1 can beef consommé
1 clove garlic, crushed
1 carrot, cut up
2 stalks celery, coarsely chopped
1/2 cup dry white wine
    (optional)

Season your pot roast with salt and pepper, and roll it in flour. Then sear it in a frying pan in hot fat as quickly as possible. The meat should be brown on all sides. Now put your meat on a rack in a heavy iron pot which has a cover, and pour the beef consommé over the meat. Add the garlic, carrot, and celery.

Bring the consommé quickly to the boiling point, cover, and let simmer slowly for 3 hours for a 4-pound roast. Baste the meat with the consommé mixture every quarter hour. Turn the meat over every other basting.

To make a delicious gravy, take out the meat, sprinkle in 1 tablespoon flour, and cook for about 5 minutes, adding a little more water if necessary. Pass the gravy through the electric blender with the vegetables in it until it has a smooth consistency.

If you want to make it the French way, add the white wine to the consommé before you put the roast in the oven. It gives a piquant flavor to the meat and gravy which is very pleasant.

At Au Danube Bleu I met the international socialite George Sebastian, who was on his honeymoon with a bride from Wheeling, West Virginia, who spoke no French. After tasting my food, they hired me away from the restaurant. The closest I would ever again come to cooking in a restaurant was when I cooked in the White House.

I will never forget my arrival with the Sebastians at their forty-acre estate in Hammamet, Tunisia. Two automobiles were waiting for us when we got off the boat in Tunis, and Sebastian chose to drive his Renault convertible himself, with his wife beside him, while I rode grandly in the back seat of the chauffeur-driven Mercedes Benz.

Flora Sebastian was on the list of Best Dressed Women of the World, and so were some of her friends. The Duchess of Windsor visited while she was still Wallis Simpson, and I served her the Sebastians' favorite chicken recipe—with wine sauce.

Later President Kennedy served this dish at the precedent-making dinner at Mount Vernon in honor of Mohammed Ayub Khan, the President of Pakistan.

POULET SAUTÉ CHASSEUR

Salt and pepper to taste	1 cup chicken consommé
1 3-pound fryer, cut into 8 pieces	1 cup dry white wine
1/4 pound butter	2 tablespoons brandy
2 tablespoons olive oil	1/4 cup tomato paste
1/2 pound raw mushrooms,	1/2 teaspoon chopped tarragon
sliced	Parsley
3 shallots, finely chopped	

Salt and pepper the pieces of fowl, and sauté them in the butter and olive oil until golden brown.

Then take the pieces of meat out of the fat, and sauté the mushrooms and shallots in the same hot grease. When they begin to turn a golden color, pour in the consommé, white wine, and brandy. Let simmer,

uncovered, until the liquid is reduced about one-third, then add the tomato paste and tarragon, and immediately return the chicken to the pan.
 Simmer, covered, until tender—about 30 minutes. Add salt and pepper to taste.
 Serve the chicken with its own wine sauce. Sprinkle with parsley. Serves 4.

In Tunisia I learned to make couscous, which I served several times at the White House. I was delighted to hear that Jacqueline Kennedy also enjoyed couscous in her travels and had ordered it made once at the White House:

COUSCOUS ARABE

1 2-1/2-pound chicken
3 pounds lamb shoulder
3 teaspoons salt
Pepper to taste
Chicken fat
8 small carrots, cut in half
  lengthwise
8 medium onions
2 cloves garlic, mashed
2 tablespoons tomato paste
1/4 teaspoon saffron

1/2 teaspoon powdered cloves
1/4 teaspoon cinnamon
1 teaspoon caraway seed
3 small hot green peppers
8 small sweet green peppers (do
  not remove seeds)
8 2-inch square chunks pumpkin
1 medium cabbage, quartered
1 cup farina
2 cups water

Cut up the chicken into small chunks with the bones, and then cut up the lamb shoulder into 1-inch cubes. Season with the salt and pepper. Brown all the meat at the same time in smoking hot chicken fat. When the meat is brown, add the carrots, onions, garlic, tomato paste, saffron, cloves, cinnamon, caraway seed, and hot green peppers.
 Cover with water, and simmer with a lid on for 45 minutes. Then add sweet green peppers, pumpkin, and cabbage.
 Cook slowly for an additional 45 minutes, adding boiling water to keep the ingredients submerged and more salt if necessary.
 While the couscous is cooking, prepare farina balls:

FARINA BALLS

Steam the farina in the 2 cups water until it is sticky—15 to 20 minutes. Let it cool and shape into little balls about 1 inch in diameter. Reheat the balls when the couscous is ready. The natives eat the farina dumplings with their hands, dipping each one into the stew liquid but you can serve it as a side dish or as a dumpling on top of the couscous.

For some reason the natives serve couscous with the meat completely hidden by the vegetables. First cut the cabbage into smaller pieces. The meat is placed on the bottom of a large shallow earthenware bowl. All the vegetables are lined up across the top. The colors are pretty to see because you have the pumpkin orange, the green of the cabbage, the white of the onions, etc. Serves 8.

I think the guest who it thrilled me most to see at the Sebastians was Somerset Maugham. He was a quiet man who listened more than he spoke. He saved his words for his stories.

The Veal Périgueux I served the famous English novelist was to become one of the favorite main courses of President and Mrs. Eisenhower for formal occasions in the White House.

VEAL PÉRIGUEUX

3 pounds veal
1/2 pound cooked smoked ham
1 small can truffles
1-1/2 teaspoons salt
Pepper to taste

2 thin slices salt pork
1/2 can chicken consommé
Melted butter
1/2 tablespoon flour

I like to cut my own veal roast from a whole leg of veal so that there is no bone. Your butcher can cut you a long, narrow piece from the veal cutlet area of the leg.

To prepare the meat, first make slits lengthwise through the meat to insert strips of ham and truffles. Use a sharp thin knife—the thinnest you have—and then thread the strips of ham and truffles through by pushing them with your fingers. Make six strips of your ham and tiny slices of your truffles. This will give your veal a beautiful mottled effect when you slice it to serve. The truffles are black; the ham is pink. Veal, which is almost colorless, needs to have such color added.

Season the roast with the salt and pepper, and wrap it with the salt pork, which you tie in place with a string. Pour the chicken consommé over the surface. Bake at 375° for 1-1/2 to 2 hours. Your meat will be brown enough because the salt pork practically melts during the roasting. Baste frequently with the consommé at the bottom of the pan, and as it diminishes, skim off the fat from the salt pork and brush your roast with melted butter. This will enhance the flavor of your gravy.

Make gravy of the liquid at the bottom of your roaster. Add 1/2 tablespoon flour for a thin gravy, and cook on top of the stove for 5 minutes, adding more consommé if necessary. Serves 6.

Lamb is the most important meat in Moslem countries, and I learned all the basic lamb dishes while at the Sebastians'. Thus I was prepared to make them for Moslem chiefs of state when they visited at the White House.

Let me give you just one of the lamb dishes now. (Boulangère, incidentally, means bakery style in French.)

LEG OF LAMB BOULANGÈRE

Garlic, slivered	5 teaspoons salt
1 7-pound leg of lamb	6 potatoes, sliced
6 onions, sliced	Chopped parsley
Salt and white pepper to taste	

Insert tiny slivers of garlic under the skin of the meat in many places, and others more deeply buried into the meat closer to the bone. Then rub the leg with the 5 teaspoons salt. Bake in a roasting dish, uncovered. You will need a roasting dish much larger than your leg of lamb because you will be adding slices of potatoes and onions. In France we serve leg of lamb rare, but in America it is served well done, so bake it 30 minutes for each pound in a 300° oven. Every quarter hour, baste your roast with water and natural juices, because the lamb has enough flavor by itself. For the last three-quarter hour, bake the sliced potatoes and onions in the same baking dish so that they absorb the delicious flavors of the meat. Be sure to baste them too, and sprinkle with salt and white pepper.

Serve the whole leg of lamb on a platter, slicing the meat first and placing it back in its position on the bone. Arrange the potatoes and onions alternately in a large circle around the meat and garnish just the vegetables with parsley. Serves 6.

Probably the most famous woman to taste my cooking at the Sebastians' was Greta Garbo. I thought her voice was very intriguing but I could not say she was the greatest beauty I have seen, though there was something haunting about her face.

In honor of the great Garbo I served a French version of a Scandinavian delicacy, Omelette à la Norvégienne.

Jacqueline Kennedy, too, was very fond of *omelette* desserts at the White House and for one of them, Omelette Surprise Pompadour, you will find the recipe with the luncheon menu served to General Douglas MacArthur.

OMELETTE À LA NORVÉGIENNE

Sponge cake
1/2 cup finely chopped mixed
  candied fruits
1/2 cup kirsch liqueur
1-1/2 quarts strawberry ice
  cream

8 egg whites
2 cups granulated sugar
Powdered sugar
3 tablespoons Cointreau or good
  brandy

This dessert gets its name from the fact that it is cut into the shape of an oval omelet and not because it is made with eggs. As a matter of fact, it is made with sponge cake as its base. Cut a thin layer of sponge cake—about 1 inch thick—to fit the bottom of your round or oval serving dish. This dish must be metal because it must go in the oven for 3 minutes.

Sprinkle the top of the sponge cake with the candied fruits, which have been soaked for 2 hours in the Kirsch. Now, leaving a 1/2-inch margin around the edge of your cake, build a mound of the strawberry ice cream to a height of 3 inches in the center and tapering sharply at the edges. Place immediately in the freezer. Keep in the freezer at least 1 hour.

When the soup is being served at the beginning of dinner, prepare the finishing touches for the Omelette à la Norvégienne. Beat the egg whites with granulated sugar until they form stiff peaks. Take the ice cream omelet from the freezer, and first cover the entire surface of the ice cream with meringue, using a spatula. Then pour the rest of the meringue into a pastry bag with a star point tube, and build a beautiful design over the entire surface, leaving an indentation at the top for the Cointreau. When all the meringue has been used, shake powdered sugar all over, and pop into a 500° oven for 3 minutes so that the sugar will brown a little bit.

Now pour the Cointreau into the indentation on top, ignite with a match, and carry into the dining room flambée. Serves 6 to 8.

Looking back, I see that it was the Sebastians, really, who started me on my journey to the White House by sending me to England to learn English so that I could converse properly with Mrs. Sebastian. Without English, I would never have been able to get a job with the American Army when World War II came.

By the time World War II ended, I was married and the father of a little girl, Janet, and my employer was an American general and several high-ranking Army officers who were headquartered at the Villa le Roc on the French Riviera. The villa was lavish, having been the former home of a member of British royalty, but my life was very lonely because my wife and baby could not be with me. So to be together as a family, I accepted a position with the first secretary of the American Embassy in Prague, my wife's home town.

Walter Birge was a wonderful human being. He was also a connoisseur of fine food, and one of the dishes I served him, I later served at the White House:

STUFFED PORK CHOPS RYSAVY

6 large pork chops, 1-1/2 inches thick
2 stalks celery, chopped fine
1 medium onion, chopped
1/4 pound butter
1 pound fresh mushrooms, chopped
1 clove garlic, crushed
1 teaspoon salt
Pepper to taste

1/2 cup chicken consommé
2 tablespoons bread crumbs
Flour
Butter
Another medium onion, chopped
1/2 cup white Bordeaux wine
Another cup chicken consommé
1/2 tablespoon flour
1/2 cup heavy cream
Chopped chives

Slit the pork chops horizontally to the bone to make a pocket for the stuffing. For stuffing use the celery, the first onion sautéed in half the butter, the mushrooms, garlic, salt, pepper, and the first 1/2 cup consommé.

Cook the stuffing until the liquid is almost gone—about 15 minutes. Then let it cool slightly, add the bread crumbs, and mix thoroughly. Stuff the chops, and close the slits with toothpicks so that the stuffing does not run out.

Then roll the chops in flour, brown quickly in the remaining butter in which you have sautéed the other onion, and add the Bordeaux and second 1/2 cup consommé. Let the chops simmer 1 hour; then remove the chops, and add the 1/2 tablespoon flour and cream, stirring constantly until thick.

Add the remaining stuffing, and pass through the blender until you have a creamy sauce to pour over the meat, garnishing with chives. Serves 6.

Another thing which Walter Birge liked and which I later made at the White House, were *Croissants,* or Crescent Rolls. I served them at the White House for company breakfasts:

CROISSANTS
(Crescent Rolls)

1-1/2 cakes fresh yeast	1-1/2 cups lukewarm milk
1/4 cup lukewarm milk	1/2 cup slightly softened butter
4 egg yolks	Another 1/2 cup slightly
2 tablespoons sugar	softened butter
2 tablespoons shortening, melted	2 egg yolks
3/4 teaspoon salt	2 teaspoons water
3 cups sifted flour	

Dissolve the yeast in the 1/4 cup lukewarm milk. While waiting for the yeast to rise to the top—about 5 minutes—put the 4 egg yolks in a mixing bowl with the sugar, shortening, salt, and flour.

Pour the yeast mixture on top of the flour, and start beating while adding the 1-1/2 cups milk. Beat with a wooden spoon for 3 or 4 minutes until the dough is smooth; then put it aside in a cool spot for 30 minutes.

Flour a board, and roll the dough 1/4 inch thick. Then take 1/2 cup slightly softened butter, and dab pieces all over the top. Fold the dough from the sides to the center and then fold over once more to make four layers.

Wrap the dough in a cloth, and let it rest for 30 minutes in the refrigerator. When the time is up, roll it again so that the butter becomes a part of the dough and makes it flaky in the baking. Dab on the second 1/2 cup butter as before. Fold the dough in the same way so that you again have four layers, and again let it rest for another 30 minutes in the refrigerator. It is best to prepare the dough the night before if you want the crescents for breakfast.

In the morning roll out the dough to a 1/4-inch thickness, and cut into triangles with 4-inch sides. Start at the bottom end, and roll so that you have a point in the center. As you place them on a greased baking sheet, twist them into a new-moon shape, from which they get the name crescent, and brush with the 2 egg yolks mixed with 1 teaspoon of water. When the egg is dry, cover with a cloth, and place in a warm spot to rise for about 30 minutes. Bake in a 375° oven until brown—about 20 minutes. Makes 18 croissants.

This is the way the First Family served them for guests at the White House, but Walter Birge liked each triangle covered with chopped walnuts and cinnamon-sugar before rolling. It takes about 1 cup chopped nuts and 1/2 cup cinnamon-sugar to fix them à la Birge.

It was Birge who inspired me to want to be an American. I asked to be registered under the quota, but before my number came up, the Communists took over Czechoslovakia. With Walter Birge's help, I escaped and soon found myself cooking for friends of his in Georgetown, Washington, D.C., the Count and Countess de Limur.

Then, even with a family, I determined to see America, and I headed west. In Hollywood, I worked for the famous "Jay" Paley of CBS and then for motion-picture director Henry Hathaway, whose home was a Grand Central Station with movie stars like Gary Cooper, Louis Jourdan, and Van Johnson always passing through.

One Hollywood favorite that I later made many times at the White House and that is still being served there is Tournedos Rossini, or, as the Nixons call it, Filet Mignon Rossini. When I prepared it at the White House for the Eisenhowers I used bacon instead of salt pork.

TOURNEDOS ROSSINI

1 1-1/2 inch-thick filet mignon
  per person
1 slice salt pork
Salt and pepper to taste
Butter
1 1-4 inch slice *pâté*
  de foie gras

1 slice truffle
Fresh white bread, in round
  pieces
1/2 tablespoon Marsala wine
Chopped parsley

Wrap the outer edge of filet with a thick slice of salt pork, and season with salt and freshly ground pepper. Then sauté rapidly in butter for 3 minutes on each side.

While your meat is being sautéed, have a second pan on top of the stove warming 1/4-inch slices of *pâté de foie gras*—1 slice for each filet—in butter. Also warming with the *foie gras* will be 1 slice of truffle per filet.

When the meat is done, take the filets out of the pan, and use the juices to fry round pieces of fresh white bread cut with a large cookie cutter to the same size as the filets.

As soon as the toast circles are brown, set them in a warm silver serving dish and place a filet on each round. Then comes the *foie gras* in the center of the filet, and on top of that is the thin slice of truffle. If you have any drippings left in the bottom of the pan, use them, with additional butter, to make 1 teaspoon sauce per filet. Now add to the hot butter—or butter and drippings combination—1/2 tablespoon of Marsala per portion. Heat almost to the boiling point, and pour over the meat immediately. Garnish with parsley.

When Hollywood lost its charm, I rolled back to Washington, D.C., little realizing that I would soon be rolling into the nation's most important residence—the White House itself.

It happened because I had gone to work for industrialist William A. M. Burden and then had switched to his friends the George Garretts, when Mr. Burden moved to New York.

At the Burdens', I had perfected my recipe for Chicken Tarragon, which I would later be serving at the White House. It was the favorite recipe of Burden, and it was later a great favorite of First Lady Jacqueline Kennedy, who served it, under its French name, Poulet à l'Estragon:

CHICKEN TARRAGON

1 2-1/2-pound fryer, cut into 6 pieces	10 small white onions
Salt and freshly ground pepper to taste	1 cup chicken consommé
	1 cup dry white wine
Flour	5 stems tarragon with leaves attached
1/4 pound butter	

Season the chicken with salt and pepper, and roll in flour. Brown the chicken in the butter to a golden color. Add the onions to the pan, and cook until they are light brown. When the onions are golden color, pour the chicken consommé over the meat and immediately follow with the wine and tarragon. Tie the stems together so that later they can be removed. If you cannot find fresh tarragon, you can find it in jars pickled in vinegar. Use 7 strands or stems if they come from a jar. Simmer the chicken for 45 minutes, and take out the tarragon cluster. The Chicken Tarragon is ready to serve with the natural sauce at the bottom of the pan. However, if you have some extra fresh tarragon leaves, your sauce will be still better if you run them through the blender with the wine-consommé sauce which comes from your pan. Reheat, pour over the chicken, and garnish with more tarragon leaves. Fresh tarragon leaves make a prettier garnish than canned. Serve with plain rice. Serves 4.

At the Garretts', I was busy with my pastry tubes again, stuffing puff paste delicacies. Now came a twist of fate. On the golf course, President Eisenhower had asked his friend John L. Hennessy, vice-president of the Hilton Corporation, to find him a French chef who could also handle pastry. John Hennessy asked Herbert C. Blunck, general manager of the Washington Statler Hotel, who just happened to be invited to one of Mrs. Garrett's teas.

He ate my puff paste. He ate my petits fours and a very intricate Viennese torte made of eight layers—each one a mere 1/4 inch thick—which is too complicated for any but the most professional cook. He quizzed me a bit and took me soon after to meet Mr. Hennessy and I was *in.*

Now let's turn to the menu I promised you for one of President Nixon's first formal dinners. As you see, it features the Rossini main course.

PRESIDENT NIXON'S
FORMAL DINNER
TO HONOR THE CHIEF JUSTICE OF THE UNITED STATES
AND MRS. WARREN

Wednesday, April 23, 1969

Crab Meat Impérial

Filet Mignon Rossini
Cocotte Potatoes
Asparagus Hollandaise

Caesar Salad

Brie Cheese
Mousse Nesselrode

CRAB MEAT IMPÉRIAL

1 egg	1/4 cup finely chopped red
2 tablespoons mayonnaise	pepper
2 teaspoons Worcestershire sauce	2 teaspoons softened butter
1/2 teaspoon salt	4 medium crab or scallop shells
1/4 teaspoon white pepper	2 tablespoons butter, in bits
1 pound fresh crab meat	
1/4 cup finely chopped green	
pepper	

In a deep bowl, beat egg lightly with a wire whisk. Add mayonnaise, Worcestershire sauce, salt, and pepper, and beat until mixture is smooth. Add the crab meat, and the peppers, and toss lightly but thoroughly.

Preheat oven to 375°. With a pastry brush, spread the softened butter over the crab shells.

Spoon the crab mixture into the buttered shells evenly, mounding the centers lightly. Dot the tops with the bits of butter. Bake in oven for 15 to 20 minutes. Then put under hot broiler for 30 seconds to brown the tops. Serve immediately directly from the shells. Serves 4.

See Index for Hollandaise Sauce.

COCOTTE POTATOES

6 large potatoes	Salt and white pepper to taste
3 tablespoons butter	

Peel the potatoes, and scoop out little balls. Melt butter in a cocotte—a flameproof casserole with cover. Add the potato balls, cover, and bake in oven at 425° until done. Season with salt and white pepper, and serve.

CAESAR SALAD

2 medium heads romaine lettuce
1 egg
1 clove garlic
1/8 teaspoon salt
1/8 teaspoon freshly ground
  black pepper

1/3 cup olive oil
4 tablespoons lemon juice
1/2 cup freshly grated Parmesan
  cheese
6 to 8 flat anchovies (optional)
12 to 14 croutons

Separate heads of lettuce, and wash leaves under cold running water. Dry each leaf, then wrap in a dry kitchen towel, and chill.

Plunge egg into rapidly boiling water for 10 seconds, remove, and set aside. Rub sides of a large salad bowl with garlic, break the chilled lettuce into serving-size pieces, and put into bowl. Add salt, pepper, egg, and olive oil, and toss the lettuce. Add lemon juice, and mix again until lettuce is thoroughly coated.

Add the cheese and anchovies, and mix once more. Scatter croutons over the top, and serve on chilled plates. Serves 6 to 8.

MOUSSE NESSELRODE

4 egg yolks
2/3 cup powdered sugar
1 cup boiling milk
1 teaspoon vanilla
1 envelope unflavored gelatin

2 tablespoons cold water
1/2 cup chestnut puree
1 cup heavy cream, whipped
1/2 cup crumbled candied
  chestnuts

With a wire whisk beat the egg yolks together with sugar. Pour in boiling milk flavored with vanilla. Stir, and put back on heat. Stir gently with a spatula (not a beater) until it is almost to the boil, but not boiling. Set aside. Add gelatin which has been soaked in the cold water for 5 minutes. After gelatin has been stirred into mixture, strain through a fine sieve, and add chestnut puree.

Let cool, and very lightly fold in whipped cream and chestnuts.

Transfer to a round charlotte mold and chill overnight in refrigerator. Decorate with additional candied chestnuts and whipped cream before serving. Serves 4 to 6.

3

FOOD FANCIES—LIKES AND DISLIKES OF THE PRESIDENTIAL FAMILIES THROUGH HISTORY

Nothing is more fascinating to me than to learn the food peculiarities and likes and dislikes of the First Families.

When I hear that President Nixon is not fond of lamb and his wife, Pat, is not fond of veal, I smile as a thousand-and-one tidbits of history from the White House kitchens and my own experiences cooking there spring to mind.

And I can see the problems of working out the Nixon menus. With chicken winning many times as a compromise.

Of course, one thing that pops into mind immediately is how different First Lady Pat Nixon is from First Lady Jacqueline Kennedy, who would have been almost incapacitated in her social life if she could not serve veal in its many succulent forms or lamb. For example, spring Lamb à la Broche aux Primeurs is what she served when Princess Grace came to call.

But on the other hand, Pat Nixon and Jackie Onassis share a common love of chicken. That is Pat Nixon's favorite, and Poulet à l'Estragon, you will recall, is what First Lady Jackie served on another special occasion, when her sister, Princess Radziwill, was visiting the White House. (See Index.)

Pat Nixon served Chicken with Mushroom Crêpes at her first White House luncheon for Cabinet wives, and when the family eats alone, chicken is perhaps the most frequent main course. Pat likes barbecued chicken, hot chicken salad, and even Enchiladas de Pollo—enchiladas with chicken.

Whenever Jackie Kennedy ate at home with the family, she would order her favorite veal dish—Roast Veal Filet with Tarragon.

46

JACQUELINE KENNEDY'S ROAST VEAL FILET

1 5-pound filet of veal rump
Pork lard, cut into fine strips
1 bay leaf
Pinch of thyme
2 whole cloves
1 thin slice garlic
2 blades tarragon leaves or pinch
    of dried tarragon

2 onions, peeled and quartered
2 cups beef consommé
2 fresh mushrooms, peeled and
    chopped
1-1/2 cups Béchamel Sauce
    (below)
1-1/2 tablespoons butter
Finely chopped chervil

Remove all the sinews from the veal rump. Lard it through with the strips of pork lard. Place the meat in a large casserole, and add the bay leaf, thyme, cloves, garlic, tarragon, onions, and beef consommé.

Bring the mixture to a boil. Then cover and simmer gently for 1 hour, or until the roast is done. Remove the veal to a deep roasting pan.

Pour over the meat 1/2 cup of the strained liquid in which the meat was parboiled, add the mushrooms, and roast in a moderate oven until the meat is well browned on all sides, basting frequently. Remove the pan from the oven, cut the meat in half crosswise, and keep it hot.

Strain the liquid from the pan through a sieve, and reduce it over a bright flame to about 1/2 cup. Mix this sauce with the Béchamel Sauce, to which the meat and the butter have been added. Heat almost to the boiling point. Place the meat on a serving platter, in the sauce, and sprinkle chervil on top. Serves 8 to 10.

BÉCHAMEL SAUCE

2 tablespoons butter
2 tablespoons flour
3/4 cup milk

3/4 cup chicken consommé or
    bouillon
Salt and white pepper to taste

In a small saucepan, melt the butter. Add the flour, making a roux of the mixture. Then add the milk and the consommé or bouillon gradually, and season with salt and white pepper. Let simmer 5 minutes, stirring constantly. Makes about 1-1/2 cups sauce.

PAT NIXON'S BARBECUED CHICKEN

1/2 cup melted butter
Juice of 2 lemons
1 teaspoon garlic salt
1 tablespoon paprika

1 tablespoon oregano
Salt and pepper to taste
2 small chickens, cut into halves

Combine all ingredients except chicken. Marinate chicken for 3 to 4 hours in sauce.

Barbecue, basting often with remainder of sauce, or bake in the oven at 325° for 45 minutes, basting often. Serves 4.

Another chicken favorite, which Chef Andraeas of Key Biscayne and Palm Beach frequently served the President when he vacationed at Key Biscayne before buying his own place there, is chicken prepared with cheese and smoked ham, the Cordon Bleu way:

PRESIDENT NIXON'S FAVORITE BREAST OF CHICKEN, CORDON BLEU

Breast of 3-pound or larger
    chicken, boned and split into
    two
Salt and white pepper to taste
2 slices Swiss cheese
2 slices smoked ham
3 to 4 tablespoons flour

1 egg, beaten with 1 tablespoon
    milk
3 tablespoons bread crumbs
Enough cooking oil to fry chicken
1 can bouillon or beef broth
1 generous tablespoon sour
    cream

Beat each breast with meat mallet to flatten. Season with salt and pepper. Now place slice of cheese and ham on top of each breast, roll all into a tight roll, and secure with a toothpick.

Coat the roll with flour, and dip in the egg and milk mixture. Dust with bread crumbs. Fry at 375° for 25 to 30 minutes until golden.

Remove breast from pan, and drain on paper towel.

Drain oil from cooking pan, and pour in a can of bouillon or beef broth to mix with drippings. Return to fire, and simmer 2 minutes.

Thicken the juices with a little flour; let cook slowly a few more minutes until it again boils and thickens. Add sour cream, blend well, and serve with the cooked chicken breast. Serves 2.

It is amusing to me that President Nixon and former President Lyndon Johnson, on opposite sides of the political fence, share a love of Mexican food. Both spent their honeymoons in Mexico.

LBJ became so addicted to hot Mexican food that jalapeno peppers were a must in the White House kitchen.

The whole Nixon family is hipped on Mexicano food. Julie Nixon Eisenhower on her twenty-second birthday celebrated with tacos and for his 30th Wedding Anniversary, her father called for tacos, too.

Nixon friends who like to try the foods that the President enjoys at San Clemente at his so-called California White House drive to a particular restaurant in the area that features a Mexican dinner called "The Nixon Special."

Included, of course, are the tacos, made just as the President liked them there—with the tortillas heavily filled with ground beef, generously doctored with hot sauce and spices, melted cheese, and shredded lettuce.

Now let's compare two chili recipes that will go down in culinary history:

RICHARD NIXON'S MEXICAN HAMBURGERS WITH CHILI

CHILI SAUCE

2-1/2 cups finely chopped onions
2 teaspoons minced garlic
2 tablespoons vegetable oil
3 tablespoons chili powder
1 tablespoon flour
2 teaspoons ground cumin
2 tablespoons ground coriander

2 teaspoons oregano or marjoram
2 19-ounce cans tomatoes
1 cup water
1/4 cup sugar
4 teaspoons salt
2 squares (ounces) unsweetened
  chocolate

In a heavy 10-inch skillet cook onion and garlic in oil until the onion is golden and transparent. Meanwhile, in a small bowl, combine the chili powder, flour, cumin, coriander, and oregano or marjoram. Add to the onion, and cook 2 minutes.

Now stir in the tomatoes and the water. Bring to a boil, and add the sugar, salt, and chocolate. Stir until chocolate melts, and then simmer for 1-1/2 hours.

HAMBURGERS

1 pound ground beef	1-1/2 teaspoons salt
1 egg, beaten	2 tablespoons butter, melted
2 tablespoons flour	
3/4 cup crushed cornflakes or	
corn soya flakes	

Preheat oven to 350°. Mix lightly the beef, egg, flour, cornflakes, and salt. Form into 1-inch balls, and brown in skillet in butter. Transfer to casserole, and cover with the Chili Sauce. Bake 20 to 30 minutes. Serve with rice and red beans. Serves 5 or 6.

LYNDON B. JOHNSON'S
PEDERNALES RIVER CHILI

4 pounds coarsely ground chuck or round steak	1 teaspoon comino seed
1 large onion, chopped	6 teaspoons chili powder (more if needed)
2 cloves garlic, crushed	2 No. 2-1/2 cans tomatoes
5 shakes liquid hot sauce (or more, to suit taste)	2 No. 2-1/2 cans kidney beans
1 teaspoon ground oregano	2 cups hot water
	Salt to taste

Put meat, onion, and garlic in large heavy boiler or skillet. Sear until light-colored. Add hot sauce, oregano, comino, chili powder, tomatoes, beans and hot water. Bring to a boil, lower heat, and simmer about 1 hour. Add salt and more liquid hot sauce, to taste toward end of cooking. As fat cooks out, skim.

Serve with a side dish of jalapeno peppers if you want to eat them LBJ's favorite way, but they might be too strong if you tend toward ulcers. Sometimes the President ordered the chili made without beans to cut calories. Serves 8 to 10.

Another chili recipe that President Johnson relished was one made by a family friend—Scooter Miller. (See Index.)

FDR liked all kinds of seafood, and there is a story told by Lillian Rogers Parks, the White House maid whom I knew when I worked there, about how upset the President was when he could not find a lobster that had been saved for him for a midnight snack. When Eleanor Roosevelt was leaving the White House, the skeleton of that lobster was found in the attic, where some hungry household worker had probably left the remains.

Eisenhower was not much of a seafood lover, except for trout, and I was glad of that because it is the one food I do not eat. President Truman didn't care for fish either. However, had I worked for Franklin D. Roosevelt, John F. Kennedy, or George Washington I would have had to steel myself to the stream of fish that flowed across their table. FDR even ate it for breakfast. His favorite dinner fish was salmon:

FDR'S FAVORITE SALMON RECIPE

3 pounds fresh salmon
2/3 cup vinegar
1-1/2 tablespoons salt
2-1/2 tablespoons butter
2-1/2 tablespoons flour
1/2 teaspoon salt

1/4 teaspoon white pepper
1-1/2 cups milk
1/2 cup heavy cream
2 hard-cooked eggs
Chopped parsley

Put the salmon in boiling water to cover, to which you have added the vinegar and salt. Cook until salmon is tender.

To make the sauce, melt the butter in a double boiler, and stir in the flour and seasonings. Then remove from fire. Pour in two-thirds of the milk and cream, which you have warmed, at once; add the rest slowly, stirring constantly, and cook until thickened. Finally, mash the eggs, and add to the sauce. Pour sauce over the fish, and sprinkle with parsley. Serves 6.

PRESIDENT KENNEDY'S
BAKED SEAFOOD CASSEROLE

1 pound crab meat
1 pound shrimp, cooked and
    deveined
1 cup mayonnaise
1/2 cup chopped green peppers
1/4 cup minced onion

1-1/2 cups finely chopped celery
1/2 teaspoon salt
1 tablespoon Worcestershire
    sauce
2 cups crushed potato chips
Paprika

Mix all ingredients except potato chips and paprika as though making a seafood salad. Fill a baking pan, and completely cover with potato chips. Sprinkle with paprika, and bake at 400° for 20 to 25 minutes. Serves 12.

I discovered Mrs. Eisenhower's secret passion—anything with mint flavor. The average person encounters mint flavor in the form of jelly or sauce on maybe a dozen occasions a year. "Mrs. E." loved mint served wherever it could be slipped in—sprinkled in with orange slices for an orange Roquefort salad; built into a gorgeous dessert, her very favorite, Frosted Mint Delight, a crushed pineapple and mint concoction which I will tell you about later; Minted Apricots for a side dish with lamb chops; and even a mint-chocolate pie.

Mamie Eisenhower's second dessert flavor was caramel. It was her favorite frosting on petits fours, her favorite flavoring in custard, and I even concocted a special apple caramel dessert that goes well with such meats as roast pork.

She was not the only First Lady who liked caramel. Dolley Madison made a delicious caramel layer cake, and Lou Henry Hoover even made Caramelized Tomatoes:

MRS. HOOVER'S CARAMELIZED TOMATOES

Slice the tomatoes in half. Make a little hole in the center of each half to hold the following ingredients:

2 teaspoons granulated sugar	Dash of salt
1 teaspoon dark brown sugar	1 tablespoon butter

Place the tomatoes in a shallow, buttered baking dish, and bake in a hot oven until the sugar is caramelized and the tomatoes are tender.

Sauerkraut has been a White House favorite through the years. Warren Harding liked it served with almost any kind of meat, but especially Vienna sausage. FDR liked it served with pigs' knuckles. Once, when Churchill was his guest, FDR ordered pigs' knuckles served. Although the Prime Minister did not share the President's yen, he manfully tried to seem enthusiastic.

He could have stood the sauerkraut, Churchill confided later to a friend, if it hadn't been, "for those damned pigs' knuckles leering at me." Here is one of FDR's favorite sauerkraut recipes:

FDR'S SAUERKRAUT WITH PORK

1 3- to 3-1/2-pound pork roast	3 teaspoons caraway seed
Garlic slivers	4 cups sauerkraut

Before roasting pork, make slits in meat, and insert garlic, using an amount of garlic to taste. While meat is roasting, add caraway seeds to cold sauerkraut to marinate. Roast in 350° oven for 2-1/2 hours. When roast has been removed from pan, skim off fat, add the sauerkraut with caraway seeds to the pan, and heat until ready to serve. Serves 6.

President Buchanan liked sauerkraut fixed with pork and sour cream:

PRESIDENT BUCHANAN'S SAUERKRAUT WITH PORK

2 pounds lean pork, cubed	2 pounds sauerkraut
3 large onions, cut up	Salt to taste
1-1/2 tablespoons paprika	1-1/2 cups sour cream

Brown the pork. Set aside. Sauté the onions, and add to the pork along with the paprika. Barely cover with water, and simmer about 1-1/2 hours.
Add the drained sauerkraut and salt to taste. If too juicy, blend in a sprinkling of flour to slightly thicken. Add sour cream just before serving, and blend thoroughly through all ingredients. Serves 6.

President Eisenhower seldom had ham, and when he did, it was usually baked in milk.
President Hoover, on the other hand, loved broiled ham with mustard as well as ham with currant jelly.

PRESIDENT EISENHOWER'S HAM STEAK IN MILK

1 1-1/2-inch-thick slice of ham	1 small onion
Milk	12 whole cloves

Cover the ham with the milk in a baking dish. Put into the milk the onion into which the cloves have been stuck.

Bake at 350° for 1 hour. Then take out ham and onion with its cloves, and you are ready to make a delicious gravy. Slice the ham at an angle, like flank steak for serving, making thin slices about 1/2 inch thick. Serves 2 or 3.

HAM STEAK GRAVY

Sprinkle flour in the milk which remains at the bottom of the baking dish, and cook for a few minutes to take away the floury taste. Then run the gravy through the blender for a few minutes, and you have a light cream sauce to serve with your ham.

PRESIDENT HOOVER'S RECIPE FOR BAKED HAM

1 smoked ham	Currant jelly
2 or 3 cups dark brown sugar	Bread crumbs
2 or 3 cups vinegar	

Boil the ham in water to which sugar and vinegar have been added. When tender, remove from water and let cool. Then skin the ham. Coat it with a layer of currant jelly mixed with bread crumbs, and brown it in the oven. Slice and serve.

President Washington preferred fish to meat. It was said this was due to his ill-fitting false teeth which made meat hard to chew. He also liked soups, especially vegetable soup:

GEORGE WASHINGTON'S VEGETABLE SOUP

1/2 cup potatoes, sliced julienne	3 cups rich beef stock
1/2 cup carrots, sliced julienne	Salt and pepper to taste
3 tablespoons butter	Slices of white bread, cut into
1/2 cup onions, thinly sliced	small squares

Fry the potatoes, carrots, and onions together in butter. Put them in the beef stock to which you have added the seasonings and cook until the vegetables are tender. Just before serving the soup, fry the bread squares and float them on top. Serves 4.

That was a simple recipe by comparison with the vegetable soup another Presidential soup fancier made for himself and his friends. To see "General Ike" approach the cooking of his soup, you would think he was getting ready to go into battle. You had to have all the troops ready:

PRESIDENT EISENHOWER'S VEGETABLE SOUP

Bones of uncooked chicken
Large beef soup bone, split so
    that marrow can escape
1 2-pound chunk beef soup meat,
    left on the bone
1-pound chunk lamb stew meat,
    left on the bones
1-1/2 teaspoons salt
1/2 teaspoon black pepper
1 clove garlic and whole onion,
    sliced
2 medium onions, sliced
3 stalks celery, cut up

3 medium carrots, diced
1 cup fresh peas
4 cups diced tomatoes
1/2 cup canned corn
1 cup shredded cabbage
2 medium potatoes, diced into
    small pieces
1 small turnip, diced
1 cup barley
1 teaspoon Worcestershire sauce
10 or 12 nasturtium stems, if
    available

Place bones, meat, salt, pepper, garlic, and whole onion in a large iron or heavy aluminum pot in about 4 or 5 quarts of water, and boil all day until the meat drops off the bones. Add water as needed.

Strain the soup stock through a colander, making sure to get all the juice you can, including the marrow that was in the bone. At this point pick out a few of the firmer pieces of meat, cut them up, and reserve them for when you are ready to finish making the soup. Let the soup stock rest in refrigerator at least overnight, and when you are ready to finish making it, skim off about half of the grease or fat that has risen to the top.

Now you are ready to finish the soup as President Eisenhower did. Prepare the vegetables that will go into it. Add the vegetables to the soup stock in the order in which they are listed in recipe, allowing each to cook two or three minutes before adding the next.

While the vegetables are boiling, cook the barley in a separate stew pan, stirring occasionally. When barley is done, add it, the Worcestershire sauce, and the meat chunks you have reserved to the soup.

Also, in a separate saucepan, boil the fresh nasturtium stems, cut up in tiny pieces, for a few minutes until tender and add to the soup. Soup is ready to be served. Serves 14 to 16.

For a third gourmet soup, try Thomas Jefferson's Beef Soup.

Jefferson felt just as strongly about soup as Ike did, and in fact, in Jefferson's own handwriting there are his "Observations on Soups" in which he says:

"Always observe to lay your meat in the bottom of the pan with a lump of butter. Cut the herbs and vegetables very fine and lay over the meat. Cover it close and set over a slow fire. This will draw the virtue out of the herbs and roots and give the soup a different flavour from what it would have from putting the water in at first. When the gravy produced from the meat is almost dried up, fill your pan up with water. When your soup is done, take it up and when cool enough, skim off the grease quite clean. Put it on again to heat and then dish it up. When you make white soups, never put in the cream until you take it off the fire. Soup is better the second day in cool weather."

Here is Thomas Jefferson's recipe:

THOMAS JEFFERSON'S BEEF SOUP

1 shin bone or soup bone which still has a lot of meat on it	2 celery stalks
	1 small cabbage
3 tablespoons butter	Any other vegetables in season
4 onions	Another 3 tablespoons butter, melted
2 turnips	
2 parsnips	Salt and pepper to taste

Cut the meat from the bone in small pieces, and fry in 3 tablespoons butter. Stir until it is lightly browned.

Cover meat with water, adding bone, and let come to a boil. Skim any film from surface of liquid, and simmer slowly until meat is tender and falls apart, adding water if necessary.

Cut vegetables into small pieces, reserving cabbage until later, lightly heating them in the melted butter until well glazed. Cover with some of the broth from the soup, and cook slowly until thoroughly done. Season with salt and pepper to taste. Mix with meat and stock to serve. When the soup is almost finished, fry the cut-up cabbage, and place it in the pot last. Toward end of cooking add more salt and pepper if necessary. Soup is done when the cabbage is done. Serves 8 to 10.

President Kennedy was definitely a soup man. You could hardly find a soup he didn't like—if it was creamed. Cream of chicken soup was probably his favorite, but it was closely followed by cream of tomato soup, cream of asparagus, and cream of mushroom.

PRESIDENT KENNEDY'S
CREAM OF CHICKEN SOUP

1 10-1/2-ounce can condensed cream of chicken soup	2 teaspoons chopped parsley
1 soup can milk	Whipped cream
	Paprika

Follow the directions on the can of chicken soup for heating the soup and milk. Pour into individual soup cups, and sprinkle with parsley. Place a tablespoon of whipped cream and a dash of paprika on top. Serves 4.

But there is one soup, which is not a cream soup, which President Kennedy loved. It is French onion soup, as made by "Mama" Young, who is the mother of the owner of Paul Young's, the restaurant where the Presidential party ate after the inaugural ball on January 20, 1961.

Here from "Mama" Young is the soup that warmed the Presidential palate on that cold inaugural night:

PRESIDENT KENNEDY'S FAVORITE ONION SOUP

3 medium onions, finely sliced	Salt and pepper to taste
4 tablespoons butter	French bread
1 tablespoon flour	Shredded Swiss cheese
2-1/2 pints beef stock	Additional butter

Cook the onions and butter in a heavy pot. When they are browned, sprinkle with flour. Allow to brown a little longer; then add the beef stock and the salt and pepper. Cook for 15 minutes. Slice the bread 1/4-inch thick, butter lightly, and then brown in oven. Put onion soup in casserole, and put croutons on top, then a layer of Swiss cheese and a small piece of butter. Put under broiler until golden brown. Serves 6.

Now let's take a look at a favorite White House soup of years gone by:

DOLLEY MADISON'S WINE SOUP

1-1/2 pounds soup beef
Veal knuckle
Soup greens
2 medium carrots, sliced
1 medium turnip, quartered
2 medium onions, sliced

Salt to taste
1/4 teaspoon red pepper, or
  more if desired
2 quarts water
2 cups sherry

Combine all the ingredients except the sherry, and cook slowly, covered, about 5 hours. Strain and return clear liquid to pot. Cool and skim grease off top. Reheat to serve, adding sherry at last minute. Serves 8 to 10.

President Lyndon Johnson liked okra combined with dill, which he used as a relish. It was made at the LBJ Ranch and kept stocked at the White House:

LBJ'S DILLED OKRA

1 teaspoon dillseed
1 quart fresh okra, washed
1 hot green pepper (jalapeño)
1 hot red pepper

2 cloves garlic
1 quart white vinegar
1 cup water
1/2 teaspoon uniodized salt

Place 1/2 teaspoon dillseed in bottom of a 2-quart sterilized jar. Pack okra as tightly as possible in the jar, without bruising. Sprinkle remainder of the dillseed over the top, and press peppers and garlic among the okra. Bring to a boil the vinegar, water, and salt, and pour over the okra. Seal jars, and allow to stand 2 weeks. Before serving, chill in refrigerator. Makes about 2 quarts.

Fruit whips were long a favorite at the White House. Both President Franklin Roosevelt and Ike liked prune whip. This was the recipe in use at the White House kitchen:

PRESIDENTIAL PRUNE WHIP

1 cup prune puree
2 teaspoons lemon juice
1/2 envelope unflavored gelatin
1/4 cup water

4 egg whites
2/3 cup sugar
1 teaspoon vanilla
1 cup heavy cream

President Eisenhower liked this served cold. I made it with prune puree, which is simply prunes cooked, pitted, and strained.

Run the puree through the blender with the lemon juice and the gelatin, which has been dissolved in the water. When the mixture has a smooth texture, take it off the blender and add the egg whites, which have been stiffly beaten with the sugar and vanilla. Put the mixture in a round mold.

The President liked this plain with cream in a side pitcher. It is also very nice served with whipped cream decoration after it is unmolded. Serves 4.

Another variation is a *Rum Custard Topping,* made with instant vanilla pudding in which you use 1 cup milk instead of the 2 mentioned in the directions and to which you add 2 tablespoons rum and 1/2 pint whipped cream as soon as the pudding starts to thicken. The whipped cream is merely folded in lightly. If you mix too much, the topping will become too liquid.

Both President Hoover and President Jefferson liked whipped fruit desserts, but their favorite was *Apricot Whip.* I made the Hoover apricot whip once but prefer the prune whip. The apricot whip was made the same way as the Presidential Prune Whip except instead of the vanilla, season the apricots with 2 drops almond extract and 1 tablespoon grated orange rind. It is served with whipped cream sprinkled with chopped almonds.

President Truman loved ice cream, while Eisenhower was fonder of sherbets. One way that Truman enjoyed his ice cream most was as a topping on Ozark Pudding:

HARRY TRUMAN'S OZARK PUDDING

3/4 cup sugar
1 egg
1-1/2 teaspoons baking powder
2-1/2 tablespoons flour
1/4 teaspoon salt

1/2 teaspoon vanilla
1/2 cup chopped nuts
1/2 cup chopped apple
Vanilla ice cream

Combine sugar and egg, and beat until creamy. Mix the baking powder, flour, and salt, and stir into the egg mixture. Finally add the vanilla, nuts, and apple. Bake in a medium oven (350°) for 30 minutes. Serve hot or cold with ice-cream topping. Serves 6.

Pound cake has always been a favorite at the White House. In the days when Dolley Madison was Jefferson's hostess, she served his favorite pound cake and wine when guests came to call. It is interesting to compare Jefferson's pound cake with that of Mrs. Truman:

JEFFERSON'S POUND CAKE

1 pound butter
1 pound powdered sugar
12 eggs, separated
1/2 teaspoon nutmeg

1/4 cup grated lemon peel
1/2 cup brandy
1 pound flour

Cream the butter and sugar; add the egg yolks, nutmeg, lemon peel, and brandy. To this mixture add, alternately, the flour and stiffly beaten egg whites.
Bake in oven at 350° for about 1 hour.

MRS. TRUMAN'S POUND CAKE

1 pound butter
1 pound sugar
9 eggs, separated

1 teaspoon lemon extract
1 pound flour

Cream the butter and sugar. Add egg yolks, lemon extract, and flour. Finally add stiffly beaten egg whites. Bake at 325° for about 1 hour.

Homemade ice cream is practically a lost art, but the Lyndon Johnsons single-handedly—their cook Zephyr's hand—revived it with a flavor they made famous by their love of it. That was peach ice cream made with Texas fruit:

LBJ PEACH ICE CREAM

3 eggs
1 cup sugar
1 quart heavy cream
1 pint milk

1 tablespoon vanilla
1/2 gallon peaches (or
   strawberries, etc.), mashed
   with sugar to sweeten

Beat eggs and sugar. Add cream and milk. Cook over low flame until it boils. Cool. Add fruit. Chill before freezing in electric or hand-turned freezer. Makes 1 gallon. Serves 20.

It was as exciting as solving a puzzle to discover the likes and dislikes of the First Family so that I could slant my cooking to their tastes. Some people like to gossip about reputations. I like to gossip about food.

I loved the thought as I fixed gingerbread for President Eisenhower, which he liked with applesauce, that Dolley Madison made it, too, and used powdered sugar instead.

MRS. EISENHOWER'S GINGERBREAD WITH APPLESAUCE

1/4 cup butter
1/4 cup lard
1/2 cup sugar
1 egg, beaten
1 cup dark molasses
2-1/2 cups flour

1-1/2 teaspoons baking soda
1/2 teaspoon salt
1/2 teaspoon ground cloves
1 teaspoon ginger
1 teaspoon cinnamon
1 cup hot water

Cream the butter, lard, and sugar. Then add the egg, followed by the molasses. The dry ingredients—flour, soda, salt, cloves, ginger, cinnamon—are then added, and finally the hot water. Beat in an electric mixer for several minutes, pour into buttered baking dish, and bake in a slow oven (325°) for 30 minutes.

APPLESAUCE TOPPING FOR GINGERBREAD

8 tart apples
Juice of 1 lemon

2 drops red vegetable coloring

Peel apples, and cut into little pieces. Put in a saucepan, and add the lemon juice. Cover and simmer until apples are soft, but be careful not to let the apples burn. Then pass through a sieve. Add red vegetable coloring, and you are ready to serve it as a topping to the gingerbread. You will notice that there is no sugar. At the White House we did not add sugar, but you can do so if you want to.

MRS. MADISON'S GINGERBREAD WITH POWDERED SUGAR

1 cup molasses	2-1/4 cups flour
2/3 cup beef drippings	4 teaspoons ginger
1-1/4 teaspoons baking soda	1 tablespoon cinnamon
1/4 cup hot water	3/4 cup almost boiling water

Combine the molasses, the beef drippings, and the soda, which has been dissolved in the hot water. Then sift the flour with the ginger and cinnamon.

Pour the almost boiling water into the liquid mixture, and beat in the flour mixture. It would be "cheating" on history to use an electric mixer, since the "elbow grease" of a slave was the only laborsaving invention of the time, so round up a couple of slaves to help you beat the batter and take turns for about 10 or more minutes. Time will move very slowly.

Bake in greased baking dish for 30 minutes, or until a straw from a broomstick comes out clean. You would really need a wood-burning stove to do this recipe justice so that you could have an uneven temperature for its baking. But if you want to "hedge" a little on history, you can try 350°. I must admit I "hedged" plenty when I made it at the White House and used 1/2 cup lard for "drippings."

I wonder if President Lincoln ever tasted Dolley Madison's recipe for gingerbread. He liked cakes and cookies heavily seasoned with ginger.

Carl Sandburg quotes Lincoln telling about the time Lincoln's mother made him very happy by baking him three gingerbread men. Abe took them out of the house and went to sit under a hickory tree to enjoy them. Along came a boy poorer than he and said, "Abe, gimme a man?"

Abe gave him one and settled down to eat his second gingerbread man slowly in order to savor it. But the other boy crammed his gingerbread in his mouth and, finishing it in two bites, demanded another.

Abe reluctantly passed it over, saying, "You seem to like gingerbread."

"Abe," said the greedy boy, "I don't s'pose anybody on earth likes gingerbread better'n I do—and gets less'n I do." Which was certainly the case with poor Abe, too.

So when Lincoln's birthday rolls around again, why don't you bake some gingerbread men or ginger cake in his memory?

If it wasn't ginger-flavored, Abe wanted fruit flavors. Lincoln's fondness for fruit was also shared by FDR, who liked berries, fresh or in pie. Lincoln often annoyed his wife by asking for only a fruit salad when she had planned an elaborate meal.

Even when it came to cake, Lincoln's favorite was one which had the flavor of fruit in the icing:

LINCOLN'S ALMOND CAKE

1/2 pound butter	1 cup chopped blanched almonds
2-1/4 cups sugar	1-1/2 teaspoons vanilla
3 cups flour	1/2 teaspoon salt
2-1/2 teaspoons baking powder	6 egg whites
1 cup milk	

Cream the butter and sugar. Then sift together the flour and baking powder. Add this to first mixture, alternating with the milk, in small amounts at a time. Now add the almonds and vanilla. Add the salt to the egg whites, beat them very stiff, and fold them into the mixture. Bake in three cake pans in moderate oven.

LINCOLN'S CANDIED FRUIT ICING

2 cups sugar	1/2 cup chopped candied cherries
1 cup water	
4 egg whites, stiffly beaten	1/2 cup chopped candied pineapple
1 teaspoon vanilla	

Boil the sugar and water over a low flame until syrup spins a thread. Then pour very slowly into the egg whites. Beat mixture until smooth and almost stiff enough to spread. Add the vanilla, cherries, and pineapple. Spread between layers and on cake.

It seems as if every President and his Lady had a specialty they particularly liked.

Many have heard about Lady Bird Johnson's favorite chocolate cake, the one that was served German Chancellor Ludwig Erhard when he visited the LBJ Ranch. It was a very appropriate cake to serve:

LADY BIRD'S TEXAS GERMAN CHOCOLATE CAKE

1 cup butter or margarine	1 teaspoon vanilla
2 cups sugar	2-1/2 cups sifted cake flour
4 egg yolks	1 teaspoon baking soda
4 ounces German sweet	1/2 teaspoon salt
chocolate	1 cup buttermilk
1/2 cup boiling water	4 egg whites, stiffly beaten

Cream butter and sugar until light and fluffy; then add egg yolks, one at a time, beating after each. Melt chocolate in boiling water, and cool; then add it and vanilla to creamed mixture, stirring well. Sift flour, soda, and salt, and add alternately with buttermilk to the mixture, beating until smooth. Fold in egg whites, and pour into three deep 8- or 9-inch cake pans. Bake at 350° for 30 minutes or more, until inserted toothpick comes out clean.

With it goes a lovely coconut pecan frosting:

LADY BIRD'S COCONUT PECAN FROSTING

1 cup evaporated milk	1/2 cup butter or margarine
3 egg yolks	1 teaspoon vanilla
1 cup sugar	1-1/2 cups flaked coconut
1 cup chopped pecans	

Mix together milk, egg yolks, sugar, butter, and vanilla. Cook, stirring constantly, until thickened—10 to 12 minutes. Add coconut and pecans, and beat until thick enough to spread. Makes 2-1/2 cups.

Truman liked buttermilk, just as Nixon does. And both FDR and Kennedy shared an interest in that great American institution, the hot dog.

FDR hated coconut, and Harry Truman would rather not eat salads.

Many of the Presidents were nibblers. Coolidge, who looked undernourished, constantly nibbled nuts between meals. So did Franklin Roosevelt and Truman. Kennedy kept a bowl of fruit—mostly apples and grapes—in his office for between-meal snacks.

When Dolley Madison wanted to please her husband, she served a round of beef with a rich garlic gravy and boiled cabbage. This was followed by ham with more boiled cabbage. For dessert, her husband liked an upside-down apple cake made with heavily spiced apples and brown sugar. Just like the average American husband, most of our Presidents have liked apple pie. FDR liked his made with especially tart apples. Eisenhower liked a deep-dish apple pie made from his wife's recipe or a variation of apple pie with a sharp cheese lining:

MAMIE EISENHOWER'S DEEP-DISH APPLE PIE

12 large tart apples, pared and thinly sliced
2/3 cup sugar
2-1/2 tablespoons lemon juice

1/4 teaspoon nutmeg
Pinch of cinnamon
4 tablespoons butter, melted
Piecrust

Season the apple slices with sugar, lemon juice, nutmeg, and cinnamon. Add the butter, and pour into a deep 8-inch Pyrex dish. Cover with regular piecrust, and bake in a 350° oven for 45 minutes.

The First Family liked their deep-dish apple pie served warm with a pitcher of cream on the side.

Once I tried to make a different topping for the deep-dish pie—the fancier French puff paste basted with egg yolk—but the word from the First Lady was that she preferred the American-style piecrust.

APPLE PIE WITH SHARP CHEESE LINING

Standard two-crust pie dough for 9-inch pan
2/3 cup sharp American cheese, coarsely grated
8 medium tart apples, peeled and sliced

2/3 cup light brown sugar
1/2 teaspoon lemon rind
Pinch of salt
1 tablespoon melted butter

Make the standard pie dough, and line a 9-inch pan. Spread the cheese on the piecrust. Then on top of this pour the filling, which consists of apples, sugar, lemon rind, salt, and butter. The apples will provide their own moisture. Bake with top crust, starting with a 400° oven for 10 minutes and reducing to 350° for about 40 minutes.

President Nixon relishes lime flavor. In fact, the President's favorite pie is Key lime pie as made by Chef Erwin Andraeas, of the Key Biscayne Hotel.

After the President won the Republican nomination in 1968, he held a
luncheon at the hotel, at which the chef served this special treat:

PRESIDENT NIXON'S FAVORITE
KEY LIME PIE

1 can sweetened condensed milk	1 baked pie shell
3 egg yolks	1/2 pint heavy cream
2-1/2 ounces lime juice	1 teaspoon sugar

Blend the condensed milk and egg yolks on low speed until well mixed.
Add the lime juice, and blend just enough to combine the juice with the
egg and milk mixture.

Pour into pie shell, and place in the refrigerator.

Beat cream with sugar until whipped, and pile it on the pie. Serve after
pie has been refrigerated for 2 hours.

4

$\gg\gg\gg\gg\lll\lll$

BREAKFAST WITH THE PRESIDENTS

I have always thought it would be fun to breakfast with each President. If you had breakfast with Calvin Coolidge, you might find him having a haircut while he ate. It was his way of not wasting a minute's time.

I love the story about the man who was invited to the White House three times under three different Presidents—McKinley, Theodore Roosevelt, and Taft. Twice it was for lunch and once for breakfast, and each time he was served the same thing—corned beef hash. If he had come during the Eisenhower years when I was cooking at the White House, he would probably have had hash again—but this time quail hash.

President Nixon is an up-and-at-it man who needs a hearty breakfast when he is on the go. His breakfast at such times is:

PRESIDENT NIXON'S HIGH-ENERGY BREAKFAST

Orange Juice
Cold Wheat Cereal
Sweet Roll
Glass of Milk   and   Cup of Coffee

Actually, by the time the President has had this breakfast, he has already worked off some of the calories, running in place in his bedroom for at least a 300 count.

A Sunday breakfast innovation of the Nixons is to hold Sunday services at the White House and invite all the worshipers for a small breakfast with them. This is a stand-up brunch served in the State Dining Room, where the long tables are set up with orange juice, sweet rolls, blueberry muffins, brioche, and coffee.

Before I tell you how to make blueberry muffins and the Sunday Service Brioche, from the Nixons' own recipes, let me tell you what it is like at the Sunday morning White House worship services.

67

Let's take January 24, 1971, as a typical Sunday service. Each time a minister from a different denomination is invited to conduct the service, but this time the minister was a Quaker, like the President. He was T. Eugene Coffin, minister of the East Whittier Friends Church in Whittier, California, the President's boyhood home.

The service was held in the East Room, and afterward, over coffee and blueberry muffins, Ethel Waters, who was guest soloist, reminisced with the President's guests about her days on Broadway.

The day she sang, there were approximately 280 guests, including White House personnel, the Nixon family, Cabinet officers, dozens of Congressional leaders and their families, and even some members of the diplomatic corps.

Now for those White House recipes:

NIXON'S SUNDAY SERVICE BRIOCHE

1 package yeast	1 cup soft butter
Lukewarm water	1 teaspoon salt
2 to 3 tablespoons sugar	7 eggs
Approximately 4 cups sifted flour	1/2 cup milk, scalded and cooled

Soften yeast in 1/3 cup lukewarm water. Add 1 teaspoon sugar and 1 cup flour. Mix and then knead until smooth. Put ball of dough in a bowl, and cover with lukewarm water. Let rise until ball floats in water, about 1 hour or less.

Put remaining flour in a large bowl. Add the ball of dough, half the butter, remaining sugar, salt, and 2 eggs, slightly beaten. Mix well with hands, adding enough milk to give a soft, nonsticky dough. Turn out onto a lightly floured board, and knead until smooth. Work in the remaining butter and 2 more eggs. Repeat the kneading. Lift the dough, and slap or bang it on the table until it is very smooth. Add 2 more eggs, work them into the dough, and repeat the kneading and banging on the table. Shape the dough into a ball, and place it in a greased bowl. Cover and let rise in a warm place (80° to 85°F) until double in bulk. Punch and stir the dough down. Shape into a ball; place in a greased clean bowl. Cover tightly with foil, and chill overnight or slightly longer.

To shape the brioche, turn the dough out onto a floured board. Cut off about a sixth, and reserve for topknots of buns. Divide remainder of the dough into twenty portions, and shape each into a ball. Place in greased brioche pans or muffin tins.

Cut reserved dough into the same number of small balls. Dampen a finger slightly, and make a depression in the center of each large ball. Place a small ball in each of the depressions. Cover and let rise in a warm place until double in bulk, or about 1 hour.

Preheat oven to 450°, and place rack near bottom. Lightly beat remaining egg, and brush over the tops of the brioche. Place in oven, and bake until well browned, about 15 minutes. Makes 20.

CHEF HALLER'S SUNDAY BLUEBERRY MUFFINS

2 cups sifted flour
2 tablespoons sugar
2-1/2 teaspoons baking powder
1/2 teaspoon salt
1 egg, well beaten

1 cup milk
1/4 cup butter, melted and
  cooled slightly
3/4 cup whole fresh blueberries

Preheat oven to 400°.

Sift together the flour, sugar, baking powder, and salt. Mix the egg, milk, and butter. Add the liquid mixture to the dry ingredients, and stir only until the flour is moistened. Do not beat the batter until smooth. Add the blueberries (if frozen, thaw and drain). Spoon into well-greased muffin tins, filling the cups about two-thirds full. Bake about 25 minutes, and serve immediately. Makes 20 to 24 two-inch muffins.

Breakfasts have been a festive time at the White House in the past, too. When Nellie Grant, the daughter of President U. S. Grant, was married to the Britisher Algernon Sartoris, the President entertained at a wedding breakfast at which the menu featured woodcocks and snipes on toast.

Coolidge gave stag breakfasts for his Cabinet and other guests, a combination of entertainment and work or briefings. The menu usually was buckwheat cakes and Vermont maple syrup.

Herbert Hoover also gave stag breakfasts, and often Mrs. Hoover had a separate breakfast for some of their wives. Lou Hoover's favorite breakfast was soufflé.

President Eisenhower thought cornmeal pancakes were a real breakfast treat, smothered with maple syrup or light molasses.

One of the strangest of his favorite foods, I thought, was quail hash. I had never heard of it before. Ike liked it for breakfast, dinner, or lunch. Actually, I don't know why it is called hash, because it has no potatoes:

PRESIDENT EISENHOWER'S QUAIL HASH

1 Quail for each serving	1 teaspoon salt
1 onion, quartered	1/4 teaspoon freshly ground
1 carrot, sliced	pepper
2 stalks celery, sliced	2 teaspoons sherry
1 bay leaf	Toast
1 pinch thyme	Chopped parsley

Use 1 quail per serving, and if they are small, then 1-1/2 per serving. For 4 servings, cover the meat with water in which you have placed the onion, carrot, celery, bay leaf, thyme, salt, and pepper. Boil over a medium flame for 40 minutes, or until tender. Bone the quail, and slice the meat julienne. Make a light cream sauce, using the quail stock and adding the sherry.

Add the quail to the sauce, and serve on toast. Top with parsley. Whether it rightfully deserves the name of hash or should be called creamed quail, I can't say, but I can report that it is delicious.

Ike was also fond of corned beef hash, which I used to make a trifle more interesting by baking in the oven:

PRESIDENTIAL CORNED BEEF HASH

1 medium onion, chopped	2 tablespoons green sweet
3 tablespoons melted butter	pepper, chopped fine
2 cups coarsely diced corned beef	1 tablespoon red pimento,
2-1/2 cups diced cold boiled	chopped
potatoes	Poached eggs
Salt and pepper to taste	

Sauté the onion in the butter. Then combine with the corned beef, potatoes, salt, pepper, sweet pepper, and pimento. Spread evenly in a heavy baking dish or casserole or heavy iron frying pan.

Bake in a hot 400° oven for 25 minutes, and top with poached eggs just before it goes to the table. It makes a really colorful dish with its bits of red and green against the yellow and white of the eggs. Serves 4.

But the Eisenhower breakfasts that intrigue me most were the ones he had when his brother, Dr. Milton, visited him. Then they shared a breakfast which was one of their favorite foods when they were growing up in Abilene, Kansas—fried mush. With it they would have prunes, sausage, and whole wheat toast.

Much has been made of "Lemonade Lucy" Hayes, who served no hard liquor at the White House during her term as First Lady. But her abstinence went to other things as well. She served only one cup of coffee to her husband at breakfast.

President William Howard Taft, the fattest President to date—330 pounds—had a steak for breakfast almost daily.

William McKinley liked a cornmeal pancake called johnnycake, in which cornmeal is substituted for half the flour of a pancake recipe and sour milk is used instead of sweet milk. But like regular pancakes, johnnycakes are served with maple syrup.

The John Kennedys often took their breakfast together, but on separate trays with separate menus. Jackie's tray was in keeping with her constant diet: toast with honey, orange juice, coffee with skimmed milk.

Breakfast with President Kennedy was very different from the steak breakfasts of Eisenhower. It consisted of orange juice, bacon and eggs, and one—only one—cup of coffee. The eggs were normally poached in a mold. His breakfast treat for special occasions was waffles:

JOHN F. KENNEDY'S WAFFLES

1 tablespoon sugar	7/8 cup milk or 1 cup buttermilk
1/2 cup butter	1/4 teaspoon salt
2 egg yolks	2 egg whites, stiffly beaten
1 cup and 1 tablespoon sifted cake flour	4 teaspoons baking powder

Cream the sugar and butter. Add the egg yolks and beat. Then add the flour and milk alternately. This mixture may be kept in the refrigerator until you are ready to use it. When you are ready to bake it, fold in the egg whites, and add the baking powder and salt. Bake on a waffle iron. Serves 3.

President Kennedy liked melted butter and maple syrup on his waffles.

Our first President, like our thirty-fifth, preferred waffles to anything else for breakfast. Washington's were unusual in that they were made with rice and served with a combination of honey and maple syrup:

GEORGE WASHINGTON'S RICE WAFFLES

1 cup flour
2 teaspoons baking powder
2 tablespoons sugar
3/4 teaspoon salt
1 cup milk

2 egg yolks, beaten
2 tablespoons melted butter
1 cup boiled rice
2 egg whites, stiffly beaten

Combine the flour, baking powder, sugar, and salt. Then add the milk, egg yolks, butter, and rice. Carefully fold in the egg whites, and your waffles are ready for the waffle iron. Serves 4.

HONEY-MAPLE SAUCE

1/2 cup honey
1/2 cup maple syrup

1/2 teaspoon caraway seeds
1-1/2 teaspoons cinnamon

Mix the ingredients well, and heat before serving.

I love a description of George Washington at breakfast after his retirement to Mount Vernon. In "A Visit to Mount Vernon in 1798," Washington's friend, J. U. Niemcewicz, tells about Washington's early morning: "He rises at five in the morning, and reads or writes until seven. He takes his breakfast-tea with a cake of Indian corn (because of his teeth), cutting it in slices, which he covers with butter and honey." Then, Niemcewicz says, Washington would get on his horse and "see the work in the fields."

Another account of a George Washington breakfast, when he was President in Philadelphia and tending to business while eating, lists a menu of sliced tongue, toast and butter, coffee and tea.

Like the Father of Our Country, Franklin D. Roosevelt also liked a rice delicacy for breakfast, but as pancakes rather than waffles:

FDR'S FAVORITE RICE PANCAKES

1 egg yolk, beaten
1 cup milk
1/2 cup flour
2 tablespoons melted butter
Additional 1/4 cup flour

1-3/4 teaspoons baking powder
1/2 teaspoon salt
1/2 cup cooked rice
1 egg white, stiffly beaten

Add egg yolk to milk, beating well. Next beat in the 1/2 cup flour. Add melted butter. Sift the additional flour with the baking powder and salt, and add to mixture. Now fold in the rice and the egg white. Cook on hot griddle, turning each pancake once. Makes 12 griddlecakes.

President Roosevelt liked his rice pancakes served with hot maple syrup to which a bit of butter had been added.

In FDR's time, Churchill was a frequent guest at the White House, and he was famous for his gargantuan breakfasts. He ate in his room and started the day with a glass of sherry. Then came the food. First fruit: apples, pears, and other fruits served whole and a glass of orange juice and a large pot of tea as well. He sipped the tea as he consumed a breakfast of eggs and assorted meats, including ham and cold cuts.

Warren Harding served breakfast waffles with all kinds of fruit preserves:

PRESIDENT HARDING'S WAFFLES

2 eggs, separated	1 teaspoon salt
3 tablespoons sugar	2 cups flour
2 cups milk	1 tablespoon baking powder
2-1/2 tablespoons butter, melted	

Blend egg yolks and sugar. Combine with milk, butter, salt, and flour. Beat egg whites, adding with the baking powder just before baking.

Serve with various fruit preserves which have been heated with the addition of a little bit of butter. Makes 8 waffles.

Thomas Jefferson opted for pancakes instead of waffles. He called them "batter cakes" and liked fried apples served with them.

We know much about Thomas Jefferson's breakfasts from Daniel Webster who visited Monticello and partook of a regular breakfast feast—fried apples, bacon and eggs, hot breads with cold meats, and "batter cakes," which were kept coming as long as the guests could eat.

The pan or "batter" cakes were served with fried apples.

Like Jefferson, President Ulysses S. Grant also liked fried apples for breakfast. But strangely enough he liked his served with fish or steak. FDR would have joined him in enjoying broiled fish for breakfast.

Lyndon Johnson could never seem to get enough of one breakfast dish—creamed chip beef on toast. Even when he was on a strict diet, he insisted on having it, and the dietitians finally came up with a modified recipe made with skimmed milk and a bouillon cube and served on dietetic bread.

President Andrew Johnson liked the most hearty flapjacks of all—buckwheat mixed with cornmeal:

PRESIDENT ANDREW JOHNSON'S BUCKWHEAT CAKES

1 cup buckwheat flour	2 teaspoons dark molasses
1 tablespoon yeast	Enough warm water to make a
1/4 teaspoon salt	thin batter
1/4 cup coarse cornmeal	

Make a thin batter of all ingredients, beat well, and set aside in a warm place to rise—preferably overnight.

Pour the pancakes on a very hot griddle, turn once, and serve with hot molasses or maple syrup mixed with butter. Makes 12 flapjacks or pancakes.

Lyndon Johnson's favorite breakfast was one on which he dined almost every Sunday:

PRESIDENT AND MRS. LYNDON JOHNSON'S
FAVORITE BREAKFAST

Chilled Melon

Deer Meat Sausage   Scrambled Eggs
Hominy Grits

Hot Biscuits

Coffee

To make the Deer Meat Sausage the Johnson way—baked—see Index.

Harry S. Truman's breakfast turned thumbs down on eggs, waffles, or pancakes for breakfast. Instead, he called for hot oatmeal with brown sugar, orange juice, whole wheat toast, and milk.

The President who intrigued me most, breakfast-wise, was Coolidge. And not just because he had that haircut while eating or because he did a lot of official entertaining at breakfasts, because it was less expensive than serving lunch or dinner.

No. The thing that intrigues me most is Coolidge's favorite breakfast:

PRESIDENT COOLIDGE'S FAVORITE BREAKFAST

Melon
Coolidge Formula Cereal
Bacon
Coffee

The cereal is the surprise. Calvin Coolidge had it specially mixed for him—2 cups of whole wheat grain to each cup of whole kernel rye. This unusual concoction was then cooked slowly in a double boiler until the wheat started to pop out of the jackets—at least three hours. Then it was served with sugar and milk.

Mrs. Coolidge did not share his health-kick breakfast. Instead she nibbled a doughnut with her morning coffee. Calvin Coolidge also liked buckwheat pancakes, which he considered more healthful than other kinds. He would tease the family cook about them, saying, "Katherine, I couldn't eat more than a half dozen of your pancakes this morning, but keep trying. You'll be a good cook, yet."

President Cleveland frequently breakfasted on lamb chops, toast, and coffee. Steak was his second breakfast choice.

President Chester Arthur enjoyed a Continental breakfast as he dressed—coffee and croissant with a bit of cheese.

Herbert Hoover liked his breakfast ham best encased in an omelet:

PRESIDENT HOOVER'S HAM OMELET

3 eggs	2 tablespoons minced ham,
1 cup diced ham, heated in	heated in butter
butter	Salt and pepper to taste

Beat eggs, and bake in hot oven for a few minutes until done. Then pour the diced ham in the center of the omelet, and fold it over. Pour the minced ham over the top to garnish, and serve.

FDR started his day with a large breakfast, such as scrambled eggs and kippers. But, like Jefferson, his favorite breakfast dish was wheat cakes with maple syrup. Sometimes he varied this with fried cornmeal mush drenched with maple syrup.

President Monroe's favorite breakfast dish was eggs baked with tomatoes, and it's my favorite, too:

BAKED TOMATOES AND EGGS À LA MONROE

1 unpeeled tomato	2 teaspoons grated cheese
Salt and pepper to taste	2 pats butter
2 eggs	2 rounds of toast

Cut the tomato in half, and scoop out some of the center part of each half, to make a little nest. Sprinkle with salt and pepper. Drop one egg gently on each half. Sprinkle the eggs with salt and pepper and grated cheese. Put a pat of butter on each egg, and bake in the oven until the eggs are done. Serve on rounds of toast.

5

->>>->>><<<-<<<-

IT WAS FUN COOKING AT THE
WHITE HOUSE

Mamie Eisenhower seldom set foot in the White House kitchens.

Jacqueline Kennedy stayed out of the kitchen, too, but used the phone for frequent communication with chef René Verdon, whom she lured away from the Essex House in New York to cook for the White House. She was wise to do so because Chef René was in the best tradition of great French chefs.

As I said, Jackie Kennedy didn't physically enter the kitchen but after each State Dinner she would fire a volley of memos to the staff and housekeeping department telling what was good and what was bad about the dinner and the appearance of the rooms.

Pat Nixon follows in the tradition of Dolley Madison. She loves to visit and chat with Chef Henri Haller, another fine French chef brought to the White House by the Johnsons and continuing with President Nixon.

Mrs. Nixon even posed for photos with Chef Haller, and I am pleased to have some of those pictures.

I wish that I could have a picture of Dolley Madison in the old fireplace-equipped kitchens of the White House. It was said no one could keep Dolley out of there because she wanted to make sure that only the best was served her guests. Dolley Madison's reputation for setting a fine table rested on the ability of her steward, whom all the staff called "French John."

Jefferson was said to closet himself for hours with his French chef, Etienne Lemaire, discussing menus and techniques of cooking various foods. Many Presidents, even though they had family cooks for family dining, employed French chefs for their formal entertainment.

Andy Jackson, for example, was thought to be a "plain feeder" because he had been a frontiersman and soldier. But actually he went in for fine foods and had a French chef named Michael Anthony Guista.

President Chester Arthur sent for a French chef from New York when he needed a state dinner prepared.

I always enjoyed it when President Eisenhower would come into the kitchen and discuss cooking. He told me about learning to cook when he was one of several boys, with no girls to help their mother in the kitchen. Two boys would be left behind on Sundays to cook the Sunday dinner while the rest of the family went to church.

Bess Truman was the closest to "home folks" in the White House in recent years. She is the only First Lady I know of who actually took guests into the kitchen—the ladies of her Spanish class—and let them help her cook a typically Mexican dish, as part of a Spanish lesson. The dish they made was Picadillo:

PICADILLO

1 pound lean ground round
1 onion, chopped
3 tablespoons oil
2 tablespoons vinegar
3 tomatoes or 1-1/2 cups canned
  tomatoes
Pinch of ground cloves
1/4 teaspoon ground cumin,
  optional
1 teaspoon sugar
3/4 teaspoon cinnamon
2 teaspoons seasoned salt
1 4-ounce can green chile
  peppers, drained

1/2 cup seedless raisins, soaked
  in 1/4 cup hot broth or
  water
1 can whole kernel corn, drained
1/2 package Taco seasoning mix
1/4 cup slivered blanched
  almonds
1 small can pitted ripe olives, cut
  up
1 pound grated Cheddar cheese
1/2 package (11 ounces) king-
  size corn chips
Crisp lettuce

Brown meat and onion in oil. Add all remaining ingredients except almonds, olives, cheese, and corn chips. Heat to boiling; reduce heat, and simmer 30 to 45 minutes. Stir in almonds and olives.

To serve, in a buttered medium casserole, layer corn chips, picadillo mixture, and cheese, ending with cheese. Bake 45 minutes at 375°, covering casserole, until cheese is bubbly.

Shred lettuce over the top, and serve with hot buttered tortillas. Serves 8.

I could go on and on with a thousand recipes, but you will still not feel that you are living at the White House unless you work with me over some typical menus. Then you can begin to live it as I did.

So come with me into the shiny, all-stainless-steel kitchen of the White

House, and let's get started. You'll find everything is very convenient to use.

Notice that electric stove with its many burners and built-in griddle. Those are the ovens next to the stove standing three ovens high, which supplement the three ovens in the stove. We needed them. If I were baking cookies or cakes, it could easily be for a hundred people. On both sides of the stove are the broilers, and that is a steamer beside the griddle on the left.

In that steamer we could steam 40 or 50 lobsters at a time or 5 or 6 hams. Notice that row of "machinery" on that table in the center of the room parallel to the warming table.

That big electric mixer is for 40 quarts, and its little brother holds 20 quarts. The little—home-size—electric mixer is over there near the baking area for convenience.

You may be interested in the slicing machine in the lineup on the long table. I used it for julienne vegetables or coleslaw as well as for slicing hams or any kind of meat. No job is too big or too small for it. The meat grinder sits beside it, and I made my own hamburger and bread crumbs and used it for a million-and-one things. Next to it is the chopper. Finally there is the coffee grinder—we always used freshly ground coffee.

The big electric saw for cutting frozen meat sits in the corner and is mounted on wheels so that it can be rolled out for cleaning.

Next to the kitchen are two freezers and two immense refrigerators, each with six compartments. There are three storerooms to keep the supplies and a special refrigerated room in which we kept vegetables and fruit, then three deep-freeze rooms for meats and frozen vegetables.

While I slip on my white jacket and chef's "top hat," would you care to glance ahead to study a sample menu and recipes from my notebook?

For example, this one which has special significance because of the soup:

Cream of Smoked Turkey Soup
Croutons

Veal Cutlet Viennese
Rice
Chopped Spinach

Parisienne Flower Pot
Cookies

You may not realize it, but a First Lady must be a good manager. Just like millions of housewives across the country, she must know what to do with the leftovers.

We had had a little aides' party once at which I had served smoked turkey. And so, on the menu a few days later appeared Mrs. Eisenhower's suggestion of smoked turkey soup. I made enough of this for two meals and was delighted when the First Lady wanted a repeat of it two days later.

SMOKED TURKEY SOUP

Bones and leftovers of turkey	1 tablespoon farina, or *roux* of 1
3 onions, sliced	tablespoon butter and 1
4 stalks celery, cut up	tablespoon of flour
A bit of garlic	1 egg, beaten
3 carrots, sliced	Chopped parsley
2 quarts water	

Boil the bones and leftovers of turkey with onion, celery, garlic, and carrots in the water. When the vegetables are well cooked, strain the mixture, discarding the vegetables. Put the clear liquid back on the stove, add farina, and cook 5 minutes. Then, just before taking the soup off the stove, add the egg, beating vigorously with a wire beater as you pour it into the boiling soup, so that there are tiny yellow curds in the mixture. Serve the soup with a pinch of parsley.

If you want, you may leave out the farina and make creamed smoked turkey soup by adding a little *roux* of butter and flour, first blending it with a bit of stock from the turkey before adding it to the soup. Serves 6 to 8.

The soup goes well with the veal cutlet I served at the White House:

VEAL CUTLET VIENNESE

2 large thin slices veal	Bread crumbs
Salt and pepper to taste	Melted butter
Flour	4 lemon wedges
1 egg, beaten	

Pound the slices of veal, and cut them into smaller pieces. Season them with salt and pepper, and roll them first in flour, then in the egg, and finally in bread crumbs.

Fry them in melted butter until golden brown; then cover and cook slowly for 15 minutes, uncovering the last 3 minutes to let them dry. Serve them with a wedge of lemon. Serves 4.

The two vegetables were strictly American—plain rice, with just a bit of butter to keep it from sticking, and chopped spinach. With so many wonderful ways to make spinach a treat rather than a great American bugaboo, I determined to introduce my spinach soups and souffles and other recipes. After all, Rome wasn't built in a day. I couldn't try everything the first week.

The Parisienne Flower Pot is as much a matter of artwork as baking. It took me back to my student days in the province of Moravia where I went to bakery school.

There are so many amusing anecdotes about the Presidents and what they ate. The story is told about the day President Johnson had some new acquaintances as luncheon guests at the White House and offered them his favorite hamburgers.

The first guest to take a bite gasped and hurriedly reached for the water. So did the other guests right down the line. Each hamburger had been stuffed with slices of very hot jalapeno peppers by Zephyr, LBJ's family cook.

And some years before that, in the Hoover administration, another family cook had a good laugh. Katherine, who had stayed over from the Coolidge administration to take care of the Hoovers, was suddenly called on to stretch a luncheon for six to a luncheon for several dozen guests.

In a flurry of activity—she had less than one hour's notice—Katherine took the lamb chops she had laid out for the original menu and ground them up with everything else she could find in the icebox—a bit of chicken, baked ham, and sausage.

The result was croquettes, circled with rice and covered with a mushroom sauce. One of the guests was so taken by the flavor that he prevailed on the President to ask Katherine for the recipe. Katherine took a guess at the measurements and even some of the ingredients and handed over a recipe that was well named White House Surprise.

And more recently there is the story about how Chef Haller

inadvertently made the press, to his discomfort. It was when the Nixons were just moving into the White House and Traphis Bryant, the electrician of the White House, went to the airport to get the Nixon dogs.

When he got them to the White House, Bryant went to the kitchen and asked the chef to get something quickly to feed the hungry creatures. Rushed, Haller reached for the first thing he could lay hands on and fixed them a steak.

The electrician, amused, related the story to a reporter, and when the story hit the papers, Haller groaned and assured Bryant the dogs were permanently off steak, no matter what emergency might arise.

President Eisenhower, as an amateur chef, knew a lot about the lore of the White House kitchen. From him I learned that the first real cookstove to take the place of fireplace cooking, or open-fire cooking, was installed about ten years before the Civil War during the time of President Millard Fillmore. First Lady Abigail Fillmore was very suspicious of the strange contraption.

In fact, President Fillmore would be called from his office now and then over some new emergency concerning the stove, and Ike kiddingly told me not to do likewise.

I went to see the original fireplace still there, hidden away in an office on the ground floor. It is now used by the curator of the White House, Clem Conger, who appreciates its historic significance and would not have it covered up for anything. One of Conger's favorite stories is about how one day he was working in his office when the whole Presidential family came in to take a look at that historic cooking relic—Pat, Tricia, Julie, and President Nixon. "I just had to take a look at that fireplace," said the President.

Another thing I learned from the Chief was that it was Benjamin Harrison who started installing a number of so-called modern bathrooms at the White House. But they couldn't have been too modern because electricity was just beginning to be installed about then.

The Trumans used to love to come into the kitchen and poke around the pots to see what was brewing inside. They used to come in together—just browsing. I think Mrs. Truman missed the days when she had been simply a Senator's wife, free to do her own cooking in her own private kitchen.

President Zachary Taylor's wife locked herself away in the family quarters of the White House and refused to have anything to do with Washington society, so that her daughter had to act as White House hostess.

Andrew Johnson's wife did not act as his hostess either, but that was different—she was an invalid when she was in the White House—and again a daughter acted as hostess. As a chef, what intrigues me most about the Johnsons, I'm afraid, is that every morning daughter Martha would go out and milk a cow for the White House milk supply.

But the growing of livestock wasn't confined to past centuries. Calvin Coolidge once raised some chickens on the White House grounds. For that matter, James Buchanan raised grapes.

My supplies all came from the various markets, and my careful shoppers were Secret Servicemen. I actually had to keep two pantries supplied, one for the Presidential family and its entertaining and the other for state dinners and government entertaining. You can imagine how complicated that would be.

I did my own meat cutting for the most part. I would cut up a whole lamb or a veal or a side of beef.

I cut beefsteaks the way Ike liked them best—1-1/2 to 2 inches. Steak was definitely his favorite meat. We had it five times the first month I was at the White House, and the President had not taken all his meals there.

On my sixth day at the White House, I found a challenge I had been waiting for—beef stew.

I had heard all about the President's wonderful beef stew, as who hadn't? So I decided to serve the Hungarian version—a goulash. I thought the meal went off rather well, but the next morning Charles, the food butler, returned from his menu session to make a strange accusation: "You must have used onions in the stew last night!"

"Of course I used onions," I said. "What is a stew or goulash without onions?"

"Well, I'm afraid you have to find out what it is, because the First Lady had trouble sleeping last night. Onions do not agree with her."

Now he told me.

Charles also made another revelation. The First Lady did not care for garlic. Fortunately I had not had much occasion as yet to use it, except for the goulash which caused her discomfort, so I discarded it from any recipe. Furthermore, I never tried to substitute things like goulash for stew on the menu again. I set about developing my own beef stew recipe.

Here are the two stews—Beef Stew Rysavy and Beef Stew Eisenhower. I am leaving the onion and garlic in both, but if you, like the First Lady, do not care for those particular seasonings, just strike them out.

BEEF STEW RYSAVY

2 pounds cubed shank of beef	6 carrots
3 tablespoons lard	18 small white onions
3 chopped medium or large	6 potatoes
onions	4 stalks celery, cut into 1-inch
Salt and pepper to taste	lengths
1/2 teaspoon celery salt	1 tablespoon flour
1 clove garlic, crushed	Additional 1/2 cup consommé
2 cans beef consommé	1/2 cup fresh peas
1 bay leaf	Chopped parsley
1/2 teaspoon thyme	

Brown the beef in the lard. Shank is the cheapest part of the beef, yet is the best meat for a stew because it gives a stew the best flavor. It has to be cooked longer than sirloin or round. When it is brown, take it out of the pan, and sauté the onions; add salt and pepper. When the onions begin to be golden, put your meat back, and add seasonings: salt and pepper, celery salt, garlic. Add the 2 cans consommé, bay leaf, and thyme. Let simmer.

If the juices diminish too much, add more consommé.

While it is cooking, make 24 carrot shapes from any size carrots—about the size of large olives—and add the white onions. Start them cooking together in salted water. Then do the same with potatoes that you did with the carrots, making uniform little potatoes with a scoop knife, sometimes called a melon-ball scoop, and cook these, too, separately with the celery. By cooking the vegetables in this manner, you have better control of the appearance of your stew, and nothing will have that broken, mashed look.

When the meat is almost done—in about 1-1/2 to 2 hours—add a tablespoon flour with consommé, straining it into the stew to be sure there are no lumps. Add the raw peas, and cook 5 minutes. Now add all the vegetables which you have cooked separately, being careful when stirring the stew not to break them. Barely simmer for a few minutes until the peas are done. Your stew is ready to serve. Sprinkle chopped parsley on top of the stew after it is in the serving dish. Serves 6.

BEEF STEW EISENHOWER

2 pounds sirloin, top or round,
  cut into 1-1/2-inch cubes
2 tablespoons shortening or
  butter
1-1/2 cans bouillon
1-1/2 cans water
2 peppercorns
1 bay leaf
3 whole cloves
1/2 teaspoon thyme

Pinch of cayenne
1 medium clove garlic, halved
6 small Irish potatoes, halved
6 small onions
1/2 bunch carrots, cut into 1-
  inch pieces
2 medium potatoes, peeled and
  cut into eighths
Flour

Brown the beef in the shortening, then add the bouillon and water, and simmer, covered, until the meat is tender. Add a bouquet garni tied loosely in cheesecloth—peppercorns, bay leaf, cloves, thyme, cayenne, and garlic. Simmer after adding vegetables until the vegetables are tender—about 30 minutes.

Remove bouquet, and drain off liquid, which is then thickened with *roux* made of 2 tablespoons flour per cup of liquid.

Blend with the stew stock, and cook, stirring constantly until thickened. Then pour this back over the meat, and simmer just a few minutes longer.

I have tasted this stew when the President made it and found it delicious. Serves 6.

But what I liked best, as I made a stew in the White House kitchens, was knowing that stew had also been made there years before for President Jefferson. And how different it was—and interesting:

THOMAS JEFFERSON'S BEEF STEW

2 pounds round of beef, cubed
1/2 pound smoked ham, cubed
2 tablespoons butter
2 cups white wine
1/2 teaspoon grated nutmeg

8 peppercorns
3 whole cloves
1-1/2 teaspoons salt
2 stalks celery, cut into 1/2-inch
  pieces

Brown meats in butter. Add wine and seasonings, and stew, covered with water, until the meat is tender. Then add the celery, and serve when the celery is done. Serves 6 or 8.

Another inexpensive foodstuff that is no stranger to the White House kitchens is plain old hamburger. It is President Nixon's favorite meat dish. (See Index for President Nixon's Meat Loaf.) It was also a favorite of the man under whom he served as Vice President.

Why don't you try both the Nixon and the Eisenhower meat loaf recipes?

PRESIDENT EISENHOWER'S MEAT LOAF

1 pound lean pork	2 teaspoons salt
1 pound beef	A little freshly ground pepper
6 slices white bread	4 hard-cooked eggs
Milk	7 or 8 strips bacon
1/4 cup heavy cream	1/2 cup beef consommé
1 egg, slightly beaten	

I use half lean pork and half beef, ground twice through the meat grinder for better texture. The second time it goes through the meat grinder add the bread, which has been soaked in milk and squeezed fairly dry. Add the cream and beaten egg, salt and pepper, and mix all together. Have the hard-cooked eggs ready.

Roll the meat loaf rather than fill a bread loaf tin. First lay 3 or 4 strips of bacon at the bottom of a baking dish big enough so that the meat will not touch its sides. Form the loaf on a double sheet of waxed paper so that you can slide it onto the pan. Put half the meat on the paper, forming the bottom half of the meat loaf, and lay the shelled hard-cooked eggs in a straight line down the middle, molding the rest of the meat loaf on top of the eggs so that the eggs inside form a line down the center.

Slide the meat loaf on top of the bacon strips; then lay 4 extra strips across the top for flavor. Around the bottom of the loaf pour the consommé, for basting. Bake at 375° for 1-1/2 hours.

It is interesting to contrast this meat loaf with the one that Martha Washington served the first President and which I fixed several times. She used cracker crumbs, which are used in the modern ham loaf, but her meat was beef only:

MARTHA WASHINGTON'S MEAT LOAF

2 pounds ground beef
3 eggs, slightly beaten
3/4 cup cracker crumbs

1 tablespoon salt
Dash of pepper

Simply combine all the ingredients, and bake.

That was of course before the day of the oven thermometer, but 375° for 1 hour should be adequate. To keep her loaf from drying out, Martha Washington basted it with melted butter. Serves 6 to 8.

I don't know what the Father of Our Country had with his meat loaf, but on Sunday, February 27, 1955, the thirty-fourth President of the United States had baked macaroni and string beans.

String beans were served plain, boiled, and buttered for family meals and usually amandine for company or state occasions.

STRING BEANS AMANDINE

Simply pour slivered almonds, which have been sautéed in butter, over cooked French-cut string beans.

BAKED MACARONI

1/2 pound elbow macaroni,
  boiled and drained
1-1/2 cups cream sauce
1-1/2 cups grated American
  cheese
Salt and pepper to taste

1 teaspoon dry mustard
Additional grated American
  cheese
Butter
Chopped parsley

Mix the macaroni, cream sauce, 1-1/2 cups cheese, salt, pepper, and mustard. Pour into casserole, and top with more cheese and butter. Bake in 400° oven for 20 minutes.

Put under the broiler for the last 2 minutes. Top with parsley, and serve. Serves 4 or 5.

A lot of corn has flowed through the White House kitchens.

No political pun intended, but corn seems always to have been a great favorite around the White House. Teddy Roosevelt had his Indian pudding. Franklin D. Roosevelt liked fried cornmeal for breakfast. James Madison liked spoon bread the way his wife, Dolley, made it with fresh corn. It was practically the same as President Eisenhower's corn pudding, but without sugar. And Hoover frequently called for cream of corn soup.

President Kennedy was fond of corn muffins, and so was an earlier President—quite unlike Mr. Kennedy in other respects—Cal Coolidge. I hope that President Kennedy tried his predecessor's favorite recipe for these muffins, for it is a very good one:

COOLIDGE'S CORN MUFFINS

2 tablespoons baking powder   1/2 cup sugar
1 cup flour   2 eggs, well beaten
2 cups cornmeal   1 cup milk

Sift the baking powder with the flour; combine with the cornmeal and sugar. Add the eggs, which have been mixed with the milk. Bake at 400° for about 25 minutes. Makes 12.

Here is a Kennedy favorite:

JFK'S HOT CHEESE CORN BREAD

2 eggs, well beaten   1 teaspoon salt
1-1/4 cups milk   1 tablespoon sugar
1/4 cup melted butter   2-1/2 teaspoons baking powder
1-1/2 cups yellow cornmeal   1/2 cup grated sharp American
3/4 cup sifted flour   cheese

Beat the eggs, milk, and melted butter. Sift together cornmeal, flour, salt, sugar, and baking powder, and add to the egg mixture. Then add the cheese, beat well, and pour into a greased shallow pan. Bake in a hot oven (400°) about 25 minutes. Serves 6.

The Rutherford Hayes family ate a lot of corn bread, too. Here is "Lemonade Lucy's" favorite recipe for it:

LUCY HAYES' CORN BREAD

4 cups cornmeal
1 teaspoon salt
2 cups milk

1 teaspoon baking soda
1 egg, well beaten
Butter

Mix cornmeal with salt, and add to the milk, which has had the soda mixed into it. Mix well, adding the egg. Pour into very hot well-buttered corn bread pan. Bake at 425° 20 to 30 minutes. Makes 24 squares.

The Eisenhower corn pudding which is strictly Southern style, follows. It was served often at the White House:

PRESIDENT EISENHOWER'S CORN PUDDING

2-1/2 cups corn (3 ears)
3 eggs, slightly beaten
2 tablespoons melted butter
1-1/2 cups scalded milk

1-1/2 teaspoons sugar
1 teaspoon salt
A little white pepper

Cut the corn off the uncooked cob. In order to eliminate the skins of the corn, first make a knife line right through the center of each row of kernels. Then carefully scrape down the lines, being careful not to take the skin along.

Blend the ingredients. Bake in a buttered Pyrex dish in a slow oven (about 325°) until done. The Pyrex dish should sit in a pan of water. Serves 6.

LBJ never tired of corn dishes and missed them when he was put on a low-calorie diet. But whenever he could have it, he liked his own special Corn Pudding with skins of kernels retained. It is a little richer than President Eisenhower's Corn Pudding, and you can take your pick which to serve. (You may also want to compare this with President Jefferson's Corn Pudding in the chapter on Jefferson.)

PRESIDENT L. B. JOHNSON'S CORN PUDDING

2 cups milk or light cream
2 cups canned corn
2 tablespoons melted butter
1 tablespoon sugar

1 teaspoon salt
1/4 teaspoon pepper
3 eggs, well beaten

Add milk, corn, butter, sugar, and seasonings to eggs. Turn into greased casserole, and bake in moderate oven for about 45 minutes, or until pudding is set. Serves 6.

And there is one final touch of corn from out of the past:

TEDDY ROOSEVELT'S INDIAN PUDDING

8 tablespoons cornmeal
6 cups milk, scalded
1/2 cup brown sugar
1/4 pound butter
1 teaspoon salt

1 teaspoon grated lemon rind
1 teaspoon ginger
1/2 pound seedless raisins
6 eggs, beaten

Combine the cornmeal with the milk. Add the sugar, butter, and salt. Let the mixture cool. Then add the lemon rind, ginger, raisins, and eggs. Bake in a buttered casserole or baking dish for 2 hours in a slow oven. Serves 10.

6

❧❧❧❦❦❦

THE NIXONS ENTERTAIN FORMALLY

Nothing is more certain than change in style of entertaining at the White House. The social world was shocked but career-burdened, hardworking Washington officials were delighted when John F. Kennedy refused to wear a white tie and made even state dinners black tie affairs. And LBJ held the line.

But now white tie and tails are a must again in Washington. President Nixon has gained a reputation as a very formal man. The Nixon style of entertaining is very dignified, very low key, with less dancing and more conversation.

President Nixon does not dance at his White House parties but invites his guests to stay and dance. Then he and Pat quietly retire to their private quarters above the formal entertainment rooms of the White House.

Jack Kennedy would dance whenever his bad back wasn't hurting too much, but President Johnson would and could dance half the night. Guests who sought to follow the protocol of not leaving before the President did would get bleary-eyed while LBJ danced on.

The Nixons maintain a high standard of cuisine in their formal entertaining. The Kennedys and Johnsons had shortened the menus to as little as four courses at times, but now the number of courses are again six or seven, just as I served in the Eisenhower administration.

Let's take a look at how the Nixons feed their guests and then compare the menus with those served chiefs of state of the same country by Nixon's predecessors. And if you like you can prepare the same meals in your own kitchen for your VIP guests.

Until the Kennedys came to the White House, formal dinners were arranged with the tables set in an E which can seat as many as 108 or 110 guests. But the Kennedys changed this because, as Jackie explained to her friends, under the rules of protocol the same people always had the same partners to the right and left of them. The Kennedys went back to President Jefferson's trick—round tables. Jefferson felt they were more democratic, and the Kennedys felt they made for more fun conversations. The Johnsons continued the practice of breaking up the room into small conversation groups with round tables. But with the Nixons the round tables are rarely used except for informal occasions.

Nor is the guest list quite the same. At one formal Kennedy dinner, JFK sat at a round table with a guest at his right who was not even related to a high-ranking official. She was simply an interesting woman, a reporter's wife.

President Richard Nixon, on the other hand, views formal dinners as work sessions as much as social occasions and sits with the male guest of honor at his right so that they can conduct business while eating.

But first for a moment, let us see what goes on backstairs at the White House when it is known that a chief of state will be arriving. The planning begins months before the visit and involves establishing what can and cannot be fed the visitor and what entertainment would please the guest of honor, as well as his host, the President.

The choice of the main course is a very delicate matter. When President Nixon entertained the Prime Minister of Great Britain and Mrs. Harold Wilson in early 1970, duck was chosen because the Prime Minister had served President Nixon duck when the President was his guest at 10 Downing Street. Also, it was different from the roast sirloin the previous President, Lyndon Johnson, had served them.

Incidentally, the rest of the menu served Harold Wilson by President Johnson was Crab Meat Chesapeake, Artichokes White House, New Potatoes, Green Salad, Ham Circles, and Strawberry Crème York. That was a larger meal than the Johnsons served on some other formal occasions. The Kennedys, incidentally, started the trend of combining the appetizer with the fish course and serving a mousse, for example, a salmon mousse, to cut out a course. The Nixons have followed suit in practically eliminating soup as a first course.

(In this chapter, since I am no longer at the White House, and since I did not get the recipes from Chef Haller as I did for the Jackie Kennedy Onassis dinner described in the first chapter, I will tell you how I would prepare these state dinners if I *were* still chef there. But let me assure you, French cooking is still French cooking whether learned in Swiss schools as Henri Haller learned it, or as I learned it as a rolling stone all over the world.

(I went back to the White House to visit with Haller in the kitchens not too long ago and had a delightful time exchanging reminiscences with him.

The main thing I learned is that not too much changes in the kitchens of the White House.)

Now first, let's take a look at a menu that features duck. Let's see how President Nixon ordered duck prepared when he hosted a formal dinner for the President of Colombia:

FORMAL DINNER IN HONOR OF THE PRESIDENT
OF THE
REPUBLIC OF COLOMBIA, HIS EXCELLENCY
CARLOS LLERAS RESTREPO AND MRS. LLERAS

Thursday, June 12, 1969

Shrimps en Aspic

Supreme of Duckling Montmorency
Wild Rice Croquettes
Broccoli au Beurre
Salade Cressonière
Camembert Cheese
Soufflé Glacé Diplomat

Demitasse

SHRIMPS EN ASPIC

2 envelopes unflavored colorless gelatin
1/2 cup cold water
2 10-1/2-ounce cans beef consommé
3 pounds shrimp, boiled and shelled
2 envelopes unflavored red gelatin
1/2 cup cold water
1/2 cup canned chicken consommé

1 small onion, finely chopped
1/4 to 1/2 cup dry white wine, to taste, if desired
Salt and white pepper to taste
Juice of 1/2 lemon
1 tablespoon tomato paste
1 teaspoon fresh or 1 teaspoon dried tarragon
1 cup heavy cream, chilled

Soften the colorless gelatin in 1/2 cup cold water for 5 minutes; then dissolve in boiling beef consommé, and let cool until it starts coating.

Line a simple round mold with the aspic. Arrange 2 pounds of the shrimp in layers in the mold, leaving the center of the mold free. Reserve remaining shrimp for mousse.

Soften the red gelatin in 1/2 cup cold water for 5 minutes; then stir it into the chicken consommé, and simmer over low heat for a minute or two. When the gelatin is dissolved, let cool.

Cut the remaining shrimp into small pieces (about 1/4 inch), and put in the container of the electric blender. Pour the consommé, lukewarm or cool, over it, add the onion, and blend until pasty. Transfer into a bowl.

Add dry white wine.

Season the shrimp mixture with salt and pepper, lemon juice, tomato paste, and tarragon.

Set the bowl with the shrimp mixture into a larger bowl filled with ice, and stir with a spatula until it starts to thicken. Whip the cream, and fold it lightly into the shrimp mixture.

Pour the shrimp mousse into the center of the mold, cover with aspic, and refrigerate for at least 4 hours. Serves 14 to 16.

SUPREME OF DUCKLING MONTMORENCY

1 6-pound duckling	1/2 cup chicken consommé
Salt	1 level tablespoon arrowroot
3 tablespoons melted butter	1 small can pitted cherries,
1/2 cup Madeira wine	drained

Wash the duckling, and dry with a paper towel. Salt lightly, and put the duckling in a pan with the butter for about 20 minutes.

Transfer the duck into an oval earthenware cocotte (flameproof casserole with lid), and pour the Madeira, consommé, and pan drippings over the duck. Cover and put into a preheated oven at 375°.

When the duck is tender, remove it from the cocotte and thicken the remaining juices with arrowroot. Add the cherries. Carve the duck, and put back into the cocotte. Spoon the gravy over it, reheat, and you can serve it in the same dish. Serves 4 to 6.

WILD RICE CROQUETTES

1 cup thick white sauce
2 cups cooked wild rice
1/2 cup diced sautéed fresh
    mushrooms
Salt and pepper to taste

Flour
1 egg, beaten
Bread crumbs
Deep fat

To the white sauce, add wild rice and mushrooms. Stir constantly until the mixture thickens and stands away from the sides of the pan. Season with salt and pepper, and spread the mixture on a buttered flat dish to cool.

Shape the croquettes into cones, balls, or cylinders. Dip in flour, then in the egg, and finally in bread crumbs.

Fry in hot deep fat at 390° until golden brown. Serves 6.

SALADE CRESSONIÈRE
See Index for recipe.

SOUFFLÉ GLACÉ DIPLOMAT

About 16 ladyfingers
Kirsch liqueur
7 egg yolks
2 teaspoons vanilla
3/4 cup sugar

2 envelopes unflavored gelatin
3 tablespoons cold water
2-1/2 cups heavy cream, chilled
Additional 1/2 cup sugar

Sprinkle the ladyfingers with the kirsch, and let stand at room temperature.

Beat the egg yolks, vanilla, and 3/4 cup sugar in a large bowl until thick and lemon-colored.

Presoak unflavored gelatin in cold water for 5 minutes. Add the softened gelatin to the egg yolks, stir thoroughly, and transfer the mixture into a double-boiler top. Cook, stirring constantly, until the mixture thickens to coat a spoon lightly. Do not let it boil. Remove from heat, and let cool.

Whip the cream with additional sugar until stiff. Fold lightly into the egg mixture.

Prepare your soufflé mold ahead of time by tying a collar of waxed paper around the top of a 1-quart mold extending about 2 inches above the rim. Tie the waxed paper around with a string. When the soufflé is frozen and the paper removed, it looks like a hot soufflé.

Pour some of the soufflé in the bottom of the mold, put 4 ladyfingers on it, and keep alternating soufflé and 4 ladyfingers until your mold is full to the top of the waxed paper collar. Smooth the top with a spatula, and refrigerate overnight.

Carefully remove the collar before serving. Serves 8 to 10.

At every formal dinner, President Nixon tries to give his guests glimpses into his life with Pat and his way of thinking.

And sometimes Nixon's warmth toward our Latin neighbors comes out clearly as it did when he hosted a dinner for the Central and Latin America diplomatic corps.

Nixon told his guests how not only had he chosen Mexico for his honeymoon but a year later he and Pat had taken "a banana boat" cruise to Panama and other Central America countries—with Pat footing the bill.

"She was affluent," the President said with a grin, "because she had been teaching. I was just a struggling lawyer."

For his honored guests, Nixon chose an elegant menu featuring pheasant:

PRESIDENT NIXON'S FORMAL WHITE HOUSE DINNER IN HONOR OF THE CHIEFS OF DIPLOMATIC MISSIONS OF THE AMERICAS

Tuesday, April 6, 1971

Turban de Fruits de Mer en Aspic—Paillettes Dorées

Supreme of Pheasant Véronique

Wild Rice   Zucchini Sauté au Beurre

Bibb Lettuce   Fromage Port de Salut

Savarin Tropicale—Sauce Sabayon

The wines were:
Schloss Johannisberger
L. M. Cabernet Sauvignon
Piper Heidsieck

TURBAN DE FRUITS DE MER EN ASPIC–PAILLETTES DORÉES
(Mold of Seafood–Cheese Straws)

2 envelopes unflavored gelatin
1/2 cup cold water
2 cans beef consommé
Shrimp, crab meat, lobster, or
    other available seafood

Lemon quarters
Cheese Straws (see Index)

Soften gelatin in the cold water for 5 minutes. While gelatin is softening, bring consommé to boil; then dissolve gelatin mixture in consommé. Let cool until it coats spoon.

Line a simple round mold with the aspic, and arrange various seafood pieces in it. Refrigerate overnight. Unmold and serve with quarters of lemon and Cheese Straws. Serves 8.

SUPREME OF PHEASANT VÉRONIQUE

Salt and pepper to taste
1 breast of pheasant cut into two
    pieces
1 tablespoon butter

1 medium onion, quartered
1/2 cup sour cream
1/2 cup canned white grapes

Cook lightly seasoned breast of pheasant in butter in saucepan with onion. When breast is three-fourths done, sprinkle with the sour cream. When done, add the grapes.

Serve with Wild Rice (see Index). Serves 2.

ZUCCHINI SAUTÉ AU BEURRE
(Zucchini Cooked in Butter in Saucepan)

Wash and thinly slice your required amount of zucchini, and cook in a saucepan in melted butter until tender. Add salt and white pepper to taste.

The French have always brought out the best in White House cuisine. I am looking now at the menu for the state dinner at which the President and Mrs. Nixon honored the President of France and Madame Pompidou. Guests numbering 110 had been invited to the white-tie dinner in the State Dining Room. Naturally the gold flatware and the Johnson china were used.

When they reached the table, the guests found that the flowers were all red, white, and blue, the colors of both France and the United States.

FORMAL DINNER
TO HONOR THE PRESIDENT OF FRANCE AND
MADAME POMPIDOU

Tuesday, February 24, 1970

Le Saumon Lafayette

Le Contre-filet de Boeuf aux Cèpes
Les Pommes Nouvelles
Les Asperges Fraîches Hollandaise
La Laitue de Kentucky
Le Fromage de Camembert
Le Melon Glacé à la Vigneronne
Les Petits Fours

Here are the recipes:

LE SAUMON LAFAYETTE

5 peppercorns	1 6-pound salmon
1 bay leaf	Fish stock
2 slices lemon peel	Mayonnaise
1 teaspoon salt	2 envelopes unflavored gelatin
2 quarts water	Garnish of small tomatoes stuffed
1 quart dry white wine	with vegetable salad

Boil peppercorns, bay leaf, lemon peel, and salt in the water and white wine for about 5 minutes. Let cool.

Add salmon to cool liquid, and bring to a slow boil, allowing to simmer slowly 6 to 8 minutes per pound. Do not overcook. Remove salmon, and cool.

Place salmon on serving platter. Skin very carefully, and cover bared meat with mayonnaise sauce, which you prepare from mayonnaise and fish aspic made from the fish stock (boiling liquid) and mixed with the gelatin. Garnish with the small tomatoes. Serves 12.

Serve with Mustard Mayonnaise Sauce:

MUSTARD MAYONNAISE SAUCE

2 tablespoons prepared mustard
1 cup mayonnaise

1 teaspoon lemon juice
Salt and pepper to taste

Combine all the ingredients in a blender set at low speed until well combined and slightly fluffy.

LE CONTRE-FILET DE BOEUF AUX CÈPES

1 4-pound filet of beef
Salt and pepper to taste
3 tablespoons softened butter

Additional butter
1/2 pound cèpe mushrooms, sautéed

Preheat the oven to 450°. Season filet of beef with salt and pepper, and rub the softened butter on all sides of meat. Insert a meat thermometer in center of roast, and when it reaches 120° to 125° transfer the meat to a serving platter and let rest at room temperature for a few minutes.

Garnish with mushrooms, and serve with new potatoes. Cèpes are a fancy flat mushroom widely used in Europe. Serves 8.

LES ASPERGES FRAÎCHES HOLLANDAISE
(Mock Hollandaise)

2 pounds asparagus
1 cup Basic White Sauce
5 tablespoons butter

1 tablespoon lemon juice
3 egg yolks

Boil the asparagus, and serve with the following sauce:

To the white sauce (see recipe below) add the butter, one tablespoon at a time, and the lemon juice, making a mock Hollandaise. Be sure to keep beating as you pour in the egg yolks, which are put in just before serving. Leftover sauce may be reheated in a double boiler for reuse. Serves 6.

BASIC WHITE SAUCE

2 tablespoons butter
2 tablespoons flour

1-1/2 cups milk
Salt and pepper to taste

Melt butter in small saucepan. Take from stove, cool a moment, and add flour a bit at a time until smoothly blended. Start adding milk, a tablespoon at a time, until you have a perfectly smooth mixture of about 10 tablespoons milk. Put back on stove, and heat gradually, stirring constantly. Continue to stir as you gradually pour in remainder of milk. Stir and cook until it barely starts to boil. Take off at the first sign of a bubble.

(This recipe will make a little more than you need for the above recipe or measure out what you need. Basic White Sauce can be dressed up with various flavors to add taste to a meal. For Cheese Sauce, for example, simply add 1/3 cup grated cheddar to the above recipe the moment you see the bubbles and take it from the heat. Another addition is 2 mashed anchovies. The latter is good for pepping up fish dishes.)

LE MELON GLACÉ À LA VIGNERONNE

1 cantaloupe, cut in half and seeded	Sugar Port wine

Sprinkle inside of melon halves with sugar, and pour in a little port wine (or any other dessert wine). Serve well chilled. Serves 2.

PETITS FOURS

4 eggs	1 cup flour
1/2 cup sugar	4 tablespoons butter, melted
1 teaspoon finely grated lemon rind	

Place the eggs, sugar, and lemon rind in a metal mixing bowl on top of a pot of boiling water—the lower portion of a double boiler. I use a wire beater, but many women prefer hand electric mixers. I prefer the wire beater because I can maneuver it better in keeping the eggs from sticking to the sides of the hot mixing bowl.

Beat the egg mixture until it becomes warm and the sugar has completely dissolved. Then take it off the boiling water, and continue beating until it is completely cool and double in volume. Now, with a wooden spoon, slowly fold in the flour; finally, fold in the butter, which you slowly pour into the mixture in a thin ribbon. Pour your batter into a buttered and lightly floured 8-inch baking square. Bake at 350° for 25 minutes.

After it is cooled, cut into small 1-1/2-inch diamonds or squares and dip into fondant (below) to cover the complete surface, holding them on the end of a fork. Makes about 24.

The color, flavor, and variety are limited only by your imagination. Pink can be flavored with rum, maple is a desirable flavor for pale beige petits fours, mint flavor for light green, lemon for yellow, caramel for caramel color. There is also pure white, for which you can use almond extract, and chocolate, made by adding unsweetened chocolate squares to the fondant.

Using a pastry tube, decorate the top of the fondant with butter cream frosting in the shape of stars and rosettes in various colors, in keeping with the flavor. Finally place bits of fruits and nuts on the tops of some of the petits fours—almonds on top of the chocolate, candied cherry bits on top of the white, candied pineapple on top of the yellow, walnut halves on top of caramel, chilled chocolate drops on top of the pink, white rosettes speckled with mint jelly for the light green.

You may prefer to use just your favorite butter cream icing or favorite boiled icing, instead of fondant, but here is how I make fondant in which I dipped my petits fours so that they were covered on all five exposed surfaces:

FONDANT

1-1/4 cups water	Vegetable coloring
4 cups sugar	Flavoring
2 tablespoons white corn syrup	

Since you will make this for parties, I will tell you how to make it the way I made it at the White House in large enough quantity to keep some stored in the refrigerator, always on hand. It keeps for months.

Pour the water into a saucepan and add the sugar. Bring to a boil, and continue boiling, making sure that the sides of the pan are kept clean of sugar crystals—use a clean brush with cold water, and wash the brush each time. When the sugar has boiled for about 5 minutes, start testing. Twist a little piece of wire to leave an opening like the eye of a needle. Dip the "eye" into the sugar mixture and blow through it. If you can blow a bubble, the mixture is ready. Now add corn syrup, and bring to a boiling point again. Just as the mixture starts to boil, remove the pan from the fire.

I prefer to work my fondant on a marble surface. However, you can use a chilled mixing bowl. In either case, cool the surface you are about to use with ice water, leaving just a few drops in the bowl or on the marble. Pour the fondant on the surface while it is hot so that it has no time to form a crust on the top. Sprinkle a few drops of ice water on top of the fondant to prevent crusting, and let cool until it is less than lukewarm.

Then take a wooden spatula, and start to work the fondant, pulling from the outer edges to the center, again and again, until the mixture is milk-white and starts thickening—about 15 minutes.

Now the fondant is ready for use. Take as much as you need, put it in a pan to warm slightly, and add the coloring and flavoring to it—a few drops of red vegetable coloring or a few drops of green mint extract combined with green coloring, and so forth. Leave a little fondant white so that you can add almond extract to it. If the fondant is still too hard even with the addition of the few drops of liquid coloring, simply sprinkle in a few drops of water. Fondant on petits fours gives a beautiful shiny surface on which the additional decorations are like a picture in a frame.

Now, for comparison, let's see what a former President, John F. Kennedy, served a visitor from France:

PRESIDENT KENNEDY'S FORMAL DINNER IN HONOR OF ANDRÉ MALRAUX, FRENCH MINISTER OF CULTURE

1962

Consommé Madrilene Iranien

Lobster en Bellevue
Stuffed Bar Polignac
Parisienne Potatoes   Florida Asparagus
Pheasant Aspic

Cream Puffs With Nuts

Now for another comparison—what President Eisenhower served his guests from France. I remember that one of the busiest days I had at the White House was the day I served a formal luncheon for the President of France at 1 P.M. for fifty-seven people and a stag dinner for twenty persons at 8 that night. It was one of those long days for me, but I also felt sorry for the President.

PRESIDENT EISENHOWER'S LUNCHEON
FOR THE PRESIDENT OF FRANCE, RENÉ COTY

Monday, May 23, 1955

Cold Vichyssoise
Fairy Toast
Green and Ripe Olives   Celery Hearts

Veal Birds
Smothered in Mushroom Wine Sauce
Spiced Pears
Cauliflower Au Gratin
Buttered Peas
Rolls

Bibb Lettuce in Salad
Champagne   Green Goddess Dressing
Cheese Straws

Lime Sherbet Ring Mold
Brandied Peaches
Petits Fours
Assorted Nuts   Candies

Coffee

CHILLED VICHYSSOISE

4 leeks, chopped
4 tablespoons butter
2 tablespoons bacon grease
1 tablespoon flour
4 medium potatoes, diced
Dash of Worcestershire
Dash of nutmeg
Salt and pepper to taste

2 stalks celery, chopped
1 quart chicken consommé
1 cup milk
1/2 cup heavy cream
Chopped chives
Garlic salt, pepper, or
    Worcestershire to taste

Sauté the leeks in the butter and bacon grease until soft. Use part of the leek greens but not all. Then add the flour, potatoes, Worcestershire, nutmeg, salt and pepper, and celery. Pour in the chicken consommé, and boil for 30 to 40 minutes. Take off the stove, and add the milk. Then blend the vichyssoise in the electric blender until it is nice and creamy, adding the cream and any additional seasonings of garlic salt, pepper, or Worcestershire in the final moments in the blender. Serve with a topping of chives after it has chilled. Serves 6.

VEAL BIRDS SMOTHERED IN MUSHROOM WINE SAUCE

Veal cutlets for 6

1 medium onion, finely chopped

1/4 pound butter

6 medium mushrooms, chopped

Salt and white pepper, to taste

1 tablespoon chopped parsley

Mushroom Wine Sauce (below)

Cut veal cutlets such as you use for breaded veal, into individual portions; then pound each one as thin as you can without breaking it so that it can be filled and rolled like a pancake.

Since each of the little cutlets is uniformly shaped into an oval for rolling, you will have pieces of meat left over; these are ground very fine by passing through the grinder twice. For six veal "pancakes" you will need 1/2 pound ground veal, so you may need to add more meat to the grinder.

Lightly brown the onion in the butter. Add the mushrooms; simmer a few minutes; season with salt and pepper; add the ground veal. Stir until your filling is well mixed. You will have to add additional seasoning of salt and pepper and the parsley.

Now place the veal cutlets on a board, and season on both sides with salt and white pepper. Divide your filling evenly, making a little heap in the center of each cutlet. Roll each veal "pancake" like a diploma, but tie your diploma three times. Since you are in the kitchen and not in school, you do not have to use fancy ribbons but can tie your meat with a piece of string. The dish gets its name from the fact that your "diploma" will end up looking like a little bird. One string is tied tightly at the beak. The second is tied tightly to make a neck about an inch or an inch and a half from the beak. And the third is wrapped around the open end about four or five times to make the feet effect.

Now your veal birds are ready for cooking on top of the stove in the Mushroom Wine Sauce:

MUSHROOM WINE SAUCE

1 onion, finely chopped
1/4 pound butter
1 pound mushrooms, thin-sliced
1-1/2 cups chicken consommé

1 cup dry white wine
1/2 tablespoon flour
Chopped parsley

Sauté the onion in the butter. Add the mushrooms, and cook gently for 5 minutes. Add chicken consommé and wine. You can put the veal birds in immediately without any browning of the meat, and simmer for 1 hour, or until the birds are tender.

Carefully remove the birds, and let them cool a little bit so that the strings can be removed easily. Sprinkle the flour in the mushroom sauce, and let cook a few minutes to remove the flour taste. Take half the sauce and pass it through the blender to give it a creamy consistency. The rest is left as is to keep the shape of the mushrooms intact. Combine the blended sauce with the unblended. Place the birds back in the sauce without their strings, reheat, and serve with parsley sprinkled on top.

I served this dish American-style with spiced pears in a circle around the meat platter. However, in France and Prague I usually served this with plain buttered rice.

SPICED PEARS

8 canned small whole pears
1/2 cup white vinegar
1 cup brown sugar
1 whole vanilla bean (about the
  size of 1 string bean)

2 sticks cinnamon
1/2 teaspoon whole cloves
Pear syrup from the can

Place pears in a saucepan for 3 minutes in the following mixture: vinegar, brown sugar, vanilla bean, cinnamon, cloves, and the syrup from the can. Cook covered. Serve hot around the meat platter. Serves 4.

CHEESE STRAWS

Puff Paste (see Index)
Sharp American cheese, finely
  grated

1 egg yolk
1/2 teaspoon water

Use a fourth of the Puff Paste recipe in Index. In other words, puff paste made from 1/4 pound butter. Roll the puff paste, preferably on marble, to about 1/4 inch. Cover the puff paste 1/8 inch thick with the cheese, and fold the dough into thirds, bringing each end in a third of the way. Then reroll after letting the folded dough rest in the refrigerator for about 30 minutes.

This time when you again roll the dough, make it still thinner—1/8 inch—and brush the surface thoroughly with the egg yolk mixed with the water to give it a shiny surface when baked. Sprinkle with just a bit of the cheese. Now cut your rolled puff paste into long, thin, strawlike lengths, the thickness of a finger.

Bake in a 400° oven until golden brown and more than doubled in height. Cheese Straws make a wonderful flaky tidbit for your salad course. You can even serve these at cocktail parties as an appetizer just as they are. Makes 20 to 24 straws.

Canada, too, was honored in one of the first formal dinners given by President Nixon. It featured beef:

FORMAL DINNER TO
HONOR THE RIGHT HONORABLE PIERRE ELLIOTT TRUDEAU,
PRIME MINISTER OF CANADA

Monday, March 24, 1969

Timbale of Seafood Américaine

Filet of Beef Jardinière
Artichokes
Cocotte Potatoes
Bibb Lettuce

Camembert Cheese
Charlotte Monticello

TIMBALE OF SEAFOOD AMERICAINE

See Index for recipe served Jacqueline Kennedy Onassis.

FILET OF BEEF JARDINIÈRE

Filet of beef
Seasoning to taste of salt, pepper,
   and garlic powder

Buttered mixed fresh vegetables

Roast the meat in hot oven of 450° about 10 minutes per pound for very rare and 12 to 14 minutes for rare.

The finished roast is served with the buttered mixed vegetables which should be arranged in distinct heaps so as to alternate their colors.

COCOTTE POTATOES

See Index for recipe served to Chief Justice Warren and Mrs. Warren.

CHARLOTTE MONTICELLO

1 cup orange juice
Grated rind and juice of 1/2
   lemon
1/2 cup sugar
2 eggs, separated

1 tablespoon unflavored gelatin
1 tablespoon cold water
8 or 10 ladyfingers
1-1/2 cups whipped cream

Mix orange juice, lemon juice and rind, sugar, and egg yolks.

Stir over fire until mixture thickens. Add gelatin which was soaked in water; then pour over stiffly beaten egg whites. Set in pan of ice water and beat until thick enough to hold its shape.

Turn into a charlotte mold lined with ladyfingers, and chill for 4 hours. Unmold on serving dish, and decorate with whipped cream. Serves 4 to 6.

Americans have long been fascinated by royalty, so let us look at a few occasions when royalty have visited the White House and see how they dined. Too often, I regret, the menu contains either squab or some form of steak. For example, President Nixon served squab to the Duke and Duchess of Windsor:

FORMAL DINNER
TO HONOR THE DUKE AND DUCHESS OF WINDSOR

Saturday, April 4, 1970

Le Saumon Froid Windsor
La Sauce Verte

Les Suprêmes de Pigeons Véronique
Le Riz Sauvage
Les Artichauts Saint-Germain
Les Feuilles de Laitue du Kentucky
Le Fromage de Brie

Le Soufflé Duchesse
La Sauce Sabayon

LE SAUMON FROID WINDSOR

2 quarts water	1 bay leaf
6 pounds salmon	2 slices lemon peel
1 quart dry white wine	1 teaspoon salt
5 peppercorns	Thirty slices cucumbers

Boil the water. Add the white wine, peppercorns, bay leaf, lemon peel, and salt, and let boil 5 minutes; then cool.

Add the salmon to the cool liquid, and bring to a slow boil. Simmer slowly, 6 to 8 minutes per pound. Do not overcook. Remove salmon from liquid and cool. Skin carefully, and scrape off the grayish fat under the skin with a spoon, until the pink meat is evenly exposed. Place on serving platter, and garnish with cucumbers. Serves 12.

Serve with La Sauce Verte below. (Check the Index for President Kennedy's recipe for Green Sauce, which is the English title for the same thing. His version does not contain wine.)

LA SAUCE VERTE

2 ounces spinach leaves	1 quart thick mayonnaise
2 ounces parsley	2 tablespoons dry white wine
2 ounces watercress	Salt and pepper to taste
Small equal amounts tarragon leaves and chervil	

Drop spinach into boiling water, and blanch for 5 minutes together with the parsley, watercress, tarragon, and chervil.

Strain, cool, and quickly press out the water and crush in a cloth, squeezing out about 3 ounces thick juice.

Add this to remaining ingredients. Makes about 1 quart.

LES SUPRÊMES DE PIGEONS VÉRONIQUE

4 squabs	2 tablespoons melted butter
Salt and pepper to taste	2 cups hot chicken consommé
4 slices bacon	1/2 cup heavy cream
1/4 pound butter, melted	1 small can white grapes, drained
4 tablespoons flour	

Cut off breast with wings attached to squabs. Season with salt and pepper; cover each breast with bacon slice. Sauté in 1/4 pound butter in covered pan until done.

To prepare sauce, add flour to 2 tablespoons melted butter, and heat slowly. Before flour turns golden, add the hot consommé a little at a time, stirring constantly with a wire whisk. Cook for 15 minutes.

Strain through a fine sieve; add the cream and grapes.

Reheat, pour over the squab breasts on a warm serving dish, and serve. Serves 4.

LE SOUFFLÉ DUCHESSE

2 tablespoons sugar	4 teaspoons butter
Pinch of salt	1 teaspoon vanilla extract
1 cup milk	2 ounces each finely ground hazelnuts and almonds
4 tablespoons sifted flour	
Cold milk	6 egg whites
4 egg yolks	Another 2 tablespoons sugar

Add first 2 tablespoons sugar and salt to milk, and bring to boil in a saucepan. Add flour, which has been blended with a little cold milk. Stir constantly, and cook for 2 to 3 minutes.

Remove from heat; add the egg yolks, butter, vanilla, and nuts. Stiffly beat egg whites with second 2 tablespoons sugar; fold lightly and quickly into mixture.

Pour into buttered and sugared soufflé dish. Place in oven at 400° and bake for about 30 minutes.

Just before serving, sprinkle with sugar to glaze.

Serve with Sauce Sabayon.

LA SAUCE SABAYON

See Index for Chef Haller's recipe as on menu in honor of Jacqueline Kennedy Onassis in Chapter 1, or use my recipe in the next menu.

A main course similar to that served the Pompidous of France was served a royal visitor from Iran:

FORMAL DINNER
IN HONOR OF HIS IMPERIAL MAJESTY
MOHAMMED REZA PAHLAVI OF IRAN

Tuesday, October 21, 1969

Suprême of Salmon Farcie Impérial

Contre-filet of Beef Bordelaise
Pommes Macaire
Bouquetière of Vegetables
Bibb Lettuce Salad

Camembert Cheese
Poires Flambées Bar-le-Duc—Sauce Sabayon
Demitasse

SUPRÊME OF SALMON FARCIE IMPÉRIAL

1 5- or 6-pound salmon
1 pound boneless white fish,
    finely chopped
3-1/2 cups bread crumbs, soaked
    in milk and squeezed
4 tablespoons butter, melted
1 tablespoon chopped chives

1 tablespoon chopped chervil
1 tablespoon chopped parsley
Salt, pepper, and nutmeg to taste
2 eggs
1/2 cup salad oil
Lemon butter
Additional chopped parsley

Prepare the stuffing for salmon: To the chopped white fish add the bread crumbs, butter, chives, chervil, and 1 tablespoon parsley. Season with salt, pepper, and nutmeg. Blend with the eggs, and mix thoroughly. Stuff salmon, and set aside.

Put the salad oil in an ovenproof (Pyrex) serving platter, and place in a 400° oven. When the oil is hot, place the fish in it, and bake for about 20 to 25 minutes. Test with a fork to see if it flakes easily. If it does, the fish is done. Baste frequently. Pour off the fat, and serve with lemon butter to which you have added chopped parsley. Serves 10 to 12.

CONTRE-FILET OF BEEF BORDELAISE

Prepare 4-pound filet of beef as in recipe for that served President of France and Madame Pompidou on February 24, 1970 (see Index for recipe called Le Contre-filet de Boeuf aux Cèpes), except that you omit the mushrooms (or cèpes) and prepare this Bordelaise Sauce.

BORDELAISE SAUCE

3 shallots, finely chopped
3/4 cup red wine
Pan drippings from roast
1 small bay leaf
1/8 teaspoon crumbled dried
    thyme
1/8 teaspoon freshly ground
    pepper

2-1/2 teaspoons arrowroot,
    mixed in 1/4 cup red wine
Few drops fresh lemon juice
6 ounces beef marrow, cubed and
    poached in slightly salted
    boiling water

Cook shallots in the wine until reduced to one-fourth the original quantity. Add the pan drippings, bay leaf, thyme, and pepper; then thicken with the arrowroot and red wine mixture. Simmer slowly for 5 minutes, and strain. When ready to serve, finish the sauce by adding the lemon juice and beef marrow. Serves 8.

POMMES MACAIRE

4 large potatoes
Salt and pepper to taste
2 tablespoons melted butter

1 teaspoon chopped parsley
Additional melted butter

Bake potatoes in the oven, and when done, scoop out all their insides in a bowl, season with salt and pepper, and work with a fork, adding the 2 tablespoons butter and parsley. Spread this preparation in the form of a pancake on the bottom of an omelet pan containing additional butter, and brown well on both sides. Serves 4 to 6.

BOUQUETIÈRE OF VEGETABLES

1 small whole cauliflower
1 pound string beans
1/2 pound small carrots
1/2 pound brussels sprouts

1/2 pound green peas
1/2 pound pearl onions
1/2 cup melted butter

Boil each vegetable separately in salted water. When cooked, arrange on a serving platter with the whole cauliflower in the center and the other vegetables around it. Pour the melted butter over when serving. Serves 8 to 10.

POIRES FLAMBÉES BAR-LE-DUC–SAUCE SABAYON

4 cups water
2 cups sugar
2 teaspoons vanilla
Peel of 1/2 lemon
3 tablespoons fresh lemon juice
6 medium Anjou pears, peeled,
    halved, and cored

2 teaspoons arrowroot, dissolved
    in cold water
12 teaspoons kirsch liqueur,
    heated

Combine the water, sugar, vanilla, lemon peel and juice, and bring to a boil. Add pear halves, and simmer over moderate heat for 10 to 15 minutes. Remove pears from the liquid, and continue boiling until the liquid reduces to about half; then thicken with the arrowroot.

Cover pears with the thickened liquid, and pour a teaspoon of kirsch into the center of each pear half. Light when serving. Serves 12.

Serve Sauce Sabayon on the side, prepared as follows:

SAUCE SABAYON À LA RYSAVY

8 large egg yolks	2 tablespoons kirsch liqueur
1 cup sugar	Currants or strawberries
1 cup white wine	(optional)

Combine the yolks and sugar in top of double boiler above simmering water. Beat with a wire whisk until the mixture is thick and fluffy. Beating constantly, pour the wine into the mixture in a thin stream, and beat until it is about triple in volume and thickens considerably—about 10 minutes. Be careful not to boil the mixture at any time.

Remove from heat, beat in the kirsch, and serve, adding currants or strawberries to decorate the pears, if desired. Serves 12.

Like the Duke and Duchess of Windsor, Prince Souvanna Phouma of Laos dined on squab at President Nixon's table. But the recipe was different:

FORMAL DINNER
TO HONOR HIS HIGHNESS PRINCE SOUVANNA PHOUMA,
PRIME MINISTER OF LAOS

Tuesday, October 7, 1969

Suprême of Lobster Bellevue

Royal Squab Farcie Périgueux
Brussels Sprouts au Beurre
Garden Salad

Bel Paese Cheese
Soufflé au Grand Marnier
Demitasse

SUPRÊME OF LOBSTER BELLEVUE

2 envelopes unflavored gelatin
1-1/2 pounds inexpensive fish
   with bones
2 parsley roots
2 stalks celery
2 leeks
4 ounces unpeeled fresh
   mushrooms
Salt to taste

6 lobsters, cooked
8 cups cooked mixed vegetables
1-1/2 cups mayonnaise
2 truffles, finely sliced
Tarragon and chervil leaves
24 small artichoke bottoms
6 hearts of lettuce
3 hard-cooked eggs, halved

Prepare aspic jelly ahead of time: Soak gelatin in 4 tablespoons cold water for 5 minutes. Boil fish, parsley, celery, leeks, mushrooms, and salt 45 to 60 minutes. Strain through fine sieve. Add the gelatin. Let liquid cool until it starts setting.

Remove all the meat from shell of cooked lobster, and fill with 6 cups salad made of cooked mixed vegetables mixed with mayonnaise.

Decorate the slices of lobster with truffles, tarragon, and chervil leaves, and glaze with aspic jelly, arranging it neatly on top of vegetable salad in the lobster shell. Garnish around it with artichoke bottoms filled with the remaining 2 cups vegetable salad, decorated with truffles, hearts of lettuce with mayonnaise, and halves of hard-cooked eggs.

Add more aspic jelly with a spoon over the garnishes.

Refrigerate before serving. Serves 6.

ROYAL SQUAB FARCIE PÉRIGUEUX

4 ounces foie gras
3 medium truffles
3 tablespoons butter
1-3/4 cups cooked wild rice

Salt and pepper to taste
6 squabs, cleaned
1/3 cup melted butter
2/3 cup boiling water

Dice foie gras and truffles. Sauté in 3 tablespoons butter. Mix with rice; add salt and pepper.

Stuff the squabs, and truss. Season with salt and pepper. Brush squabs with melted butter, and bake about 45 minutes in hot oven (400°). Baste every 6 minutes with the boiling water to which melted butter has been added. Serves 6.

BRUSSELS SPROUTS AU BEURRE

2 pounds brussels sprouts   4 tablespoons melted butter

Boil brussels sprouts in salted water, about 15 minutes, or until tender; drain, and dry. Sauté sprouts in butter until light brown. Serves 6.

SOUFFLÉ AU GRAND MARNIER À LA RYSAVY

6 to 8 ladyfingers
1/4 cup Grand Marnier
2 tablespoons butter
2 tablespoons flour
Dash of salt
1/2 cup hot milk
1/2 teaspoon vanilla extract

5 egg yolks
4 tablespoons granulated sugar
6 egg whites
Additional 1 tablespoon
   granulated sugar
Powdered sugar

Sprinkle ladyfingers with Grand Marnier to moisten. Let stand for 30 minutes.

Melt butter in saucepan, add flour and salt, and cook slowly until the roux starts to turn golden. Stir in hot milk. Cook slowly for 5 minutes, stirring constantly. Add vanilla.

Beat egg yolks with the 4 tablespoons sugar, and add to the sauce.

Beat egg whites until stiff, with additional 1 tablespoon sugar added during last few minutes of beating. Fold egg whites carefully but thoroughly into the mixture.

Pour half the mixture into a buttered and sugared soufflé mold, and cover with ladyfingers. Fill the dish with the rest of the soufflé mixture.

Smooth the top with spatula, and bake in moderately hot oven (375° to 400°) for 18 to 20 minutes, or until it is well puffed and browned.

A minute or two before removing from oven, sprinkle a little powdered sugar on top for glaze. Serves 6.

Serve at once with Grand Marnier Sauce:

GRAND MARNIER SAUCE

1 cup heavy cream
1 tablespoon sugar

4 tablespoons Grand Marnier

Chill cream, and whip, but not stiff, only semi-whipped to the consistency of sauce. Add sugar and Grand Marnier. Serves 6.

Now let's see how Nixon's predecessor, President Johnson, entertained a royal lady:

PRESIDENT JOHNSON'S
FORMAL DINNER HONORING HER ROYAL HIGHNESS
PRINCESS MARGARET AND LORD SNOWDON

Pompano Amandine

Boned Squab Stuffed With Wild Rice
Artichokes With Pureed Filling
Green Salad

Brie Cheese
Praline Glace

President Johnson was more a steak man as witness the menu he set before Greek royalty:

PRESIDENT JOHNSON'S
FORMAL DINNER IN HONOR OF HER ROYAL HIGHNESS
PRINCESS IRENE OF GREECE

Crab Meat Crêpes Irene

Tournedos
Saffron Rice Pilaf
Spinach Ring
Salad Greens

Brie Cheese
Strawberries Monticello

Tournedos (Héloïse) had also been served to a South American chief of state by John Kennedy:

DINNER
IN HONOR OF THE PRESIDENT OF THE
REPUBLIC OF PERU AND SEÑORA DE PRADO

September 19, 1961

Salmon Mousse
Tomato and Cucumber Salad

Tournedos Héloïse
Roast Potatoes
Green Beans with Almonds

Assorted Cheeses
Crackers

St. Honoré Cake

Demitasse

TOURNEDOS HÉLOÏSE

1-1/2-inch thick filet mignon	Croutons
for each person	Artichoke bottoms
Butter	Creamed chopped mushrooms

Sauté the steaks in butter; place them on croutons which have been sautéed in butter. On each steak place an artichoke bottom which has been cooked and filled with creamed chopped mushrooms. Serve very hot.

GREEN BEANS WITH ALMONDS

See index for String Beans Amandine

ST. HONORÉ CAKE

A St. Honoré cake is a complicated dessert which is, indeed, fit for a president or a king. It is made of two kinds of dough and it may seem like a lot of work to serve a vanilla pudding, but it is well worth the effort for a party in delighting the eye, as well as tempting the palate.

A St. Honoré cake is constructed rather than poured into a cake pan to be baked, although, in a manner of speaking, it is a cross between a pie and a cake in shape, since the cake is only the form in which the filling is poured.

To make a St. Honoré cake, you first must make a flat, circular layer of dough, baked on a baking sheet. For the sides, and to hold in the filling, little balls of choux paste are used for their picturesque effect, placed in a circle around the edge of the cake layer, just as if they were the sides of a piecrust.

Then the filling is made, rich with whipped cream, and *voilà*, St. Honoré Cake:

Dough for bottom of cake shell:	1/8 teaspoon salt
1/2 pound butter	2 eggs
1/2 cup sugar	1 beaten egg
1 egg yolk, slightly beaten	For the coating:
1 teaspoon grated lemon rind	3/4 cup sugar
1/2 teaspoon vanilla	1/4 cup water
3 cups flour	For the filling:
For the choux paste:	1 package instant vanilla pudding
1/4 cup butter	mix
1/2 cup water	1 cup milk
1/2 cup flour	1 pint heavy cream, whipped

To make the dough, cream the butter and add the sugar. Then add the egg yolk, lemon rind, vanilla, and flour. Roll dough into a ball, and place in refrigerator until cold. Then roll the dough 1/8 inch thick, and cut into a round circle the size of a plate. This must be smaller than the plate on which you will serve it. Prick the dough with a fork in many places to keep it from rising too much. Place on a baking sheet.

Now make your choux paste, which is a cream puff dough. Bring the butter to a boil in the water. Then, while it is still on the stove, add the flour and salt, stirring rapidly until the dough ceases to stick to the bottom of the pot. Take the pan off the fire, and put the dough into an electric mixer. While your beater is at low speed, add the 2 eggs, one at a time, beating 4 minutes after each egg.

Using a pastry bag, with a tube as thick as a finger, lay a ring of choux paste around the edge, brushing the top with beaten egg. Bake the cake bottom and its ring of choux paste in a hot oven (425°) for 30 minutes.

At the same time, make 15 small balls of choux paste, about half the size of walnuts, and also bake them on the baking sheet.

When the bottom layer, with its choux paste edge, and the choux paste balls are baked, set them aside to cool.

Now make a coating for the small balls: Boil the sugar and water to make a syrup, until the temperature reaches 286°. Dip the choux paste balls into the mixture and place them around the border of the cake, on top of the edging of choux paste.

Now for the filling of the cake: Make the vanilla pudding, using only 1 cup of milk instead of the 2 cups called for on the package. Then fold in the whipped cream. Using a tablespoon, instead of a pastry tube, place this mixture in the center of the cake. Shape it to form large peaks. Serves 8.

President Nixon has followed in the Kennedys' footsteps in honoring talented and creative people at the White House. Here, for example, is the menu he served a longtime star of the music world:

FORMAL DINNER
TO HONOR DUKE ELLINGTON

Tuesday, April 29, 1969

Coquille of Seafood Neptune

Roast Sirloin of Beef Bordelaise
Potatoes Parmentier
Mushrooms Provençale

Salade Cressonnière

Cheddar Cheese Mousse
Glace Nougatine

COQUILLE OF SEAFOOD NEPTUNE

1 teaspoon chopped shallots	2 teaspoons chili sauce
1 teaspoon dry mustard	2 cups diced cooked lobster
1 teaspoon Worcestershire sauce	1 cup bay shrimps, cooked
Juice of 1/2 lemon	Crisp lettuce
Pinch of white pepper	2 hard-cooked eggs, sliced
Salt to taste	Chopped parsley
1 cup mayonnaise	6 radishes, coarsely chopped

Mix together shallots, mustard, and Worcestershire sauce; then add lemon juice, pepper, and a little salt. Add mayonnaise and chili sauce, stir to mix again, and add lobster and shrimp. Serve on 6 individual shells over crisp lettuce, and garnish with eggs, parsley, and radishes. Serves 6.

ROAST SIRLOIN OF BEEF BORDELAISE

Same recipe used for President and Madame Pompidou's dinner, February 4, 1970, except that you use boneless top sirloin and sautéed cèpes. See Index for recipe called Le Contre-filet de Boeuf aux Cèpes. And see Index for Bordelaise Sauce.

POTATOES PARMENTIER

6 medium potatoes, peeled and cut into balls	Salt to taste
Salted water for parboiling or butter for oven browning	Chopped parsley

Potatoes can either be parboiled in salted water for 4 minutes, then browned in a skillet with butter, or put raw into a skillet with about 3 tablespoons butter and browned in oven until evenly colored and done. Salt when they are done, and sprinkle with parsley. Serves 6 to 8.

Here is my version of Mushrooms Provençale, which is richer than Chef Haller's version and omits the tomatoes:

MUSHROOMS PROVENÇALE

1 pound mushrooms, stems
    removed
4 tablespoons butter
Salt and pepper to taste

1 tablespoon chopped shallots
1 clove garlic, crushed
Chopped parsley

Wash and dry mushrooms. Melt butter in a heavy skillet. Season mushrooms lightly with salt and pepper, and sauté them in the butter until brown. Remove mushrooms from skillet, and add to the butter the shallots and garlic. Sauté for 2 minutes, return the mushrooms to skillet, and cook a few minutes longer, shaking the skillet to reheat them evenly. Sprinkle all with parsley, and serve. Serves 4.

SALADE CRESSONNIÈRE

1 clove garlic, cut (optional)
2 bunches watercress, washed,
    dried, and stems removed
1/2 cup olive oil

2 tablespoons lemon juice or
    white vinegar
Salt and pepper to taste
Dry mustard

Rub salad bowl with garlic, and toss greens in a dressing made with the olive oil and either lemon juice or white vinegar plus seasonings. Serve on chilled plates. Serves 4.

CHEDDAR CHEESE MOUSSE

1/4 cup half-and-half
1/2 pound sharp, well-aged
    Cheddar cheese, finely
    grated

1 cup heavy cream
1 teaspoon Worcestershire sauce
1 teaspoon kirsch liqueur

Mix half-and-half and cheese in electric blender, adding about 1/2 cup cheese at a time. Place this mixture in top of double boiler over hot, but not rapidly boiling, water. Heat and stir until the mixture is smooth and all the cheese is melted. Remove from heat, and cool at least 10 minutes. In the meantime, whip the heavy cream until stiff, and season it with the Worcestershire sauce and kirsch. Fold the seasoned whipped cream lightly into the cheese mixture. Pour into a mold or bowl that has been rinsed in cold water and chill until firm (best overnight). Unmold and serve. Serves 6 to 8.

GLACE NOUGATINE

4 egg yolks
1 cup sugar
1 cup milk
1 cup light cream
1 teaspoon vanilla extract

2 cups whipped cream
1 cup pulverized Praline (below)
    or caramelized almonds
Additional whipped cream
Additional Praline

Beat egg yolks in double boiler until light and lemon-colored. Gradually beat in the sugar and stir in 1/4 cup of the milk. Heat remaining milk and the light cream until very hot but not boiling. Gradually stir milk mixture into the egg mixture, and cook over hot, but not boiling, water, stirring constantly, until mixture coats the spoon or spatula. Add vanilla and cool. Fold in the whipped cream and praline or almonds. Place mixture in a 1-quart ice-cream mold, and freeze at least 6 hours. Unmold and decorate with whipped cream, sprinkle with praline, and serve. Serves 6 to 8.

PRALINE FOR GLACE NOUGATINE

1 cup sugar
1 cup blanched almonds

1 tablespoon water
Butter

Mix sugar and blanched almonds in a heavy iron skillet. Add water, and cook over medium heat until sugar is melted and amber-colored. Grease a large plate with butter, and pour mixture onto it. Cool until it hardens, and then crush with mallet, but do not make it too fine.

And here the menu served one of America's outstanding artists:

FORMAL DINNER
IN HONOR OF ANDREW WYETH

Thursday, February 19, 1970

Suprême of Filet of Sole Véronique

Breast of Pheasant Smitane

Wild Rice Croquettes
Green Beans Amandine
Bibb Lettuce Salad

Brie Cheese
Vacherin Glacé aux Fraises

SUPRÊME FILETS OF SOLE VÉRONIQUE

1 tablespoon butter
1/2 small onion, finely chopped
8 filets of sole
Salt and pepper to taste
3/4 cup white wine
1/2 cup water

3/4 cup Basic White Sauce (see
   Index)
1 cup canned small grapes,
   drained
2 tablespoons whipped cream

Melt butter in pan; add onion. Season the filets with salt and pepper, roll and skewer them with wooden picks, and arrange in pan. Sprinkle them with wine and water, and cover. Bring to boil. Remove filets, place on dish, remove skewers, and cover with waxed paper. Continue cooking liquid until reduced to 3/4 cup. Add Basic White Sauce and grapes.

Fold in whipped cream, and pour sauce over the fish.

Brown under a hot broiler, and serve. Serves 8.

BREAST OF PHEASANT SMITANE

1 breast of pheasant, cut in two
4 tablespoons butter
Additional 2 tablespoons butter
1 medium onion, quartered
1/2 cup finely chopped onion

1 bay leaf
2 tablespoons flour
1-1/2 cups heavy cream
2 tablespoons fresh lemon juice
Salt and pepper to taste

Cook the pheasant with 4 tablespoons butter, seasonings, and quartered onion in heavy saucepan until done. Add a bit of water, if necessary.

In another saucepan, warm additional butter for about 10 seconds over medium heat. Add the finely chopped onion and bay leaf. Stir constantly and cook until the onions are soft.

Add flour, and continue stirring until it is golden. Be careful not to burn; lower heat accordingly. Add cream, stir with wire whisk, and cook over moderate heat about 10 minutes. Strain through a fine sieve into another small pan. Press hard with the back of a spoon on the onions to extract all their juice before discarding them.

Mix lemon juice and salt and pepper into the sauce. Pour over the breasts of pheasant and serve. Serves 2.

WILD RICE CROQUETTES

See Index for recipe as on menu June 12, 1969, for President of Colombia Carlos Lleras Restrepo.

GREEN BEANS AMANDINE

1-1/2 pounds green beans	3 tablespoons melted butter
1 quart water	2 ounces slivered almonds
1 teaspoon salt	

Wash and stem beans. Bring to boil water with salt. Add beans gradually, so water continues to boil. Cook the beans for 18 to 20 minutes until tender, but still crisp. Drain and put in a pan with butter. Sprinkle with almonds, heat, and serve. Serves 6.

VACHERIN GLACÉ AUX FRAISES

8 egg whites	2 cups sliced fresh strawberries
1 pound powdered sugar	1 cup whole strawberries
4 cups whipped cream	

Mark buttered and floured baking sheets with round circles, the size desired for meringue layers. Beat egg whites very stiff; blend in most of the powdered sugar. Fill a pastry bag, using a large plain tube, and form meringue layers in the marked circles. Sprinkle with remaining sugar. Bake in a very slow oven—250°, or until tinged with gold. Stack two or more layers with whipped cream to which you have added sliced strawberries. Decorate the top with whipped cream and whole strawberries. Chill and serve. Makes 24 large or 48 medium meringue circles. Serves 12 to 19.

Occasionally, as when the guest of honor comes from an Iron Curtain country which frowns on formal attire, an informal dinner is held instead for the important foreign visitor:

INFORMAL DINNER
TO HONOR NICOLAE CEAUSESCU, PRESIDENT OF THE COUNCIL
OF STATE OF THE REPUBLIC OF ROMANIA,
AND MRS. CEAUSESCU

Monday, October 26, 1970

Suprême of Sole Bosniaque

Roast Filet of Beef St. Germain—Sauce Périgourdine
Carrots au Beurre
Bibb Lettuce Salad — Bel Paese Cheese

Blanc Mange—Sauce Framboise

The wines were: Bernkasteler Doktor, Louis M. Martini Pinot Noir,
and Louis Roederer Cristal

SUPRÊME OF SOLE BOSNIAQUE

Carrots
Leeks
Green celery stalks
6 filets of sole
Salt and pepper to taste
1 cup dry white wine
2 tablespoons butter

1 bay leaf
Another 2 tablespoons butter
2 tablespoons flour
1 cup heavy cream
2 egg yolks, if necessary
Parmesan cheese

Cut carrots, leeks, and celery stalks into julienne strips to make about 1 cup. Boil vegetables in salted water. Strain and save the liquid.

Sprinkle the filets lightly with salt and pepper, and poach them in 1 cup of the vegetable liquid, wine, first 2 tablespoons butter, and bay leaf in a flameproof dish covered with waxed paper in medium-hot oven for about 10 minutes.

Make very light roux with second 2 tablespoons butter and flour. Stir in the wine liquid drained from the filets (remove the bay leaf), and cook about 10 minutes, stirring constantly. Add the cream, and if sauce is too thin, add the egg yolks, but do not cook it anymore.

Arrange the filets of sole on a serving platter, put the vegetables julienne on it, pour the sauce over, and sprinkle lightly with Parmesan cheese. Just before serving, place under a hot broiler for a few minutes. Serves 6.

ROAST FILET OF BEEF ST. GERMAIN–SAUCE PÉRIGOURDINE

1 4-pound filet roast of beef	3/4 cup beef consommé
Salt, pepper, and garlic powder to	Large mushroom caps, sautéed
taste	Puree of green peas
2 tablespoons flour	

Season and roast beef in 450° oven about 10 minutes per pound for very rare and 12 to 14 minutes for rare. Add flour to the roast drippings, scrape the sides of the pan, and brown the flour. Add the consommé, simmer, and strain.

Set the roast on a long serving dish, and garnish with mushroom caps filled with puree of green peas. Serves 8.

Serve with Sauce Périgourdine:

SIMPLIFIED SAUCE PÉRIGOURDINE

2 tablespoons fresh truffles, diced	Salt and pepper to taste
1 tablespoon butter	5 tablespoons Madeira wine

Cook the truffles gently in butter. Season with salt and pepper, and drain. Dilute the juices in the pan with 1 tablespoon of the Madeira, and stir in the brown gravy which you previously made. Simmer a few minutes, and strain.

Put the truffles back in the sauce, add the remaining Madeira, and keep hot without allowing to boil.

CARROTS AU BEURRE

Whole tiny carrots	Salt and pepper to taste
Butter	

Boil carrots in salted water, and sauté in butter. Season with salt and pepper to taste, and serve.

BLANC MANGE–SAUCE FRAMBOISE

1 pound white almonds, finely
    ground
4 or 5 bitter almonds, finely
    ground
3 cups (24 ounces) filtered water

1 cup sugar
2 envelopes unflavored gelatin,
    softened in 2 tablespoons
    water

Pound ground almonds in a mortar as fine as possible, while adding, spoon by spoon, the filtered water. Press very tightly by squeezing in a cloth. Dissolve the sugar in the almond milk, and add gelatin. Bring almost to boiling point, while stirring.

Pour into oiled mold with center hole like that used for Bavarian cream. Refrigerate and serve with warm Sauce Framboise (below). Serves 6.

SAUCE FRAMBOISE

1-1/2 cups raspberry jelly
2 teaspoons arrowroot or
    cornstarch

3 tablespoons Kirsch liqueur

Melt raspberry jelly over low heat, thicken with arrowroot, and flavor with kirsch.

7

-»»‹‹‹-‹‹‹-‹‹‹-

DINING FORMALLY WITH PRESIDENTS PAST

I am glad I didn't cook in the Teddy Roosevelt administration. The "rough and ready" Teddy hung all his stuffed heads of wild animals around the walls of the State Dining Room. I much prefer Healy's thoughtful seated portrait of Abraham Lincoln that hangs above the table now.

Among the outstanding hosts of the White House were undoubtedly the Hoovers. In their first three years in the White House, they sat down alone at the dinner table just three times, according to their housekeeper, Ava Long.

An invitation to the White House is a command performance and guests are never late without letting the White House know in advance. But during the Hoover administration, dinner was once kept waiting fifteen minutes for a missing guest who had not bothered to call to say he would be late for the formal 8 P.M. sit-down state dinner.

The guest and his wife arrived at the end of the first course and were told that the President was at dinner but that they could wait and join the group for coffee. The couple left in a huff and were never invited back.

They should have stayed, had coffee, and smiled no matter how hungry they felt—and come up with a good reason for their lateness as well.

At least they didn't have to endure the stuffed feeling of which President Grant complained after every formal meal. A man of very simple taste, he nonetheless is credited with giving the most elaborate meals ever served at the White House: as many as thirty courses sometimes, with six different wines to wash them down.

It was not until Chester Arthur's administration that the formal White House meal was finally reduced to a more manageable fourteen courses. But there still were those six wines.

It is fascinating to see what Presidents of old ate. One account of President Washington dining at Mount Vernon comes from the diary of Amariah Frost of Milford, Massachusetts, who visited Mount Vernon in

128

June, 1797. Frost tells of arriving at 10 A.M. and finding Washington out on horseback, checking the work of the laborers in the fields. While waiting for Washington, Frost was served a rum punch by a servant. I could almost feel I was there when I read how "the President directed us where to sit (no grace was said). Mrs. Washington sat at the head, the President next to her at her right."

Frost goes on to say "the dinner was very good," and he speaks of "a small roasted pigg" as the *pièce de résistance*. But that was only one of many courses that Frost and several other guests sat through. Other dishes were beef, boiled leg of lamb, peas, "lettice," artichokes, cucumbers, "puddings, tarts, etc." Frost says that each person called for the drink of his preference, and the President "preferred" a glass of wine.

In contrast, when the Eisenhowers entertained the Soviet Premier and Mrs. Khrushchev, they served a very simple American meal. Curry soup, roast turkey with cranberry sauce, sweet potatoes, tossed green salad.

During the war years, the Franklin Roosevelts gave luncheons which were partially working sessions for such men as Winston Churchill and Charles de Gaulle.

Here is the menu of one such meal:

PRESIDENT ROOSEVELT'S
LUNCHEON FOR GENERAL CHARLES DE GAULLE

July 7, 1944

Jellied Bouillon

Broiled Chicken   Currant Jelly
Asparagus   Duchess Potatoes
Parsleyed Carrots
Tossed Salad

Vanilla Ice Cream   Crushed Raspberries
Angel Food Cake

Coffee

FDR's successor, Harry Truman, served Winston Churchill some of Truman's own favorite foods:

PRESIDENT TRUMAN'S
LUNCHEON IN HONOR OF SIR WINSTON CHURCHILL

January 5, 1952

Oyster Soup
Celery Hearts

Filet Mignon with Mushrooms   Asparagus with Hollandaise Sauce
Grilled Tomatoes   Hard Rolls
Hearts of Lettuce with Roquefort Dressing

Strawberry Shortcake

President Roosevelt thoroughly enjoyed visitors at the White House
because most of his time was spent in a wheelchair. Polio had ren-
dered his legs almost useless. When King George and Queen Elizabeth
were scheduled for a visit in 1939, so the story is told, FDR actually took
over the planning from First Lady Eleanor. It was just that he enjoyed it
more than she did. And he even helped work out the menu:

PRESIDENT ROOSEVELT'S FORMAL DINNER HONORING
KING GEORGE AND QUEEN ELIZABETH OF ENGLAND

June 8, 1939

Clam Cocktail

Calf's Head Soup

Terrapin   Corn Bread

Boned Capon   Cranberry Sauce
Peas   Buttered Beets
Sweet Potato Puffs
Frozen Cheese and Cress Salad

Maple and Almond Ice Cream
Pound Cake
Coffee
Wine

Problems of protocol are always around to plague the White House staff. When King George and Queen Elizabeth came to visit the Roosevelts in 1939, FDR solved the problem of entertaining royalty by having the tables of the State Dining Room arranged in a horseshoe. FDR and the queen sat on one side of the table—the outside curve—and King George and First Lady Eleanor sat on the other side—the inner curve.

FDR and the king were served by butlers simultaneously, and then Eleanor and Queen Elizabeth were served simultaneously. I always laugh when I think of that and say, "Well, that's show business." And if you don't think White House dinners are staged, you haven't been reading the newspapers.

Every moment is staged. Let me tell you how it looked to my eyes when I first arrived at the White House.

I had been at the White House just one month when President Eisenhower issued invitations for a formal dinner for an old friend, General Robert Cutler, who was retiring as special assistant to the President in charge of national security affairs. I had cooked a thousand formal dinners all over the world—Paris, Prague, Cannes, Tunisia, Hollywood—but this was the White House and I confess I had to strengthen my courage with a silent *Dieu veut*—"so God wills"—as the hour drew near.

There was one thing on my side in this military maneuver—for every White House function is a triumph of the kitchen "battlefield." The main course was Roast Veal Périgueux, and this I had served many times before.

I had been studying White House social etiquette and found it the closest one can come to customs of royalty in America. I think I was nervous mostly because of the ritual which attends a formal affair.

When the President issues an invitation to a formal dinner at the White House, it is different from a hostess inviting several couples in for dinner. The hostess appreciates an extra ten minutes to see that the cook has everything ready. But the White House expects precise punctuality. Everything is perfectly timed. The guests arrive, and the men check their coats at the cloakroom where each is handed a little envelope. It contains a small drawing of the table, marked to show where each of them will sit. It also contains the names of the partners each will have, because no man escorts his own lady to dinner.

Before the dinner there is a reception so that the President can meet any guests he does not know and greet old friends.

The couples make their way to the East Room, where hangs the portrait of George Washington that Dolley Madison saved so many years ago. Here the guests greet others of the party, and aides present men to their female partners if they are not acquainted. The guests are assembled in a line around the room according to rank and their position at the table.

At precisely the correct moment, the President enters the room with the First Lady—the President leading. With them are the guest of honor and his wife. They form a small receiving line, and the guests file by to pay their respects to their host and hostess and meet the honored guests, even if they have just met two hours ago at a conference. A military aide stands with the President and another with the First Lady to make any introductions that are necessary. Even for people the President has met, it helps to have an aide present because no President can possibly have at his fingertips the names of all the people that he has met in a year or a lifetime. Many guests spend their moments with the President reminding him of where they met him last.

When the President has greeted everyone, the Marine Band strikes up a march and the President leads the way to the State Dining Room with the wife of the guest of honor. The First Lady is escorted by the guest of honor. Every male guest takes the lady the White House has assigned him and has the duty of escorting his dinner partner back to her husband or friends after the affair is over.

Incidentally, at the White House when someone says, "The redcoats are coming," nobody runs. It just means the red-jacketed Marine musicians have arrived and are setting up their music.

It was always a thrilling moment for me to see the guests enter the dining room to martial music. Of course, I was behind a screen that stands between the pantry and dining room and could not be seen.

There was only one President who ignored the unwritten rule that the President's wife is not her husband's dinner partner. That was William McKinley, who insisted that his wife, Ida, sit beside him because she suffered nervous attacks and might suddenly need his help.

The table at which the guests sit at a state occasion glows with gold rampant upon a field of white. The tablecloth itself is "spanking white," as Americans say, and maids have given it its final pressing on the table. But the flatware is gold instead of silver, dating back to the Harding administration. The guests sit on gold chairs, and the china is heavily etched with gold to match the gold service. Gold vases hold huge displays of flowers. Pink roses were Mamie Eisenhower's favorite flower—but the flowers varied according to the favorite colors of the honored guests.

Dinner consisted of six courses for a formal affair. A formal luncheon was four courses.

The shape of the table varies with the number of people. A horseshoe shape can hold 104 persons. The straight table is used for groups of 44 or less. An "E" can hold 110.

For 80 guests we would have 15 or 16 butlers to serve. We always brought in outside help both for serving and for helping in the kitchen for these special occasions. The people had been as thoroughly checked for security as I, or any other regular White House employee, had been.

At a formal dinner Charles, the head butler, and his brother John, the second butler, always served the President and the First Lady and the guests of honor. I would put a little piece of parsley on the President's platter so that they would know it was his, after he went on his diet. Before that, he ate everything exactly like everyone else.

When the guests sit down, there is no food on the table. Just napkins, place cards and the table service. But as soon as the President is seated, the butlers enter—one for every seven guests—bearing platters of the first course. In come, simultaneously, several other butlers to pour the wine and the water. Soup is served already poured into small individual bowls, but all other food is passed on silver platters for the guests to help themselves. It is, of course, beautifully garnished and arranged.

When the soup is removed from the right side, the same butler who removes it places a warm plate served from the left side. The President is always served first, even ahead of the First Lady.

For the main course, the butlers work in pairs, one holds the tray with the meat and the gravy in separate containers, while behind him stands the other butler with vegetables—one platter on each arm. Meanwhile, still another butler is serving hot rolls. No butter is served at a formal meal. The rolls are already buttered. Bread and butter plates are not used for state dinners, but for less formal occasions.

Dessert is served in the same way as other courses. We never had individual dessert portions already placed on individual plates. The guest served himself from the platter.

Coffee is not served in the dining room at a formal dinner. The White House follows European style, and coffee is served in another room—the Red Parlor for the ladies, the Green Room for the men. Then the guests often listen to a music recital. Frequently the President invites outstanding people from the world of show business, and they perform for the other guests. There is even pomp and ceremony in the way the musicale is handled. The ladies rejoin their escorts in the Blue Room after coffee, and the whole company forms a procession to the East Room, where the entertainment takes place.

The kitchen is on the ground floor of the White House, and the food is brought upstairs to the pantry for serving in the State Dining Room on the great round and oval silver trays. I inspected each tray before it went into the dining room, standing by with my garnishes and my ever-present pastry tube. The butlers emerged from behind the large standing screen, since a door would have been too clumsy.

Sometimes it would be eleven at night before I would leave the White House, full of the triumph of a meal well done.

President Eisenhower was not the first President to employ a French chef. President Arthur did so, too. He was noted for his fine entertainment, although his sister had to act as hostess, since his wife did not live to see him elevated to high office.

Jefferson had a French chef named Julien. Kennedy's French chef was René Verdon. Washington, incidentally, had a chef with almost my own name—Fraunces.

Sometimes as I passed the dining table I thought of President Hoover, who always used the State Dining Room, even when he ate in solitary splendor. Hoover had been the son of a blacksmith too poor even to send him to college. Young Herbert raised many a callus working his way through college by manual labor, and his strength brought him right up to the highest job in the land.

The Eisenhowers did not go in for the tremendous receptions that used to be given for 1,400 and 1,500 persons in one night by the Trumans. The largest affairs that I experienced were the lawn parties for veterans which topped the 1,000 mark. But for inside parties, the number was kept as small as possible, and President Eisenhower preferred the intimacy of stag dinners.

President and Mrs. Truman would have to take a coffee break to rest themselves from the hours of standing in a receiving line. Coolidge once distinguished himself by disposing of a line of 2,000 persons nonstop in one hour. The guests were not happy.

The Kennedys made a few innovations, to do away with rigid White House formality. For example, they did not stand in a receiving line, but walked around the room greeting their guests.

Back in the early days of the White House before the days of electricity, the hour of dining was 4 in the afternoon, and the meal would go on for hours through some ten courses. But now the hour for a formal dinner is set for 8 P.M.

As the guests assembled in the East Room, I sometimes thought of those days and how the White House must have looked then. The first reception at the White House was held on New Year's Day, 1801. President John

Adams holds that honor. I think he would turn over in his grave if he knew what a fuss is still being made about the fact that his wife used the East Room, the current reception hall, for drying her laundry. After all, when he was second President of the United States, the capital city was such a swampy, desolate place that Congressmen didn't even bring their wives to live in Washington.

The White House, or "President's Palace" as it was then called, was practically unfurnished, and the treasury of the young Republic was too bare to make big outlays for fancy furniture. In Abigail Adams' defense, it should also be pointed out that it was the winter of 1800 when the first First Lady to live in the White House moved in, and there really was no other way to dry the clothes but in the house.

It was her son, John Quincy Adams, who is credited with innovating the custom of drinking toasts at the White House.

I mentioned the garden parties for veterans a moment ago. These have been going on for many years, and once when the Hoovers gave the party, playful soldiers absconded with the silverware, which they took as souvenirs for their nurses at their veterans' hospitals and later sheepishly returned.

In Andrew Jackson's day White House entertainment suffered its worst era. Guests really "made themselves at home," spitting tobacco juice on the draperies and casually coming and going by way of the windows. Once when the President received a cheese and invited everyone to have a piece at a sort of open house, it took the servants a month to clean the rugs.

Gracious living in the White House reached a high under President Hoover, who ordered only the best of everything.

One President tried to do away with the protocol of traditional White House formal entertainment. That was President Jefferson, who felt that democracy should extend into the White House dining room because in America everyone was equal to everyone else. The results were hardly gratifying. Many women got angry at him, but the table Mr. Jefferson set was of such quality that few who were invited rejected his invitations.

When I came to the White House, I already knew about the *affaire* Dolly Gann-Alice Roosevelt Longworth over precedence—whether the sister of the Vice President outranked the wife of the Speaker of the House.

As I got ready for the first formal dinner I would serve in the White House—a dinner "for 80 at 8:00"—I thought of how President Eisenhower would be following the customs of almost two centuries and how, when the evening was over, the pageantry would continue in the manner in which the guests would leave.

First the President and his Lady would retire. Then the ranking guests would have to go before it would be permissible for any other guests to leave. How inconvenient for everyone, I thought. Suppose the ranking guest does not want to go? Yet he knows that others are trapped. When the head of a foreign government is visiting, the President and First Lady solve the delicate problem by escorting the guest of honor to the front door of the White House so that, in effect, both leave the party together.

And how about the lesser guest who has something he simply must do, but he cannot leave? It is *de rigueur* for him to stay.

I would leave it to history—future history—to decide whether the current system of protocol must go. I had my first formal dinner to think about.

DINNER FOR GENERAL ROBERT CUTLER

Saturday, March 12, 1955

Prosciutto Ham and Melon

	Cream of Celery-Clam Soup Rysavy	
Sherry	Cheese Straws	
	Green and Ripe Olives	Curled Carrots

	Bouchée Victoria
Sauterne	with Maine Lobster
	Tomatoes and Cucumbers Marinated

	Roast Veal Périgueux
Red Burgundy	Cauliflower Sautéed
	String Beans Amandine
	Bread Sticks
Champagne	Endive in Salad
	Green Goddess Dressing
	Toasted Club Crackers

Charlotte
Strawberry Sauce
Assorted Nuts   Coffee   Candies

Prosciutto ham is an Italian ham which is cured but served raw, sliced paper thin. I served this frequently on the French Riviera in the old days.

The ham imparts a delicate flavor to the melon and is quite salty. You can buy it in Italian specialty stores.

The recipe for Roast Veal Périgueux is in Chapter 2. The recipe for Cream of Célery-Clam Soup Rysavy is in Chapter 12.

BOUCHÉE VICTORIA WITH MAINE LOBSTER

Patty shells
4 2-pound lobsters (for 8 people)
Court Bouillon (below)
1/4 pound butter

2 tablespoons flour
1/4 cup heavy cream
2 tablespoons sherry
Chopped parsley

I used my own puff paste patty shells (see Index) but you can use the patty shells that you get at the bakery shop.

Cook the lobsters in the Court Bouillon, which is a French way of saying "vegetables with water and wine," used as a stock for cooking seafoods.

Place the lobsters in this boiling mixture, and cook for 20 minutes. Then take the lobsters out, shell them, and save the red eggs (roe), if any, and the green tomalley, which will be used later to color the sauce.

Take the lobster shells, crush them, and put them all back in the bouillon to simmer for another hour. The shells will give a nice color to the broth, and the bits of lobster which remain will add flavor.

While the shells are cooking, dice your lobster in bits of 1/2 inch or less. Now make a *roux* of the butter and flour, keeping the *roux* white. Add a cup of fish stock to the *roux*, to make a creamy sauce. Now strain the stock that remains. You probably will have needed to strain some of the cup of stock which you added to the *roux*, since the stock diminishes as it boils. You can save the remaining fish stock in a paper container in the freezer to use for future fish dishes.

To your cup of creamy sauce add the heavy cream and sherry. Put your sauce in the top of a double boiler, because the cream and sherry should not come to a boil. Gently fold in the cubed lobster, being careful not to crush it, and if your mixture is too thick, add a little more of the lobster stock you have strained.

Fill your patty shells just before serving, and top with a sprinkling of parsley. Serves 8.

COURT BOUILLON

2-1/2 quarts boiling water
5 teaspoons salt
2 carrots, sliced
4 stalks celery, sliced
2 medium onions, sliced
1 sprig parsley

1/2 teaspoon thyme
2 bay leaves
7 peppercorns
2 cups dry white wine
Seafood

In the boiling water to which you have added the salt, cook the following vegetables and spices loosely tied in a cheesecloth bag: carrots, celery, onions, parsley, thyme, bay leaves and peppercorns. After cooking for 1 hour, add the wine and whatever seafood you desire to use.

CHARLOTTE WITH STRAWBERRY SAUCE

1 envelope unflavored gelatin
1/4 cup water
1 cup milk
4 egg yolks
1/2 cup sugar
1 teaspoon vanilla
1 pint heavy cream, whipped

12 to 15 ladyfingers
1 cup whipped cream
Whole strawberries
Crushed strawberries
Sugar
Fresh orange juice

Soak the gelatin in the water. Let the milk come to a boil. While the milk is heating, beat the egg yolks with the 1/2 cup sugar and vanilla in the electric mixer until it can be poured in a ribbon. Now pour the boiling milk slowly into the egg yolks while they are beating, to prevent the yolks from cooking. Just before you stop the electric mixer, pour in the gelatin mixture to blend it thoroughly with the egg mixture.

Strain and let cool in the refrigerator. When it starts to thicken, fold in the cream, and pour the mixture into a round mold or melon mold, which you have lined with ladyfingers. Leave in the refrigerator for about 4 hours or more. Unmold by dipping mold into warm water. Place on a serving dish with the molded side up, and decorate with the additional whipped cream, using your pastry tube, and whole strawberries spaced around the outer edge.

A separate serving dish of crushed strawberries, with sugar and fresh orange juice added to it, accompanies the charlotte to the table. Serves 6.

There is a quaint poem someone showed me one day at the White House which dates back to the 1700's when Jefferson was a young man. It shows how universal is the interest in food and how never-changing. It was published, incidentally, in a magazine of the day called *Gentleman's*. Let me give you just the first two stanzas:

A RECIPE FOR SOUP

Take a knuckle of veal,
    You may buy it or steal;
In a few pieces cut it,
    In a stewing pan put it.

Salt, pepper and mace,
    Must season your knuckle;
Then what's joined to a place,
    With other herbs muckle.

"Muckle," as you may have guessed, was another word for much or many. But not all White House entertaining of the great involves a large number of guests. For example, when, in 1956, President Eisenhower entertained Prime Minister Nehru of India, only seven were present at the luncheon which I served before the President took Nehru to the farm at Gettysburg for a quiet visit. There were the President and Mrs. Eisenhower, their son, John, and his wife, Barbara, Mrs. Eisenhower's mother, Mrs. Doud, and of course, the guest of honor, Prime Minister Nehru, and his daughter, Madame Indira Gandhi, who stayed behind to visit with Mrs. Eisenhower. Because of the Prime Minister's Hindu religion, we served no wine.

LUNCHEON
FOR PRIME MINISTER NEHRU OF INDIA

Sunday, December 16, 1956

Oysters on the Half Shell
Toasted Sea Biscuit

Roast Leg of Lamb
Mint Sauce   Gravy

Mashed Potatoes
Thyme Peas
Rolls

Savarin with Fruit
Coffee

OYSTERS MIGNONETTE

Oysters on the half shell
1/2 cup vinegar
1/2 cup water

1/2 cup finely chopped onion
Freshly ground black pepper and
salt

I served the oysters with Sauce Mignonette. This is simple to make. To the vinegar and water, add onion and a generous seasoning of pepper and a little salt. The oysters, of course, are dipped into the sauce as they are eaten.

THYME PEAS

Peas
1 teaspoon thyme

1/4 cup beef consommé
Butter

Cook your peas as usual, and while they are cooking, make your herb dressing in a separate pan. Cook the thyme in the consommé for 5 minutes. Then strain the liquid, add a generous portion of butter, and pour over the peas. This is a good way to give a little pep to a commonplace vegetable.

Now here is a menu served to another celebrated guest:

PRESIDENT KENNEDY'S LUNCHEON
IN HONOR OF GENERAL DOUGLAS MACARTHUR

July 20, 1961

Consommé Rubis à la Moldavia

Stuffed Cornish Hen with Wild Rice
Sauce Périgourdine

MERINGUE

4 eggs   1/8 teaspoon salt
For each egg: A pinch of cream of tartar
2 tablespoons sugar
1/2 teaspoon vanilla or lemon
   juice

Put eggs in bowl, and beat with whisk or egg beater. When soft peaks start to form, add sugar gradually, vanilla or lemon juice, salt, and cream of tartar.

In contrast with what the Nixons served the Duke and Duchess of Windsor, here is what the Coolidges fed the Duke of Windsor when he was the very eligible twenty-five-year-old Prince of Wales:

PRESIDENT COOLIDGE'S
FORMAL LUNCHEON IN HONOR OF THE PRINCE OF WALES

Fruit Cup

Bouillon
Fairy Toast

Speckled Trout

Broiled Chicken

Peas   Bermuda Potatoes

Mixed Salad
Cheese Biscuits

Ice Cream with Strawberry Topping

Cakes

Coffee

Salted Almonds   White Rock

President Eisenhower used formal luncheons a lot for entertaining. Partly because of his health, he did not like to entertain at night. The choice of dishes was quite sumptuous, even though it was only a luncheon. Members of Congress were served roast pheasant.

PRESIDENT EISENHOWER'S
CONGRESSIONAL LUNCHEON

Monday, March 7, 1955

Hot Madrilene
Sliced Lemon

Queen and Ripe Olives   Celery Hearts
Melba Toast

Roast Pheasant
Wild Rice
Bread Sauce   Gravy
Buttered Brussels Sprouts
Rolls

Tossed Salad
with Hearts of Palms
Sour Cream Roquefort Dressing
Toasted Whole Rye Wafers

Orange Sherbet Ring Mold
with Brandied Peaches

Cookies
Assorted Nuts   Candies
Coffee

ROAST PHEASANT WITH BREAD SAUCE

Pheasant (1 for every 2 guests)	Salt pork, thinly sliced
Salt and pepper to taste	1 cup chicken consommé
1 bay leaf	Sprinkling of flour
Pinch of thyme	1 cup dry bread crumbs per
3 slices onion	person
1 stalk celery	Butter

I counted one pheasant for every two guests because only the breast of pheasant would be served at this occasion. However, the whole pheasant is roasted. The rest can be used later.

Season the inside of the pheasant by rubbing with salt and pepper and by placing inside the bay leaf, thyme, onion, and celery.

Now season the top of the pheasant with salt and pepper, and cover the breast section with thin slices of salt pork tied in place with a string. Place on a rack in a roasting pan, and cover with aluminum foil. Only the top of the bird is covered with aluminum foil so some consommé is needed under the rack to keep the steam rising up to the underside of the bird and for frequent basting. I wrap the aluminum foil so that I can easily draw it aside to baste the breast section.

Bake in a 375° oven until done—about 1-1/2 hours. Take off the string and the salt pork, and brown the bird, uncovered, in the last few minutes.

From the remaining liquid at the bottom of the roaster make the gravy, adding to it the vegetables which have been cooked inside the pheasant. Add just a sprinkling of flour to thicken it, and strain after it has cooked about 20 minutes to blend in the flavors of the vegetables.

Now to serve the pheasant: brown about 1 cup bread crumbs per pheasant in butter. Place the crisp buttered crumbs in a pile in the center, and lay the half breasts in pairs on each side of the crumbs, laying partially on the crumbs. Then when each person serves himself, some of the buttered crumbs come along with the breast, giving a little crispness which is pleasant.

BREAD SAUCE FOR ROAST PHEASANT
(Each Pheasant)

1 cup milk	Pinch of white pepper
1/4 cup fine bread crumbs	2 tablespoons butter
1 small onion, with 5 whole	1/4 cup coarse dry bread crumbs
cloves stuck in it	Additional 1/2 tablespoon butter
1/4 teaspoon salt	

Put the milk, the fine crumbs, and whole onion with its cloves in the top of a double boiler; simmer for about 30 minutes. Add salt, pepper, and 2 tablespoons butter. Brown the coarse crumbs in additional butter. The onion is removed when the sauce is finished and it is ready to be served. The toasted crumbs are sprinkled on top of the sauce when it is in the serving bowl. The sauce is passed at the same time as the gravy. Serves 2.

WHITE HOUSE
SOUR CREAM ROQUEFORT DRESSING

2 cups mayonnaise	2 tablespoons lemon juice
1 cup sour cream	6 ounces Roquefort cheese
1/2 cup wine vinegar	

Combine, in the blender, the mayonnaise, sour cream, vinegar, lemon juice, and Roquefort cheese. Let blend several minutes until the dressing is nice and creamy.

ORANGE SHERBET RING MOLD WITH
BRANDIED PEACHES

Use a ring mold to mold your sherbet, allowing at least 2 hours to refreeze the sherbet in the freezer. Just before serving, put your mold in warm water for a moment, unmold in a round serving dish, and fill the center with drained brandied peaches, decorating the top of the sherbet only with a pattern of whipped cream, using your pastry tube.

To brandy the peaches, if you have not been able to buy any ready-made at the market, simply take a can of peach halves, drain the juice, add an equivalent amount of brandy to the juice, and bring your peaches to a boil in the brandied liquid. Just as soon as they come to a boil, remove instantly from stove and cool. Before the brandied peaches can be served in the sherbet ring, they must be drained and ice cold.

A dry cookie is the best kind to serve with the brandied dessert. I served a sugar cookie.

Now for comparison see the simplicity of an important state luncheon served by President Kennedy:

PRESIDENT KENNEDY'S
LUNCHEON
FOR COUVE DE MURVILLE, MINISTER OF FOREIGN
AFFAIRS OF THE FRENCH REPUBLIC

September 15, 1961

Cold Curried Soup

Filet of Sole
Pureed Potatoes
Spinach

Tomato and Cucumber Salad

Cream Puffs with Chocolate Sauce

Demitasse

COLD CURRIED SOUP

1 package frozen green peas	Salt and pepper to taste
1 10-1/2-ounce can chicken soup	1/2 cup heavy cream (optional)
1 teaspoon curry powder	

Cook frozen green peas in the chicken soup. When they are cooked, add curry powder, and mix in the blender. Season to taste, and let cool. You may add cream if you wish. Serves 4 or 5.

FILET OF SOLE

See Index for recipe.

PUREED POTATOES

6 medium potatoes   1 teaspoon salt
3 tablespoons butter   1/2 cup heavy cream

Cook the potatoes about 40 minutes. Mash them in the electric mixer. Add the butter, salt and cream, and beat until they are light and creamy. Serves 4 to 6.

SPINACH

See Index for recipe.

CREAM PUFFS WITH CHOCOLATE SAUCE

1/2 cup water   2 eggs
1/4 cup butter   Vanilla-flavored whipped cream
1/2 cup sifted flour   Powdered sugar
Pinch of salt   Chocolate sauce

Heat the water and butter, and bring to the boiling point. Then add the flour and salt. Cook and stir the batter until it leaves the sides of the pan and forms a ball. Remove from fire. Beat in the eggs, one at a time, and mix well. Make small puffs with your pastry bag on a greased baking sheet. Bake them in a hot oven (400°) about 30 minutes. Then reduce the heat to 350° and bake them 5 more minutes.

When the puffs are cool, make a gash in the side of each one, and fill with whipped cream sweetened with sugar. Serve with chocolate sauce. Makes 8 large or 16 small puffs.

The **VIP** treatment accorded heads of state is also given to the President's own official family—the Vice President and the Cabinet members—and the Chief Justice of the Supreme Court. It is also granted the Speaker of the House of Representatives.

Here is the dinner Ike served Chief Justice Warren.

PRESIDENT EISENHOWER'S
FORMAL DINNER
TO HONOR CHIEF JUSTICE WARREN

Tuesday, January 29, 1957

Hot Tomato Juice with Whipped Cream
Dry Sack

Fairy Toast
Hearts of Celery   Assorted Olives
Château
Climens
1937

Lobster Thermidor
Sliced Cucumbers Marinated in French Dressing
Boston Brown Bread Sandwiches

Puligny-
Montrachet
1952

Roast Rock Cornish Game Hen
Pâté de Foie Gras, Wild Rice Dressing
Crab Apple and Watercress Garnish
Creamed Zucchini
Sliced Pickled Beets
Bread Sticks

Pol Roger
1945

Tossed Bibb Lettuce in Blue Cheese
Toasted Club Crackers
Frozen Rum Pudding Melon Mold
Butterscotch Sauce
Ladyfingers

Assorted Nuts   Candies
Coffee

Cigars   Cigarettes
Liqueurs

FAIRY TOAST

Slice white bread as thin as you can and cut off the crusts to make perfect squares. (I use a square sandwich-type loaf of bread so that I have a smaller square.) Let the slices dry for 30 minutes. Then 1 hour or so before serving place them in a 400° oven with the door open and toast until they are golden brown on one side. They are so thin you do not need to turn them over.

LOBSTER THERMIDOR

3 2-pound lobsters
Court Bouillon (see Index)
6 tablespoons butter
2 tablespoons flour
1/2 cup heavy cream
3 tablespoons sherry

2 tablespoons grated Parmesan cheese
Additional cheese, salt, and white pepper, if needed
Melted butter

Cook the lobsters as you did for *Bouchée Victoria*, in the Court Bouillon.

Let the lobster cook 20 minutes in the boiling stock. Then split the lobster horizontally so that you have a top shell and a bottom shell. Only the shell body and tail are served stuffed.

Remove the meat from the body, the claws, and other portions, throwing back into the stock all the shells which you break, and let simmer to strengthen your stock.

Only the body-tail section is set aside and not cooked further.

To strengthen the flavor, also place the green tomalley back into your stock.

Let simmer for 2 hours. Then strain. Now make a creamy sauce. For 3 lobsters, make a *roux* of the butter and flour, adding 1-1/2 cups of the strong lobster stock. Just before taking from the stove, thin your thick sauce with the cream and sherry. Add Parmesan cheese. If you need to, add salt and white pepper. When your sauce is finished, fold in the lobster meat, which you have diced, and heap in the lobster shells. Sprinkle with more Parmesan cheese and melted butter, and place under the broiler for a few minutes until the cheese melts and the surface is brown. Serves 6.

ROAST ROCK CORNISH GAME HEN WITH PÂTÉ DE FOIE GRAS AND WILD RICE DRESSING

3 1-1/4 to 1-1/2-pound Cornish
   hens
Salt and pepper to taste
1/2 pound wild rice
1/2 cup light cream sauce, made
   with chicken consommé
   (see Index for Basic White
   Sauce and substitute consommé
   for milk)
1 cup diced foie gras
Butter

For the gravy:
Necks and giblets of the birds
1 onion, chopped
1 clove garlic, minced
1 stalk celery, cut up
1 carrot, cut up
3 tablespoons flour
1-1/2 cups broth

To garnish:
Spiced whole crab apples
Watercress
Turnip "flowers"

If the Cornish hens are a little more than 1 pound apiece, you will need one for every two persons. However, sometimes for stag dinners we served smaller hens whole, and each person received a whole stuffed bird.

Cut each bird down the middle so that you have two perfect halves. I sliced them frozen in our special saw for cutting frozen meats, but the average housewife should wait until they have defrosted or have her butcher do the splitting. Season the inside of each half with salt and pepper, and you are ready for your stuffing, or dressing.

To make the dressing, cook the wild rice in salted water. Now make the cream sauce, using consommé. You will need 1/2 cup. When you have made a light sauce, add to it the *foie gras* (goose livers) which you can buy canned. Fold this into the rice, being careful not to mash the *foie gras*, and add salt and pepper to taste.

Now stuff your individual servings of bird. Place the bird on aluminum foil which has been buttered, so that the rice will not stick to it. Brush the tops of the birds with butter, salt, and pepper, and fold the aluminum foil around, leaving the tops open. Bake in a 375° oven for 30 minutes, basting frequently. When the birds are almost done, raise the oven temperature to 450° for a few minutes, to brown. Serves 6.

To make the gravy for the Rock Cornish hen, use the neck and giblets of the birds, which have also been cooked with vegetables—onion, garlic, celery, and carrot. Do not use too much water because you will want a strong stock. Cook until vegetables start to disintegrate. Strain and add to this the liquid remaining from baking the hens. Let cook a little longer, and add to it a paste of flour and a little broth, stirring constantly until the gravy loses its floury taste. Strain and serve.

The hen halves are served on a platter with the dressing side down. (I place a little paper panty on each leg bone.) In a circle around the silver tray place the crab apples, which are a pretty red. (You can buy them at any grocery store.) On one end of the platter place a little bouquet of watercress in which sits a cluster of modernistic "flowers" made with turnips. Try your hand at carving bits of turnips into daisies standing on toothpicks. Serves 6.

FROZEN RUM PUDDING MELON MOLD

1/3 cup rum	Whipped cream
1-1/2 quarts vanilla ice cream	Marrons

Stir rum into ice cream and pour into a melon mold. Leave overnight in the deepfreeze, or for at least 3 hours. Before serving, unmold, and decorate with whipped cream and glazed chestnuts, which are called *marrons* and can be purchased in specialty stores. Serves 6.

BUTTERSCOTCH SAUCE FOR FROZEN RUM PUDDING MELON MOLD

1 package instant butterscotch pudding mix	1/2 cup heavy cream, stiffly whipped
1/2 the milk in package directions	Additional milk, if necessary

Use butterscotch pudding to which you add only half the amount of milk suggested in the directions. As the pudding begins to set, fold in whipped cream. Just before you serve, if the sauce is too thick, add just a bit more milk to make it the proper consistency for topping your frozen dessert.

LADYFINGERS

4 egg yolks
1/2 cup granulated sugar
6 egg whites, stiffly beaten

Another 1/2 cup granulated sugar
1 cup sifted flour
Powdered sugar

Beat the egg yolks with the first 1/2 cup sugar. Then beat the egg whites with the additional sugar, stiffly enough to form peaks. Now fold in the whites to the yolks, using a wooden spoon, and finally fold in the flour. Put in a pastry tube or bag with a medium round point. Make your ladyfingers on ungreased white or brown paper, about 2 or 3 inches long. Sprinkle with powdered sugar out of a shaker before you put them into an oven of 375° until they are light brown—about 12 minutes. When they are cool, you can peel the paper right off, or while they are still warm you can remove them with a spatula. Makes 75.

Embarrassing things are forever happening at White House dinners and receptions, but they happened with greater frequency, it seemed, in the Lyndon Johnson administration. That was because he insisted on bringing together persons of widely diversified backgrounds, like labor leaders and business tycoons who would end up politely snarling at each other.

But it was during a dinner that included movie star Joan Crawford and Justice William O. Douglas' new, twenty-two-year-old bride that the worst possible thing happened. Joan Crawford eyed the young Mrs. Douglas with what some called "condescension" and loudly explained that what was in front of her was a finger bowl, reaching across the table to "help" her with it.

An elaborate state luncheon was served in honor of the President of Italy. The menu, with the appropriate wines, follows:

PRESIDENT EISENHOWER'S LUNCHEON FOR THE PRESIDENT OF ITALY AND SIGNORA GRONCHI

February 28, 1956

Consommé à la Royale
Fairy Toast

Celery Hearts   Queen and Ripe Olives

Broiled English Filet of Sole

Graves Select   Maître d' Hôtel Butter
1949   Danish Tomatoes

Broiled French Lamb Chops
Minted Apricots
Parsleyed Potato Balls
String Beans Julienne

Rolls

Pol Roger   Bibb Lettuce in Salad
Dry Special   French Dressing
Cheese Straws

Lemon Icebox Dessert
Assorted Nuts   Candies

Coffee

LEMON ICEBOX DESSERT

1 envelope unflavored gelatin	Rind of 1 lemon, grated
1/3 cup cold water	3 egg whites
3/4 cup milk	Another 1/3 cup sugar
1/3 cup sugar	1 cup heavy cream, whipped
3 egg yolks, beaten	Additional whipped cream
Juice of 1 lemon	Chopped red maraschino cherries

Soften the gelatin in the water. While it is softening, let the milk come to the boiling point with the first sugar. Pour the milk over the egg yolks, beating vigorously as you pour. Now add the lemon juice and rind. Beat a little more, and then add the softened gelatin. Let cool in the refrigerator. Beat the egg whites with the additional sugar until they are stiff, and add to the gelatin mixture as soon as it starts to set. Finally fold in 1 cup whipped cream (the size should double) and pour into a mold. This is best when it has been left to chill overnight in the refrigerator.

When you unmold your lemon icebox dessert just before serving, decorate it with whipped cream passed through your pastry tube, and sprinkle with maraschino cherries. Serves 4 to 6.

Now let me show you how President Kennedy entertained Amitore Fanfani of Italy five years later:

PRESIDENT KENNEDY'S LUNCHEON FOR THE PRESIDENT OF THE COUNCIL OF MINISTERS OF THE ITALIAN REPUBLIC, AMITORE FANFANI

June 12, 1961

Homard en Bellevue

Roast Sirloin Richelieu
Potatoes Château
Stuffed Tomatoes with Mushrooms
Braised Lettuce

Bombe Vésuvienne
Petits Fours

Demitasse

HOMARD EN BELLEVUE

See Index for Lobster Bellevue.

ROAST SIRLOIN RICHELIEU

Sirloin of beef   Broiled mushrooms
Pork fat

Lard the sirloin of beef with strips of pork fat, and pan roast it over high heat on top of stove to brown quickly and seal in the juice. Baste it with a few tablespoons of its own cooking juice. Then place it in the oven and roast, allowing 14 minutes per pound. Garnish with mushrooms. Allow 1/2 pound of meat per person.

POTATOES CHÂTEAU

Potatoes   Chopped parsley
Clarified butter

Cut the potatoes in the shape of large cloves of garlic. Cook them slowly
in clarified butter in a heavy iron pan until they are brown all over.
Sprinkle parsley on top, and serve.

STUFFED TOMATOES WITH MUSHROOMS

4 tomatoes   1/2 pound mushrooms, finely
Salt and pepper to taste   chopped
2 tablespoons chopped onions   Pinch of chopped parsley
4 tablespoons butter

Make a circular cut around the stem end of the tomatoes; remove this
part and squeeze the tomatoes to remove the water and seeds without
spoiling their shape. Season with salt and pepper, place in an oiled baking
dish, and bake for 5 minutes in a very hot oven. Stuff the tomatoes with
the following mushroom stuffing: Heat the onions in the butter; add the
mushrooms; brown until almost all the liquid has evaporated; season with
salt and pepper, and finish with a pinch of parsley. Bake the stuffed
tomatoes 20 minutes in a hot oven. Serves 4.

BRAISED LETTUCE

Boston lettuce   Onion slices
Salt and pepper to taste   Bouillon
Pork fat   Any kind of meat gravy

Blanch clean Boston lettuce about 10 minutes in salted boiling water.
Drain; cool in water. Then press the water out. Cut each head in half;
season with salt and pepper, and place side by side in a sautéing pan
containing pork fat and onions. Brown over the fire; then pour in enough
bouillon to cover the heads of lettuce halfway. Cover the pan with
aluminum foil or thin brown wrapping paper, and braise in the oven until
dry. Serve with meat gravy poured over the heads.

PETITS FOURS

See Index.

One would think different Presidents would fete leaders of the same country similarly. Not at all. Let us look at how four Presidents feted German leaders.

This is the menu for the dinner given by President Johnson for Chancellor Ludwig Erhard of West Germany:

PRESIDENT JOHNSON'S
FORMAL DINNER HONORING CHANCELLOR LUDWIG ERHARD
OF WEST GERMANY

Vichyssoise

Lobster Thermidor
Berny Potatoes
Creamed Spinach

Green Salad

Mousse of Roquefort

Strawberries Romanoff

Wines served were:

Inglenook Pinot Chardonnay
Dom Pérignon 1955

Just as the Nixons and Kennedys felt particularly at home with the Irish, President Johnson was especially relaxed when he entertained official guests from Germany. Chancellor Erhard, he even took to the LBJ Ranch.

When Willy Brandt, then mayor of Berlin, was in this country, President Johnson entertained him at the White House and an even more simple menu—although delicious—was chosen:

PRESIDENT JOHNSON'S
DINNER HONORING WILLY BRANDT,
MAYOR OF BERLIN

Melon Balls in Wine

Leg of Lamb White House
Puree Favorite
Braised Endive

Chocolate Mousse
Demitasse

Wines served were:

Bernkasteler Schlossberg Spätlese Doktor Thanisch 1961
Inglenook Cabernet Sauvignon
Piper Heidsieck 1959

Here is the much more elaborate meal I prepared when Ike feted
Chancellor Konrad Adenauer.

PRESIDENT EISENHOWER'S
LUNCHEON FOR CHANCELLOR
DR. KONRAD ADENAUER

Monday, May 27, 1957

Chilled Vichyssoise
Melba Toast

Hearts of Celery   Assorted Olives

Filet of Sole Meunière
Coleslaw   Tomatoes and Cucumbers

Beaune-   Broiled New York Sirloin
Grèves   Pepper Relish
1952   Spanish Corn   Buttered Spinach
Rolls

Spring Salad with Artichoke Hearts
French Dressing
Cheese Straws

Lemon Sherbet Ring
Fresh Strawberries
Rum Sauce
Petits Fours
Assorted Nuts   Candies
Coffee

CHILLED VICHYSSOISE

See Index for recipe.

FILET OF SOLE MEUNIÈRE

Filets of sole
Milk
Salt and white pepper to taste
Flour
Butter

Few drops lemon juice
Chopped parsley
1 tablespoon capers
Lemon wedges

Soak the filets in milk, which has been seasoned with salt and white pepper, for 5 or 10 minutes. Drain on a paper towel, roll in flour, and fry in butter until golden brown. Then put them on a silver serving dish, and squeeze over them a few drops lemon, some parsley, and the capers. Just before serving, heat the butter remaining at the bottom of the pan until it is smoking hot, pour over the fish, and send it to the table with a few wedges of lemon.

SPANISH CORN

2 packages frozen corn
1 green pepper, diced
1/2 can pimento, drained and
    diced

Butter
Salt and white pepper to taste

Cook the corn, and in a separate pan parboil the green pepper. Add the green pepper and the pimento after you have drained and buttered the corn. Season with salt and white pepper, and serve. Serves 6 to 8.

Let us consider now the menu President Kennedy served Chancellor Adenauer four years later.

PRESIDENT KENNEDY'S LUNCHEON IN HONOR OF DR. KONRAD ADENAUER, CHANCELLOR OF THE FEDERAL REPUBLIC OF GERMANY

April 12, 1961

Avocado Pear Belle Aurore

Roast Beef Brabant Style
Potatoes Nancy
String Beans Amandine

Salad Lorette

Raspberry Bombe Glacée

Demitasse

AVOCADO PEAR BELLE AURORE

2 avocados	1 cup diced celery
Lemon juice	1 cup crab meat
Salt	1/2 cup mayonnaise

Cut the avocados lengthwise into halves, and remove the seeds. Sprinkle with lemon juice and salt. Combine the celery and crab meat with the mayonnaise to moisten. Fill the center of the avocados with this mixture, and serve. Serves 4.

ROAST BEEF BRABANT STYLE

Roast beef   Braised celery
Salt and pepper to taste   French green beans

Wipe the meat with a damp cloth, and sprinkle with salt and pepper. Place it on a rack in the pan, and roast, uncovered, in a slow oven (300°), allowing 35 to 40 minutes per pound. Garnish the meat with celery and beans.

POTATOES NANCY

2 cups cooked diced potatoes   Salt and pepper to taste
2 cups white sauce (see Index   Buttered bread crumbs
  for Basic White Sauce)

Mix the potatoes, white sauce, and seasoning, pour it into a greased baking dish, cover with the bread crumbs, and bake in a hot oven (450°) for 15 minutes. Serves 6.

STRING BEANS AMANDINE

See Index for recipe.

SALAD LORETTE

Use the same amounts of endive, hearts of celery, and cooked beets, all sliced julienne. Season with French dressing.

Let us go back a half century now to look at the elaborate dinner held for the brother of the Emperor of Germany in 1902. That was Prince Henry of Prussia and the host was President Theodore Roosevelt. As a pretty and vivacious young girl, Alice Roosevelt was very much a part of the official gathering:

PRESIDENT THEODORE ROOSEVELT'S
FORMAL DINNER IN HONOR OF PRINCE HENRY OF PRUSSIA

February 24, 1902

Huîtres sur Coquille
Croûtes Panachées

Potage Consommé Brunoise
Céleri Frise

Terrapin à la Baltimore
Filet de Boeuf Hambourgeoise
Chapon à l'Ambassadrice
Asperges Sauce Mousseline
Punch
Sorbet Impérial
Canard Canvasback Pooti
Hominy   Salade de Saison

Glace
Cerises Fondantes   Petits Fours
Marrons Glacés
Café

When I read war news of Vietnam, my mind goes back to the time I served a Vietnamese who came to this country seeking help for his country back in 1957. Many will remember the name. I am remembering now that dinner which President Nixon attended as Vice President. It was on Wednesday, May 8, I prepared a formal dinner for the President of Vietnam, His Excellency, Ngo Dinh Diem, and after it was ready, I wandered into the State Dining Room reading the place cards of the names and faces that I would surely miss in the years to come: Vice President and Mrs. Richard M. Nixon, Senator and Mrs. Lyndon B. Johnson, Minority Leader Joseph W. Martin, and others, all around the table set for sixty-three guests.

I studied the gold chairs and the gold vases and the gold "silverware" and the gold china. I thought of the care that had been given even to choosing the pink flowers—carnations and snapdragons—because pink was the favorite color of the guest of honor.

Who knew what momentous decisions had been made in the minds of great men at this very table? Who knew which chefs had helped make history by preparing a meal that sat so lightly on the stomach that it stimulated the thinking of a famous mind?

The menu for this occasion had been worked out with the First Lady.

PRESIDENT EISENHOWER'S DINNER
FOR PRESIDENT NGO DINH DIEM OF VIETNAM

Wednesday, May 8, 1957

Pâté de Foie Gras in Aspic of Port Wine
Melba Toast

Dry Sack

Cream of Green Pea Soup
Croutons
Hearts of Celery   Queen and Ripe Olives

Château
Climens
1942

Crab Meat Mornay
Sliced Tomatoes and Cucumber Marinated
Bread and Butter Sandwiches

Beaune-
Grèves
1952

Roast Long Island Duckling with
Dressing, Apple Rings, Gravy
Wild Rice with Mushrooms
Buttered Asparagus
Finger Rolls

Pol Roger
1945

Bibb Lettuce in Salad
Green Goddess Dressing
Cheese Crescents

Frosted Mint Delight
Petits Fours

Assorted Nuts   Candies

Coffee

Cigars   Cigarettes

PÂTÉ DE FOIE GRAS IN ASPIC OF PORT WINE

4 tablespoons butter
3/4 pound goose liver (foie gras)
1 jigger dry port wine
1-1/2 envelopes unflavored
  gelatin ·
1/3 cup water
Salt and pepper to taste
1 cup heavy cream, whipped

1/2 cup chicken consommé
Additional 1 envelope unflavored
  gelatin
Another 1/2 cup consommé
Additional 1/2 cup dry port wine
Truffles (from pâté de foie gras
  cans)

Serve these individually molded in the little tins which mold individual gelatin desserts or salads. Blend in the electric mixer the butter and goose liver. If you buy these in the can, take out the truffles and save them for the decoration on top of the aspic. Now add to the ingredients in the blender 1 jigger port wine and the 1-1/2 envelopes gelatin, which has been dissolved in the water. Blend until light and fluffy, and then add salt and pepper. The whipped cream is added after removing from the blender; it is merely folded in before pouring into the individual molds. This mixture is encased in little shells of port wine jelly.

To make the port wine jelly, take the first additional 1/2 cup consommé and dissolve the additional gelatin in it. Then add the second 1/2 cup consommé and the additional port wine. Pour this liquid into your six little molds, and place in the freezer. As soon as it starts to adhere to the sides, pour out the liquid centers, and save at room temperature for later use. Now, using a pastry tube, fill the centers of the molds with, first, the sliced truffles at the bottom, and second, the pâté de foie gras, which you squeeze through your pastry tube. Fill the molds almost to the top, and then pour in the remainder of the port wine jelly to seal in your foie gras filling completely.

When you unmold this first course, just before serving, it will be very attractive with the tiny truffles in a pattern under the glaze of the jelly. Serves 6.

CRAB MEAT MORNAY

Patty shells
4 tablespoons butter
2 tablespoons flour
Salt and pepper to taste
1 cup chicken stock or
  consommé

1/4 cup heavy cream
1/2 cup sherry
1 pound crab meat

I served this course in a large shell made of Puff Paste, which I described in an earlier chapter (see Index), but the easiest way for a housewife to make this dish is simply to buy the little patty shells. You may take your choice. But here is how to make the crab meat filling:

First make the Mornay sauce, melting the butter and blending it with the flour, salt, and pepper. Keep your *roux* white in color, and add the chicken stock or consommé. Let it simmer for 10 minutes, stirring occasionally, and just before taking off, add the cream and finally the sherry and the crab meat, which have been kept warm together in a double boiler. Add salt and pepper.

Pour into the patty shells, and you are ready to serve. Serves 6 to 8.

ROAST LONG ISLAND DUCKLING WITH DRESSING

1 3-pound duckling
1 large onion, chopped
1 small bunch celery, stringed
  and chopped
4 tablespoons butter

1 cup chicken consommé
Raw duckling liver
Half loaf dried bread, ground
1 clove garlic, chopped
Salt and pepper to taste

Roast the duckling in the usual way, starting with aluminum foil covering and a hot oven (375°) for 1-1/2 hours, taking off the covering for the final browning. The stuffing is very simple and has no sage or thyme. Its secret lies in using a lot of celery. First, sauté the onion and the celery in butter, and then simmer them in the consommé. The liver is chopped raw and added to the bread with the garlic. Combine all the ingredients, salt and pepper to taste, and stuff your bird. Serves 2.

APPLE RINGS

The apple rings are sautéed in butter until they are golden brown and placed in a ring around the duckling. No sugar is needed.

WILD RICE WITH MUSHROOMS

Cook the wild rice, and for every 2 cups cooked rice add 1/2 cup chopped sautéed mushrooms. This is served at the same time as the duck. Serves 4.

Unfortunately I do not have a complete menu from the Lincoln administration, but there are many old newspaper accounts about how lovely and "elegant" everything was and how beautiful snuffboxes were exchanged as gifts between the host and guest of honor. I don't think Abe Lincoln ever made use of any snuffbox he received.

At one formal Lincoln dinner, pheasant, venison, and terrapin, as well as turkey stuffed with truffles, were served.

The largest formal dinners in White House history were given by the President who had the simplest tastes, but was a victim of his time and his wife's social ambition. Ulysses S. Grant was happiest with plain hash or fried fish. But he had to endure formal dinners that lasted for hours and contained from twenty to thirty courses.

The Grant state dinners were such an endurance contest to sit through that the President came up with the quaint idea of getting up midway in the meal to walk around a bit and have a glass of Roman Punch. This was made by pouring champagne, spiked with rum, over crushed frozen lemonade (see Index).

One such meal described by a reporter at the time listed among many other courses—Vegetable Soup, Croquet of Meat, Filet of Beef, Partridge, Potatoes, Mushrooms, various vegetables and salads, Roman Punch and six wines, Rice Pudding, fruits that included pears and quinces, Ice Cream, Chocolate Candy, Nuts, and Coffee.

Thank goodness I wasn't there!

8

JEFFERSON, THE FIRST
WHITE HOUSE GOURMET

Thomas Jefferson was probably the greatest gourmet we have ever had in the White House. Maybe that's because he was a widower and substituted an interest in food for the usual domestic life. Surely he spent an inordinate amount of time talking about food, planning his menu, and growing unusual crops. He kept a little book which told him when his various favorite foods would be in season. And he drew charts of his gardens.

Typical entries might say:

"May 16. First dish of peas from earliest patch."

"June 4. Windsor beans come to table."

"June 13. A fifth patch of peas come in."

"July 13. Last dish of peas."

Thomas Jefferson's wife, Martha, never lived in the White House, for he had been a widower for almost two decades when he became President. His hostesses were his daughters, Martha and Maria, and on some occasions he called on Dolley Madison, the wife of his Secretary of State. Dolley was destined to become the next First Lady.

Many Jefferson recipes were written in his own handwriting. One of the cherished possessions today at Monticello is a collection of those marvelous recipes. James A. Bear, Jr., curator of Monticello, takes pleasure in relating how Thomas Jefferson preferred his foods cooked.

For example, Jefferson liked rabbit stew cooked with chunks of bacon, onions, red wine, and seasonings. He liked catfish soup boiled with lean ham and half a dozen peppercorns. And he liked vegetables served as a porridge—carrots, parsnips, turnips, and onions seasoned with thyme, parsley, and lots of butter—boiled to a shapeless mass and strained through a colander.

Amusingly, one recipe directs, "Take four calves feet and wash without taking off the hoofs. . . ."

My favorite comment about Jefferson is that of President John F.

Kennedy at a dinner for Nobel Prize winners in April, 1962, which he said was undoubtedly the greatest congregation of great minds ever assembled under one roof, except perhaps when Thomas Jefferson dined alone.

In epicurean circles there still exists a cult of Jeffersonian cookery. April 13—Jefferson's birthday—is a special occasion for toasting Thomas Jefferson. Every year, on April 13 or as close to Jefferson's Birthday as can be arranged, descendants of Jefferson and trustees of his estate, Monticello, sit down to a meal featuring his favorite dishes, a menu which changes every year. They dine in the very dining room where Jefferson once presided.

There are many stories told about him—stories concerning his special friendship with a certain beautiful Mrs. Maria Cosway, stories about how he rode around on his horse checking the gardens' crops, and how he sat talking with friends in French and Italian. But mostly the talk will be of "Mr. Jefferson" and how he would be taking his food were he there.

The guests frequently tell anecdotes handed down to them from relatives and servants who knew Jefferson. For example, they quote Isaac, a slave at Monticello, who dictated some of his memoirs of the great man. There is the story of how Jefferson had a favorite clock in his kitchen at Monticello and never went into the kitchen except to wind the clock.

And how "Old Master," as Isaac called him, had three fiddles and "played in the arternoons and sometimes arter supper."

And how, when Old Master "was a-writin' he wouldn't suffer nobody to come in his room." According to Isaac, he "had a dumb-waiter. When he wanted anything he had nothin' to do but turn a crank and the dumb-waiter would bring him water or fruit on a plate or anything he wanted." And still according to Isaac, Jefferson's vegetable garden was "monstrous large; two rows of palings, all 'round ten feet high."

The guests chuckle about how Jefferson hated eavesdropping servants and went to great lengths to confound them. And how he credited his longevity to eating many vegetables and drinking wine instead of whiskey. And how when he first tasted waffles in Holland, he fell in love with them and bought a waffle iron for 1.3 florins to bring back to Monticello.

Though the scene for the Jefferson Anniversary Dinner is the dining room of his beloved Monticello, no servants or guests are dressed in Colonial costume. "We feel that would be phony," Mr. Bear explains, "I don't think Jefferson would have wanted it that way. Jefferson was a thoroughly modern man, a Renaissance man, and were he alive today, he would be dressed in the latest fashion."

But let us return to the table conversation. Jefferson would be furious when servants spread gossip from one plantation to another. He had two devices for keeping servants at a distance while he was dining with his guests. One was circular shelves which would come out of the wall at the touch of a button into the dining room and on which servants would place the food in the pantry. But when he wanted even greater privacy with no servants even in the pantry on the other side of the wall, he had servers placed beside each guest from which they helped themselves to each course.

In Jefferson's day at Monticello the invitations went out reading that "Th. Jefferson requests the favor" of so-and-so's company at dinner on such-and-such a date bringing along "any friends who may be with them." The result of this generosity was that Jefferson, who left the White House in debt, continued to have problems with his finances at Monticello. But the invitation for April 13 is strictly limited to the principals only.

Very important to the epicurean event is Helen Duprey Bullock, a historian with the National Trust for Historic Preservation, who has researched Jefferson the man and the gourmet for forty years. It is she who wrote a book about Jefferson's romance with Mrs. Maria Cosway entitled, *My Heart and My Head*. It is also she who every year works out a menu for the annual birthday celebration.

So now let us get to work reconstructing one of these meals from the recipes preserved at Monticello and tested to make sure that modern ingredients work the same as the old, when sugar was coarser, flour heavier, and butter more pungent.

This is the menu for Thomas Jefferson's 228th Anniversary Dinner, chosen to show his interest in Spanish food and to include his favorite Spanish wines:

THOMAS JEFFERSON BIRTHDAY DINNER
ON THE 228TH ANNIVERSARY OF HIS BIRTH

April 13, 1971

Gazpacho

Tio Pepe Sherry

Hot Devill'd Crab

Roast Leg of Lamb   Conserve of Currants

Château Latour

Saffron Rice   Green Peas with Mint   Corn Pudding

Asparagus Vinaigrette

Montrachet
Cheese Mold   Beaten Biscuit
Strawberry Meringues Chantilly
Pedro Ximenez
Nuts and Candied Fruits
Coffee   Brandy

JEFFERSON'S GAZPACHO

1 clove garlic
1 large cucumber, peeled and
   diced
2 green peppers, slivered
4 tomatoes, peeled and cut into
   small pieces
1 slice stale toast, grated
5 tablespoons olive oil

1-1/2 quarts chicken consommé
2 tablespoons vinegar
1 teaspoon salt
1/4 teaspoon pepper
1 cup bread cubes
Garnishes of chopped celery,
   onion, and red pepper

In a wooden bowl or on a chopping board put garlic, cucumber, green peppers, tomatoes, and grated toast. Mix together, and then add oil as if making mayonnaise. When oil is absorbed, add a little water, salt, and pepper, and pass through colander. (If you have an electric blender, use it in place of colander.) Add consommé and vinegar. Add more salt to taste. Add bread cubes, chill, and serve very cold. Garnish with celery, onion, and red pepper. Chill. Serves 6.

JEFFERSON'S HOT DEVILL'D CRAB

1 pound fresh lump crab meat
2 teaspoons fresh lemon juice
4 tablespoons butter
2 tablespoons flour
1 teaspoon prepared mustard
1/2 teaspoon grated fresh or
   bottled horseradish

1 tablespoon chopped parsley
1 cup milk
2 hard-cooked eggs, minced
1/2 cup soft grated bread crumbs
   with 2 tablespoons melted
   butter

Flake the crab meat, removing any remaining cartilage or shell. Mix with lemon juice. In top of double boiler melt the butter, and stir in flour. Add mustard, horseradish, parsley, and milk. Stir until thickened. Add crab meat and eggs. Remove from fire, and place in six buttered crab shells or coquilles. Sprinkle with buttered crumbs. Bake at 400° for 10 minutes. Slide under broiler for a few minutes to brown the tops. Serves 6.

JEFFERSON'S ROAST LEG OF LAMB

The lamb in Jefferson's household was rubbed with salt, pepper, and a combination of spices including sage, thyme, rosemary, and dry mustard. Then it was put on the spit in a reflecting oven and turned a quarter turn at a time over the coals and basted from time to time to keep it from drying.

CONSERVE OF CURRANTS

1 onion, finely minced	1 sprig parsley
3 tablespoons butter	1 cup clear soup stock
1 tablespoon flour	1 tablespoon lemon juice
1 bay leaf	1 cup currant jelly
2 cloves	Salt and pepper to taste

Sauté onion in butter until lightly browned. Add flour, bay leaf, cloves, parsley, and soup stock. When the sauce has thickened, add lemon juice, currant jelly, and salt and pepper to taste. Strain and serve in a gravy boat. Can also be used with venison.

JEFFERSON'S CORN PUDDING

6 to 8 ears green corn (for 2 cups) or 2 cups canned cream-styled corn	1 teaspoon salt
	4 eggs
2 cups milk	4 tablespoons butter

Shuck the corn and remove all silk. With sharp vegetable knife score each row of kernels down the middle; then cut corn from cob. Scrape the ear lightly to get the remaining kernels and corn "milk."

Scald milk, and pour over corn. Add salt. Beat eggs, and add to mixture. Melt butter in a casserole, being sure to cover sides of casserole. Pour mixture into casserole, and bake at 350° for 50 to 60 minutes. Serves 6.

(I like Helen Bullock's comment: "Adding sugar to this pudding is a bit like trampling on the Confederate flag, but for those who would eat alien corn, 2 tablespoons may be added. In the 18th century, a corn pudding with a cup of sugar would be served as a dessert, and a similar sweetened pudding was made of macaroni and eggs for dessert.")

JEFFERSON'S ASPARAGUS VINAIGRETTE

2 pounds asparagus   1 teaspoon lemon juice
1-1/2 quarts water   1/2 teaspoon salt

Place asparagus in a sinkful of cold water until crisp and drained of possible sand. Pick up each stalk at stem end and snap. With a little practice this trick is easily learned, and asparagus will break at point where tough portion ends and remaining portion is tender and edible. Scrape lightly with a paring knife. Tie in a bundle with string.

In the bottom section of double boiler boil water with lemon juice and salt. Place asparagus in water; invert top of double boiler to serve as lid. Water should come within an inch of tips of asparagus. The steam will cook the tips. Boil about 15 minutes, depending on freshness and tenderness of asparagus. Drain and cool. Serves 6.

VINAIGRETTE SAUCE

1/2 teaspoon salt   2 tablespoons pickle relish
1/2 teaspoon pepper   2 hard-cooked eggs, pressed
1 tablespoon prepared English   through colander with
   mustard   wooden spoon
1/2 cup olive or salad oil
1/3 cup tarragon wine vinegar
1 tablespoon chopped chives or
   mild scallions (using part of
   tops)

Mix dry ingredients; stir in oil and vinegar, alternately. Blend well. Add chives, relish, and eggs. Stir. Serve over asparagus on Bibb lettuce. Makes 1-2/3 cups sauce; serves 6 to 8.

JEFFERSON'S CHEESE MOLD

In Jefferson's day, cheese was made daily as needed, but prepared cream cheese will do very nicely.

4 ounces cream cheese
1 small carton cream-style
cottage cheese

2 tablespoons light cream

Blend the ingredients together, and pour into an oiled small mold. Chill until ready to use. Turn out onto serving plate. Serve surrounded with Beaten Biscuits:

JEFFERSON'S BEATEN BISCUITS

4 cups flour
1/2 cup butter
1/2 cup lard

1 cup milk
1 teaspoon salt

Combine ingredients, making a stiff dough, and beat for 15 or 20 minutes. (In Jefferson's day servants would beat biscuits for several hours.) Roll and cut into small rounds. Bake in oven at moderate temperature until brown. Makes 24.

JEFFERSON'S STRAWBERRY MERINGUES CHANTILLY

6 egg whites at room temperature
1/2 teaspoon cream of tartar
2 cups granulated sugar
1/2 teaspoon each vanilla and
almond flavoring
1 cup heavy cream

2 tablespoons powdered sugar
2 tablespoons kirsch liqueur or
brandy
1 quart strawberries, washed and
hulled

Beat eggs and cream of tartar with hand beater until mixture stands in peaks that are light and frothy, but not dry. Add granulated sugar very gradually, beating constantly until all sugar is incorporated and mixture, when pinched, is not grainy. Add flavorings. Preheat oven to 275°. Place heavy brown paper on cookie sheets. With pastry tube or large spoon place meringues on paper about 2 inches apart, dividing mixture into 12 portions. Shape meringues with pastry tube or spoon into round shells depressed in center. Put in oven, and bake 50 minutes. Turn off oven, and without opening it, leave meringues for at least an hour. Peel paper from meringues. If not used immediately, store in cool, dry place lightly wrapped in waxed paper.

Now whip well-chilled cream in a cold bowl, fold in powdered sugar, and add kirsch or brandy. Place a meringue on a dessert plate, fill shell with strawberries, top with whipped cream, and garnish with large strawberry on top. Serves 12.

Just for fun, and because a more interesting rice dish was served, let's compare the menu you have just seen with the Jefferson memorial dinner of 1962:

THOMAS JEFFERSON BIRTHDAY DINNER, 1962

Deviled Egg with Anchovies on Watercress

Monticello Clear Consommé with Sherry

Poached Rock Fish with Béarnaise Sauce

Old Dominion Roast Leg of Lamb   Brown Gravy
Pilau of Rice with Pignola and Pistachio Nuts
Minted Peas
Whole Gooseberry Conserve

Salad Greens   Olive and Sesame Oil Dressing

Crème Brûlée Served with Macaroons
Nuts: Pecans and Almonds
Coffee

The Crème Brûlée, which he called Burnt Cream, is at the end of this chapter.

Another recipe I want to give you from this delightful meal is Jefferson's Pilau of Rice with Pignola and Pistachio Nuts. Since everyone knows the Saffron Rice used in the 1971 Jefferson dinner, I thought this would be a greater treat for amateur chefs and housewives. Jefferson, incidentally, was so fond of rice and anxious to improve the rice he had to put up with in this country that he once smuggled in a little rice seed when he was coming back from Europe.

JEFFERSON'S PILAU OF RICE WITH PIGNOLA AND PISTACHIO NUTS

2 tablespoons butter
1/4 cup pignola nuts
4 cups cooked rice
1/2 cup blanched unsalted
  pistachio nuts

Salt and pepper to taste
2 teaspoons mace

Melt the butter slowly in a heavy frying pan, and stir the pignola nuts over a low heat until they turn a golden color. Now add the rice and then the pistachio nuts, salt, and pepper to taste. Finally, blend in the mace just before serving. Serves 8.

For all his fine tastes and lavish spending, Jefferson didn't mind using leftovers. For example, leftover mashed potatoes were served in the form of little cakes:

JEFFERSON'S POTATO CAKES

Use mashed potatoes which have been generously fluffed with cream and butter, salt and pepper. Make little cakes of the cold mashed potatoes. Roll in bread crumbs which have been seasoned with salt and pepper. Fry in butter until golden and serve immediately.

Jefferson liked every kind of green salad, and he raised a great variety of lettuce, as well as many kinds of cabbage and celery. He is said to have had five kinds of endive alone.

With his green salad he liked a garlic dressing:

MONTICELLO GARLIC SALAD DRESSING

1 large clove garlic, crushed
1/2 cup olive oil
1/2 cup sesame oil

1/2 cup wine vinegar
1 teaspoon salt
1/2 teaspoon pepper

Place all the ingredients in a 2-quart jar, and shake well. Let stand awhile before shaking again and using. Makes 1-1/2 pints.

Like LBJ and President Nixon, Jefferson, too, had a Mexican dish that he enjoyed—or at least one he thought was typical of Mexico:

JEFFERSON'S MEXICAN BEAN SOUP

2 cups black Mexican beans	1 cup wine
2-1/2 quarts water	3 slices toast, made into croutons
2 pounds short ribs of beef	Butter
Salt to taste and generous amount of pepper	

Wash beans, and add to the water with the short ribs and seasonings. Boil over low flame for 3 to 4 hours, or until beans are soft. Remove meat; pour remainder through colander, pressing beans through. Return to pot with small pieces of meat and stock; simmer another 10 minutes or so. Take from stove; add wine and pepper to taste. Serve immediately with croutons browned in butter. Serves 8 to 10.

Jefferson is credited with having brought baked Alaska to America from Paris, but it was different from the huge ice cream cakes we now pop into the oven, with ice cream under meringue. Jefferson served ice cream encased in little balls of warm pastry, one to each serving.

Many people wonder how Thomas Jefferson made his ice cream. Let me give you the recipe as it is given at Monticello. You might find it interesting to compare Jefferson's recipe with Lyndon Baines Johnson's (see Index) many years later, and try both ice-cream recipes.

JEFFERSON'S ICE CREAM

1 quart heavy cream	1 cup sugar
6 egg yolks	1 tablespoon vanilla or grated
1/2 teaspoon salt	vanilla bean

Scald the cream, and then gradually add to it the egg yolks, which have been beaten until creamy and then beaten some more while gradually adding the sugar and salt.

Leave on stove, stirring constantly until the mixture is thick. Remove from stove and strain. Now stir in the vanilla, and pour the mixture into a hand-crank ice-cream freezer, around which ice and salt have been packed in a ratio of 1 part salt to 3 parts ice.

Crank freezer until ice cream is thick. Pour out the ice cream into a mold which is surrounded with salt and ice in a ratio of 1 part salt to 4 parts ice. Place in a cold spot until it sets and serve immediately. Makes 3 pints.

Jefferson had an icehouse in which he kept things cold during the summer. The rule was that it could be opened only once a day so as not to melt the ice.

In spring he had shad caught by the barrelfuls and placed in his private pond at Monticello. He liked the fish broiled simply:

JEFFERSON'S BROILED SHAD

Slit the fish open, being careful to remove the backbone without splitting the whole fish in two. Let it lie open a bit with a sprinkling of salt and pepper on it. Then place fish under a flame, broil until tender and brown, and serve with melted butter. Serves 2 to 6, depending on size. Allow about 1/2 pound per person.

Probably the style of cooking Jefferson liked best was French, but he did not mind mixing in all kinds of American Colonial dishes, such as Virginia ham glazed with a sprinkling of sugar and Southern fried chicken.

But the way he garnished the chicken was interesting. First, cornmeal was boiled and let cool. Then with a cookie cutter, small circles were cut in the cold mush, which were then fried until golden brown and placed around the platter to garnish.

Another interesting touch is the sauce he liked poured over the fried chicken as it was being served:

JEFFERSON'S SAUCE FOR FRIED CHICKEN

1 cup heavy cream	Salt and pepper to taste
1 tablespoon butter	2 teaspoons chopped parsley

Scald the cream, then stir in the butter, seasonings, and parsley. Pour over the chicken immediately.

Jefferson and the Franklin D. Roosevelts shared a love of duck:

JEFFERSON'S ROAST DUCK

1 4- or 5-pound duck, including
   giblets
2 onions, coarsely chopped
A few fine sage leaves
1/2 teaspoon salt
1/2 teaspoon pepper
Additional pinch of salt

Flour
Melted butter
1/2 teaspoon mace
2 tablespoons catsup
5 peppercorns
1 teaspoon lemon pickle
2 tablespoons flour

Rub inside of duck with salt and pepper; then pour in onions and sage leaves. Dust outside of duck with salted flour, and roast in very hot oven about 30 minutes. Baste with butter as it roasts. Make a coating for the duck with the broth from the stewed giblets, to which you add flour, mace, catsup, peppercorns, and pickle. Strain and pour on duck. Serve onion sauce in a gravy boat, made by combining the onion mixture inside the duck with the scrapings from the bottom of the pan. Serves 4.

Teddy Roosevelt liked Indian pudding, and so did Thomas Jefferson. Here is Jefferson's recipe:

JEFFERSON'S INDIAN PUDDING

1 cup molasses
2 tablespoons melted butter
1/2 teaspoon salt

10 tablespoons cornmeal
2 eggs, beaten
1 quart milk

Stir the molasses, butter, and salt into the cornmeal. Add the eggs. Bring the milk to a boil, and very gradually add it to the molasses-meal mixture. Pour into baking dish, and bake in slow oven for 1-1/2 hours, or until pudding sets. Serves 6 to 8.

Jacqueline Kennedy's favorite dessert was also a favorite with Jefferson. It is interesting to see how Jefferson liked his Crème Brûlée, which he called Burnt Cream.

JEFFERSON'S BURNT CREAM
(Crème Brûlée)

Peel of 1/2 orange
1 quart milk
2 egg whites
6 egg yolks
6 tablespoons granulated sugar

Sprinkling of essence of lemon
2 tablespoons flour
1/4 teaspoon salt
1 tablespoon butter
Powdered sugar

Put the orange peel in the milk, and bring to a boil. Beat egg whites until light, and add the yolks, continuing to beat a little longer. Sprinkle granulated sugar with essence of lemon to taste, and add to it the flour and salt. Stir the flour-sugar mixture very gradually into the milk, and continue to stir until mixture thickens.

Now add butter, stirring until integrated. Take off stove, and strain mixture through a sieve. Pour into baking dish. Carefully sprinkle powdered sugar over the complete surface until it is about 1/2 inch thick. Place under a flame until glazed—the modern broiler does very nicely.

Chill and serve. Serves 8 to 10.

9

AT HOME WITH THE NIXONS

When President Nixon finishes work and takes the elevator to the family quarters on the second floor of the White House, he is just like any family man arriving home from a day at the office. He steps off the elevator, calls out, "Hey, everybody, I'm home," and waits for everyone to rush out to greet him.

His interest in everything going on in the second-floor family quarters even encompasses the White House help. For example, when the President found that his wife's personal maid, Fina Sanchez, wife of his valet, Manolo, was feeling under the weather, he ordered her to stay in bed and had the staff serve a tray of food to her bedside.

No wonder Nixon's valet says, "I have learned kindness from the President. He wants to make everyone happy and somehow he always knows how to do this."

Pat Nixon and the President approach everything that concerns him as a team. The President and his wife even go over the details of each dinner party they are giving—the food, the guest list, the decorations, the wines.

"I like to get his thinking on everything," says the First Lady. "He comes up with some unusual and interesting ideas." Pat admits the President has the last word on which wines will be served while she has the last word on flowers and colors to be used.

The Nixons share many little "in" jokes like calling a certain favorite family rug their "cookie rug" since they chose it because it wouldn't show Tricia's and Julie's cookie crumbs. They also share favorite foods.

How would you like to make the President's favorite menu for dining at home with his family? You'd be surprised how simple the menu is. Here it is, along with Pat Nixon's own recipes for each course:

PRESIDENT NIXON'S FAVORITE DINNER MENU, FAMILY STYLE

Broiled Grapefruit

Meat Loaf
Corn Soufflé   String Beans Amandine
Tossed Greens, with Pat Nixon's Special Salad Dressing

Angel Pie

Milk

PRESIDENTIAL BROILED GRAPEFRUIT

2 grapefruit
4 tablespoons maple or maple-
   blended syrup
Butter

Garnish of walnut half,
   maraschino cherry, jellied
   cranberry or jellied cherry
   sauce

Start heating the broiler. Halve two grapefruit, and separate sections with grapefruit knife. With kitchen shears snip out the center. Drizzle maple or maple-blended syrup on each half; dot with butter. Heat under broiler until bubbly, and serve immediately.

A walnut half, maraschino cherry, jellied cranberry or jellied cherry sauce may be placed in center for decoration. Serves 4.

PRESIDENT NIXON'S MEAT LOAF

1 pound beef
1 pound pork
1/3 cup finely chopped onion
1-1/2 teaspoons seasoned salt

1/4 teaspoon ground black
   pepper
1 8-ounce can tomato sauce
3 slices bacon

Heat oven to 350°. In a large bowl lightly mix with a fork the beef and pork (ground together) with the onion, seasoned salt, and black pepper. Add just enough tomato sauce so that the meat may be formed into a loaf, and place in a baking dish or loaf pan.

Lay the bacon over the loaf, and pour the remainder of the tomato sauce over it. Bake about 1-1/2 hours, or until thoroughly done. Serves 6.

PAT'S CORN SOUFFLÉ

2 tablespoons butter
2 tablespoons flour
1 teaspoon salt
1/4 teaspoon ground black
  pepper

1/8 teaspoon paprika
Dash of Tabasco
1/2 cup milk
1 package frozen corn
3 eggs, separated

Heat oven to 375°. Lightly butter a 1-quart casserole. In a saucepan melt the butter. Blend in the flour, salt, pepper, paprika, and Tabasco; stir until smooth and bubbling. Add the milk, and cook until thickened. Stir in a package of frozen corn thawed just enough to separate the kernels. Separate whites from yolks of eggs. Beat the whites until stiff, and beat the yolks until thick. Add the yolks to the corn mixture; then fold in the whites.

Turn into casserole, and bake 30 to 35 minutes. Serves 4.

PAT NIXON'S SPECIAL SALAD DRESSING

2/3 cup olive oil
1/3 cup red wine vinegar
1 teaspoon seasoned salt
1/2 teaspoon salt
1 teaspoon ground black pepper

1/8 teaspoon dry mustard
1/8 teaspoon paprika
2 bay leaves
3 tablespoons hot water

In a pint bottle or screw-top jar place all ingredients. Secure top, and shake well. Refrigerate until needed. Makes 1/2 pint.

PAT NIXON'S ANGEL PIE

1/2 cup finely chopped walnuts
  or pecans
2 egg whites
1/8 teaspoon salt
1/8 teaspoon cream of tartar
1/2 cup sugar

1-1/2 teaspoons pure vanilla
  extract
4 squares (4 ounces) sweet
  cooking chocolate
3 tablespoons water
1 cup heavy cream

Heat oven to 275°. Lightly butter an 8-inch pie plate. Prepare the walnuts or pecans. In a bowl, combine the egg whites, salt, and cream of tartar. Beat until foamy. By tablespoons add the sugar, beating well after each addition. Beat in 1/2 teaspoon vanilla extract, and continue beating until mixture stands in stiff peaks. Fold in nuts. Spoon into pie plate, and spread into form of pie shell. Bake 50 to 60 minutes; cool.

In a saucepan over low heat stir together chocolate and water until chocolate is melted. Remove from heat and cool until thickened; add remaining vanilla extract. In a bowl whip the cream; fold into chocolate, and spoon into cooled meringue shell. Chill at least 2 hours before serving. Serves 6.

Pat Nixon in discussing her husband's favorite meal went on to say that an alternative to meat loaf, if the President has been careful with calories for some time, is spaghetti and meat balls.

RICHARD NIXON'S SPAGHETTI AND MEAT BALLS

3/4 pound beef, ground together with 1/4 ground pork
1 cup packaged bread crumbs
1/2 cup grated Parmesan cheese
1 clove garlic, minced
1/2 cup milk
2 eggs, beaten
1-1/2 teaspoons salt
1/4 teaspoon ground black pepper
3 tablespoons olive oil
1/2 cup chopped onion
Additional 1 clove garlic, minced

2 1-pound 3-ounce cans tomatoes
1 8-ounce can tomato sauce
1 6-ounce can tomato paste
1 teaspoon basil, crushed
Additional 2 teaspoons salt
Another 1/4 teaspoon ground black pepper
2 tablespoons minced parsley
12 ounces spaghetti, cooked according to package instructions

In a bowl mix lightly with a fork the beef and pork with bread crumbs, Parmesan cheese, first garlic clove, milk, eggs, 1-1/2 teaspoons salt, and first 1/4 teaspoon black pepper. Form into 1-inch balls, and cook slowly in olive oil until well done.

In the olive oil sauté until tender and golden the onion and the second garlic clove. Meanwhile, rub through a sieve the tomatoes, and combine with tomato sauce, tomato paste, basil, the additional salt, second 1/4 teaspoon black pepper, and parsley. Add tomato mixture to sautéed onion, and simmer 1 hour. Add browned meat balls, and heat to serving temperature. Serve over spaghetti. Serves 6.

In addition to Pat Nixon's Special Salad Dressing, the Nixons are delighted with a French dressing Chef Haller makes for them:

CHEF HALLER'S FRENCH DRESSING

1 medium onion, chopped
1 clove garlic, very finely
   chopped or run through
   garlic press
1 teaspoon Dijon-style mustard
1 teaspoon Worcestershire sauce
2 egg yolks
1 teaspoon salt

Pinch of black pepper
3 tablespoons red wine vinegar
Juice of 1 lemon
6 tablespoons corn oil (or 3
   tablespoons corn oil and 3
   tablespoons olive oil)
1/2 tablespoon chopped chives

Mix onion, garlic, mustard, Worcestershire sauce, egg yolks, salt, black pepper, vinegar, and lemon juice thoroughly with a wire whisk or in electric blender. Add oil slowly, and blend well. Fold in chives. Serves 6.

Mexican food tempts President Nixon. Now and then he gets a yen for tamales prepared this way:

PRESIDENT NIXON'S FAVORITE TAMALE PIE

3 cups water
1 cup cold water
1 cup cornmeal
2 teaspoons salt
1/2 cup chopped onion
2 tablespoons butter

1 pound ground beef
2 cups canned tomatoes
2 pimentos, chopped
1 tablespoon chili powder
1/4 teaspoon black pepper
Ripe olives (optional)

Bring the 3 cups water to a boil in a saucepan. Meanwhile, combine the cold water, cornmeal and 1 teaspoon of the salt; pour into boiling water, stirring constantly. Cook until thickened; then cover and continue cooking 10 to 12 minutes, stirring occasionally.

Preheat oven to 350°. Butter a 10-inch juice-saver pie plate—one with high rim—or place pie plate in a cookie tin to protect oven.

In a large skillet, sauté onion in butter until tender and golden; add beef. Brown beef, stirring constantly with a fork. Combine tomatoes, pimentos, chili powder, remaining salt and black pepper; add to ground beef mixture, and heat thoroughly.

Line the pie plate with half the cornmeal mush. With a slotted spoon, spoon meat mixture into the center, and cover with remainder of the mush. Bake 1-1/2 hours. If desired, garnish with ripe olives. Serves 6 to 8.

Another Mexican recipe that Pat Nixon has cherished for years is an unusual treatment of chicken with raisins and green olives:

PAT NIXON'S ENCHILADAS CON POLLO
(Enchiladas with Chicken)

1 cup salad oil
6 tomatoes, peeled and chopped
1 onion, chopped
2 green peppers, chopped
1 teaspoon salt
1/16 teaspoon black pepper
1 cup chopped cooked chicken
1 tablespoon chopped seedless
 raisins

3 tablespoons chopped green
 olives
12 tortillas (canned or fresh)
2 eggs, beaten
Garnishes of shredded lettuce,
 slivered radishes, chopped
 sweet onion, sliced peeled
 avocado

Heat 3 tablespoons of the oil in saucepan. Add tomatoes, onion, green pepper, salt, and pepper. Stir while simmering 20 minutes.

Mix chicken, raisins, and olives in a bowl.

Dip tortillas in egg. Center 1 tablespoon chicken mixture on each tortilla. Roll up and fasten with toothpick.

In another saucepan heat remaining oil to 375°. Fry tortillas 3 minutes, and drain. Place on platter, and cover with tomato mixture. Garnish with lettuce, radishes, onion, and avocado. Serves 4.

Pat Nixon saves and experiments with all the chicken recipes she can find. Here is an all-time favorite:

PAT NIXON'S HOT CHICKEN SALAD

4 cups cold cooked chicken
   chunks
2 tablespoons lemon juice
3/4 cup mayonnaise
1 teaspoon salt
1/2 teaspoon monosodium
   glutamate
2 cups chopped celery

4 hard-cooked eggs, sliced
3/4 cup cream of chicken soup
1 teaspoon onion, finely minced
2 pimentos, finely cut
1 cup Cheddar cheese, grated
1-1/2 cups crushed potato chips
2/3 cup finely chopped toasted
   almonds

Combine all ingredients except cheese, potato chips, and almonds. Place
in a large rectangular dish. Top with cheese, potato chips, and almonds.
Let stand overnight in refrigerator. Bake in 400° oven for 20 to 25
minutes. Serves 8.

Whenever they have roast beef, the Nixon family insists on Mrs. Nixon's
Yorkshire pudding:

PAT'S YORKSHIRE PUDDING

Pan drippings from roast beef
2 eggs, well beaten
1 cup milk

1/2 teaspoon salt
1 cup sifted all-purpose flour

Remove the roast from the pan, and drain off most of the fat. Turn up
the oven temperature to 425° and return the pan to the oven while
quickly preparing the batter.
   Blend the eggs with milk and salt; add flour, and beat until smooth. At
once pour over hot drippings, and bake 35 to 40 minutes. Serve with the
roast beef. Serves 6.

The Nixon Family likes fruit flavors—especially citrus—even in its salads:

PAT NIXON'S CONTINENTAL SALAD

1 package lemon- or orange-
   flavored gelatin
1-1/2 cups canned grapefruit
   juice

1 (16-ounce) can or jar diced
   beets
1/2 cup sliced celery
Salad greens

Dissolve gelatin in hot grapefruit juice, and add 1/2 cup liquid drained from beets. Chill until partially thickened. Fold in beets and celery.

Pour into large salad mold. Chill until firm. Unmold on salad greens, and top with Sesame Seed Dressing:

PAT NIXON'S SESAME SEED DRESSING

1 tablespoon canned grapefruit
   juice
1 3-ounce package cream cheese

1/4 cup mayonnaise
1 tablespoon toasted sesame seed

Gradually blend grapefruit juice into cream cheese, beating until fluffy. Fold in mayonnaise and sesame seed.

A favorite Nixon salad combines avocado with the First Lady's liking for citrus fruit:

PAT NIXON'S AVOCADO SALAD

2 medium avocados
1 package lemon-flavored gelatin
1-1/2 cups hot water
3 tablespoons lemon juice
1 can No. 2-1/2 grapefruit
   sections, drained

1/2 cup chopped celery
Whipped cream and mayonnaise,
   mixed

Mash avocados. Stir into slightly thickened lemon gelatin base made with lemon-flavored gelatin, hot water, and lemon juice.

Stir in grapefruit sections and chopped celery.

Chill and unmold. Serve with a whipped cream and mayonnaise mixture. Serves 8 to 10.

Vegetables in general do not thrill the President. But here is one vegetable recipe he relishes:

PRESIDENT NIXON'S BAKED STUFFED TOMATOES

4 large or 6 medium tomatoes
3 ounces (4 to 5 slices) bacon, cut
   into small pieces
6 tablespoons olive oil
3/4 cup chopped onion
1/4 pound fresh mushrooms,
   chopped

1 tablespoon snipped chives
1 tablespoon snipped parsley
1 egg, beaten
1/2 teaspoon salt
1/8 teaspoon pepper
Bread crumbs

Remove stem ends of the tomatoes, and scoop out three-fourths of each tomato, leaving about 3/4-inch wall. Be careful not to pierce the skin if using a paring knife.

Next, partially fry the bacon in a large skillet. Add 4 tablespoons of the olive oil; then heat and mix in onion, mushrooms, chives, and parsley. Sauté for 10 minutes, stirring the mixture occasionally.

Remove the skillet from the heat, and quickly mix in the egg, salt, and pepper. Immediately fill the tomatoes, and put in oiled baking dish. Top with bread crumbs, and drizzle with remaining oil. Bake at 400° about 40 minutes. Serves 4 to 6.

As I always am when a new Presidential family comes to the White House, I was very curious to know how the Nixons stay so slim under the barrage of dining and wining guests at the White House, Key Biscayne, or San Clemente.

The secret for the Presidential couple, I soon learned, is moderation. And the cooperation of Chef Haller. When the family dines alone, it is Chef Haller who makes the suggestions as to what to serve, but Pat Nixon invariably goes over the menus. Since President Nixon does not care much for lamb and the First Lady does not particularly like veal, these two meats are not served often.

The family diet is built around chicken and beef with a few seafood dishes thrown in for variety. The President's favorite dish is his wife's meat loaf. But to keep his waistline slim, he is apt to have a lean steak or rather dry Salisbury steak quite often—both served medium rare.

Connie Stuart, his wife's press secretary, tells of often seeing the President lunch simply on "small steak—medium rare, peas, and a glass of water. No bread. No dessert."

Mrs. Nixon also is amazed at her husband's "won't power." She says, "Dick's instincts are right when it comes to food. He just instinctively stays away from high-calorie foods or eats only small portions of them."

There is nothing wrong with Pat Nixon's "won't power" either. The First Lady keeps her slim figure—and her exact weight is something she prefers to keep secret—by eating a light breakfast of toast, juice, and coffee and a light lunch. Then she can enjoy higher-calorie foods in the evening.

A typical lunch for Pat is a sandwich of sliced meat on toast, a small tossed salad, fruit, and iced tea or a glass of milk or both.

But now let's go back to the fun kind of eating when calories don't count—so much.

When Mrs. Nixon entertains close friends, a favorite party casserole is Shrimp Superb. It is versatile and can be served as an appetizer or buffet main dish:

PAT NIXON'S SHRIMP SUPERB

17 hard-cooked eggs	1/2 cup mayonnaise
1-1/2 pounds raw shrimp, or 1 pound frozen cooked, peeled and deveined shrimp	1/4 pound grated Cheddar cheese
6 ounces bleu cheese, crumbled	2 tablespoons honey
	4 ounces potato chips

Shell the eggs. Shell and devein the raw shrimp, or defrost frozen shrimp; in boiling salted water to cover, simmer 2 to 5 minutes, or until pink and tender. Start heating oven to 250°. Cut eggs into eighths, and halve shrimp lengthwise.

Put into a large bowl with bleu cheese, mayonnaise, Cheddar cheese, and honey. Mix well, and turn into a 2-quart casserole. Crush potato chips in a bag by squeezing the bag. Sprinkle the crushed chips over the shrimp mixture, and bake 1 hour. Serves 15 to 20.

The Nixons enjoy interesting breads. Nut bread has been a favorite at the White House since Dolley Madison served it many years ago to her guests. I served it to the Eisenhowers, made with walnuts, pecans, and lemon rind. The Nixons prefer theirs with orange juice, apricots, and walnuts:

PAT NIXON'S APRICOT NUT BREAD

1/2 cup firmly filled with finely
   diced dried apricots
1 egg, beaten
1 cup sugar
2 tablespoons melted butter
2 cups sifted flour

3 teaspoons baking powder
1/4 teaspoon baking soda
3/4 teaspoon salt
1/2 cup orange juice
1/4 cup water
1 cup chopped walnuts

Cover apricots with hot water. Let soak about 2 hours. Drain; whirl in blender until pureed, or mash with potato masher. Cream together egg, sugar, and butter. Sift flour with baking powder, baking soda, and salt. Add dry ingredients alternately with orange juice and water to sugar mixture. Add apricot puree and nuts. Mix well. Bake in greased loaf pan (9 by 5 inches) in oven preheated to 375° about 1-1/2 hours, or until wooden pick inserted in center comes out clean.

Serve plain with butter, or cut in thin slices and serve sandwich style, spread with softened cream cheese to which crushed pineapple has been added, if desired.

Though she likes a crisp top crust, Pat Nixon tries to eliminate a few calories by doing away with bottom crusts:

PAT NIXON'S CRUSTLESS APPLE PIE

1/3 to 1/2 cup granulated sugar
1 teaspoon ground cinnamon
1 cup water
6 medium cooking apples (about
   2 pounds), washed, cut into
   eighths, cored, and pared

1 cup sifted all-purpose flour
1 teaspoon baking powder
1/2 teaspoon salt, if desired
6 tablespoons shortening
1/2 cup lightly packed brown
   sugar

Blend granulated sugar and cinnamon in a large heavy saucepan. Stir in water and apples, bringing to a boil; then reduce heat, and cook for 10 minutes, stirring occasionally.

Sift flour, salt if desired, and baking powder together, blending thoroughly. Set aside.

Put shortening in a mixing bowl, and cream it with the brown sugar. Beat in the flour mixture, adding gradually.

Turn the apples and syrup into a greased 9-inch pie pan. Cover apples completely with the topping.

Bake at 350° about 35 minutes, or until the apples are tender and the topping is browned. Cool on a wire rack.
Serve hot or cold with whipped cream, if desired. Makes 9-inch pie.

Like many First Ladies before her, Pat Nixon likes desserts with fruit flavors, especially blueberry. Mamie Eisenhower liked blueberry pie (see Index), but Pat prefers a layered blueberry pastry:

PAT NIXON'S BLUEBERRY DESSERT

2-1/2 cups fresh blueberries or 2
   10-ounce packages frozen
   unsweetened blueberries
1/2 cup sugar
1/4 teaspoon orange peel
Dash of mace

1/8 teaspoon cardamon
1 cup piecrust mix
1 tablespoon butter
2 teaspoons lemon juice
1/2 teaspoon vanilla
Whipped cream (optional)

Place blueberries in buttered 1-1/4-quart shallow baking dish. Combine sugar, orange peel, mace, and cardamon. Sprinkle sugar mixture and piecrust mix in alternate layers over blueberries. Continue until all is used. Dot with butter. Drizzle lemon juice and vanilla over all. Bake in 350° oven 45 minutes. Serve with whipped cream, if desired. Serves 4 to 6.

The First Lady's own favorite pie is this one:

PAT NIXON'S RASPBERRY PIE

2 10-ounce packages frozen
   raspberries, thawed
2 cups vanilla wafer crumbs
1/2 cup sugar
1 teaspoon cinnamon
5 tablespoons melted butter

1 envelope unflavored gelatin
1/4 cup cold water
1/2 teaspoon lemon peel
1/2 pint heavy cream
1 teaspoon vanilla
Whipped cream (optional)

Drain raspberries, reserving 1 cup of the juice. Combine crumbs, sugar, 1/2 teaspoon of the cinnamon, and the butter; pat into a 10-inch pie plate. Bake in 375° oven 8 to 10 minutes; cool. Soften gelatin in water. Mix the reserved raspberry juice, the remaining cinnamon, and lemon peel; heat to boiling. Remove from heat; add gelatin, and stir until melted. Chill until mixture just begins to thicken.

Whip cream; add vanilla. Fold raspberries, gelatin mixture, and whipped cream together. Pour into pie shell. Chill. Decorate with additional whipped cream, if desired. Serves 6 to 8.

It is interesting to compare the soufflés that Jackie Kennedy enjoyed with Pat Nixon's favorite. Mrs. Kennedy liked a vanilla soufflé with a chocolate sauce or Soufflé Froid au Chocolat (see Index), but Pat Nixon likes hers vanilla all the way:

PAT NIXON'S VANILLA SOUFFLÉ

4 tablespoons butter   4 tablespoons sugar
2 tablespoons flour   4 teaspoons vanilla
1 cup light cream, scalded   6 egg whites, beaten
5 egg yolks

Melt butter, blending in flour thoroughly. Cook until mixture begins to color. Slowly add cream, stirring constantly. Cook about 5 minutes.

Beat egg yolks with the sugar, and stir into above mixture. Flavor with vanilla, and fold in egg whites. Pour into buttered, sugared soufflé dish, and bake at 450° for 10 to 12 minutes. Lower oven to 350° and bake about 20 minutes longer, or until a knife inserted in center comes out clean. Serve with Vanilla Sauce (below). Serves 8.

VANILLA SAUCE

6 ounces sugar   Vanilla to taste
6 egg yolks   1 pint milk

Beat sugar, egg yolks, and vanilla together. Add to the milk. Heat in top of double boiler until thickened. Take off stove, and cool before using. Makes 1 pint.

Lyndon Johnson loved pudding—any pudding. President Eisenhower enjoyed rice pudding made the English way seasoned with lemon and dotted with raisins. But President Nixon likes his much richer and chock-full of fruit. It is a particularly delicious dessert:

GLORIFIED RICE À LA NIXON

1 cup uncooked rice
2 cups cold water
1 teaspoon salt
1 tablespoon butter
1/3 cup sugar
1 8-3/4-ounce can pineapple
  tidbits

1 red apple, coarsely chopped
1-1/2 cups miniature
  marshmallows
1 cup heavy cream
1/2 teaspoon pure vanilla extract

In a saucepan combine the rice, cold water, salt, and butter. Turn the heat to high. When water just begins to boil, stir once with fork, reset heat to medium-low, cover, and simmer 18 to 20 minutes, or until all liquid is absorbed.

Measure two cups warm rice, and combine with sugar. Add the pineapple tidbits, apple, and marshmallows. Let stand 1 hour.

Whip cream with vanilla extract, and fold into the rice mixture. Serves 6 to 8.

IO

﴾﴿

AT HOME WITH THE JOHNSONS

No President except Jefferson relished a greater variety of flavors in cookery than Lyndon B. Johnson. He liked every style of cooking, and there was a saying in the White House kitchen that LBJ "will eat anything that doesn't bite him first." He was especially partial to German food, Southern style cooking and French haute cuisine, but his greatest love was special Mexican food.

At receptions at the White House, Lady Bird Johnson would sigh and shake her head as she saw her husband break his diet and reach into a bowl of fiddle-faddle. He simply could not resist the combination of nuts and popcorn held together by syrup.

It will be interesting to see what history says of President Lyndon Johnson's penchant for making a social melting pot of the White House by inviting everyone from disc jockeys to racing jockeys and from little old coffee shop owners to little old schoolteachers.

The President was hurt most, his friends say, by the hostility of the press whom he sought to befriend. LBJ invited many members of the Washington press corps to his ranch, soon after becoming President, drove them around the fields in his jeep, opened his heart and his food lockers, and sought to show them full Texas hospitality with an LBJ brand.

But the reporters came away imitating his Texas drawl and wrote amusing stories about the President as a bumpkinish, rather over-affectionate, showoffy rancher. Even the speed at which he drove when he got behind the wheel came in for comment.

LBJ later tried to hold himself aloof from the press; but it wasn't his way, and many Washington correspondents found themselves invited as guests to White House formal dinners.

Those who had worked for the President longest still talk about his fantastic generosity to them—how he would give suits as presents to loyal aides and might treat a hardworking secretary to an expensive complete makeup job by Eddie Senz in New York. When he invited the Pakistani camel driver to be his guest, while he was Vice President, it was no grandstand play. It was just LBJ being himself.

But "himself" meant the LBJ wrath as well, and Lyndon Johnson was known for spurts of temper, as well as for warmth and generosity.

Only a person like Johnson could have got away with entertaining a visiting chief of state at a giant outdoor barbecue, as he did German Chancellor Ludwig Erhard, and made it appear a perfectly natural thing to do. But for now I want to concentrate on his favorite dishes when eating at home when "home" was the White House second-floor living quarters.

It was said around the White House that to LBJ, a week without chili in some form was a week wasted. You have already seen his Pedernales chili named for the river that flows through his Texas ranch. But here is another favorite named for a friend, Scooter Miller:

SCOOTER'S DALLAS JAILHOUSE CHILI

1/2 cup olive oil	1 tablespoon comino seed
2 pounds ground beef	1 tablespoon salt
2 cloves garlic, chopped	1 teaspoon white pepper
1-1/2 tablespoons paprika	3 cups water
3 tablespoons chili powder	Cooked dry pink or red beans

Heat oil, and add meat, garlic, and seasonings. Cook slowly, covered. Add water as needed, stirring occasionally, and continue cooking for a total of 4 hours. Take cover off after the first hour, so chili will be slightly thickened. Serve with equal portions of beans. Serves 6.

The President was a great fancier of chili dips to be served at family parties. The first is his own chili recipe, and the second uses Scooter Miller's:

CHILI CON QUESO DIP

1/2 pound American cheese	Fritos
1/2 can Ro-tal tomatoes	
1 cup Lyndon B. Johnson's Pedernales River Chili (see Index), made without the beans	

Melt the cheese in the top of a double boiler. Add the tomatoes, and blend. Blend in the chili, and serve as dip with a bowl of Fritos. Serves 12.

SCOOTER'S CHILI DIP

1-1/2 pounds lean ground beef
1 tablespoon bacon or beef fat
1/4 cup flour
1/2 can beef consommé
1-1/2 onions, chopped
1-1/2 teaspoons powdered
    comino seed

1-1/2 ounces chili powder
1 scant teaspoon oregano
1-1/2 teaspoons salt
1 pound Cheddar cheese
Bowl of Fritos or quartered fried
    tortillas

Sauté the meat in just enough fat to cover the bottom of the skillet. When meat is browned, add the rest of the fat and the flour. Add heated consommé, stirring. Add onions and seasonings. Simmer for 30 minutes, stirring frequently. Increase heat, and stir continually until mixture thickens. Place mixture in top of double boiler, and add cheese in small chunks, stirring until melted. Add more salt, if necessary. Serve in a chafing dish, with Fritos or fried tortillas. Serves 25 to 30.

Strangely enough LBJ concocted his own Chinese recipe:

PRESIDENT LYNDON JOHNSON'S OWN CHINESE CHOP SUEY

1/2 pound lean pork or chicken
2 tablespoons fat
1 cup diced celery
3/4 cup diced onions
1 cup bouillon
1/4 cup mushrooms
1 tablespoon cornstarch
2 tablespoons water
1 No. 2-1/2 can bean sprouts,
    drained
1 No. 2-1/2 can mixed
    vegetables

1 teaspoon salt
1/4 teaspoon sugar
Dash of white pepper
Dash of paprika
More than a dash of garlic
    powder
Rice and crisp noodles
2 tablespoons soy sauce
    (optional)

Cut meat in small pieces, and brown in fat. Add celery, onions, and bouillon; cover and simmer for 20 minutes. Add mushrooms and paste made of cornstarch and water, and cook for 10 minutes, stirring until thickened. Add bean sprouts, mixed vegetables, and seasonings, and heat thoroughly. Serve hot with rice and crisp noodles. If desired, soy sauce may be added for flavoring. Serves 6.

The Johnsons were very sentimental and loved to remember their friends by the food they liked. One family favorite was named for the Congressman who had been Lyndon Johnson's mentor in the early days of his career on Capitol Hill:

FRIED CHICKEN À LA SAM RAYBURN

2 tender young chickens	4 heaping tablespoons lard
2 cups flour	Additional 2 tablespoons flour
Salt and pepper to taste	1-1/2 cups cold water

Cut up chicken, and dredge in flour. Season with salt and pepper. Have lard sizzling hot in big iron skillet. Fry chicken in sizzling fat until golden brown on all sides. Lower heat, and cover. Let steam until tender.

To make the gravy, loosen bits of chicken and flour left in pan. Add 2 tablespoons flour, and stir till smooth. Slowly add cold water, and stir until consistency of gravy is right. Cook up two or three times again, boiling for a minute or so at a time and turning fire down, then up again. Serves 4 to 6.

When the President's weight permitted it, he liked a biscuit made with Lady Bird's recipe with some of Mr. Sam's gravy on it. In this case, the gravy would be made with whole milk instead of water so the gravy had a light creamy look. Here is the recipe for Lady Bird's Baking Powder Biscuits, which are good for pouring gravy over, as well as serving with a meal.

Incidentally, Lyndon Johnson also liked these biscuits made tiny and served as an afternoon snack with Deer Meat Sausage (see Index.)

LADY BIRD'S BAKING POWDER BISCUITS

1 cup flour	1 teaspoon salt
2 teaspoons baking powder	1 tablespoon shortening
2 teaspoons sugar	1/4 cup milk

Mix and sift dry ingredients. Add half the shortening and all the milk, and beat. Add enough flour to knead well. Roll out on floured board. Fold over and roll again. Melt remaining shortening in baking pan. Place cut biscuits in pan, and brush with melted shortening. Bake in 400° oven about 20 minutes, or until browned.

But getting back to sentimentality, another LBJ trick was to name each course after the wife of one of the official guests so, at a formal dinner honoring the Vice President, the Chief Justice and the Speaker of the House, the menu looked like this:

Sole Nina
(named for Mrs. Earl Warren, wife of
the Chief Justice)

Pheasant Muriel
(named for Mrs. Hubert H. Humphrey,
wife of the Vice President)

Wild Rice Croquettes
Asparagus

Winter Garden Salad with Minnesota Cheese

Harriet Soufflé
(named for Mrs. John McCormack, wife
of the Speaker)

LBJ also felt a sentimental fondness for the pie he had eaten with another departed friend, Alben Barkley:

ALBEN BARKLEY'S CHESS PIE

1 heaping tablespoon flour	4 eggs
2 cups sugar	1/2 teaspoon vanilla
1/2 pound butter	

Mix sugar and flour together, add to butter, and blend until light and fluffy. Add eggs, one at a time, beating after each addition. Add vanilla, and pour into unbaked pie shell. Bake in 300ᵛ oven about 1 hour, or until knife inserted comes out clean.

LBJ liked tossed salad finely cut and easy to eat. And he liked it served with Lady Bird's French Dressing:

LBJ'S TOSSED SALAD

To suit the President, the salad had to contain five vegetables—tomatoes, onions, lettuce, green peppers, and celery.

LADY BIRD'S FRENCH DRESSING

1 cup salad oil
1 tablespoon catsup
1 teaspoon salt
1 cup white vinegar

2 or 3 cloves garlic
1 teaspoon coarse ground black
  pepper

Mix all ingredients, and shake well. Makes 1 pint.

LBJ was very fond of a fruit-carrot salad. Especially if served with his favorite dressing made with poppy seed:

LBJ'S POPPY SEED SALAD DRESSING

1 teaspoon dry mustard
1 clove garlic
1 cup salad oil
1/3 cup white vinegar

1 teaspoon grated onion (or juice)
1/4 cup sugar
1 teaspoon poppy seed
Pinch of salt

Put all ingredients in a jar, cover, and shake well. Chill in refrigerator and serve. Makes 1-1/2 cups.

Now for the salad which the President liked topped with the poppy seed dressing:

PINEAPPLE, CARROT, AND RAISIN SALAD

1 cup grated carrots   Mayonnaise to moisten
1 cup crushed pineapple, drained   Lettuce
1/4 cup seedless raisins

Carefully mix all ingredients except lettuce. Serve on crisp beds of lettuce. Serves 4.

Like his predecessor, Jack Kennedy, LBJ was fond of seafood. Here is his favorite:

PRESIDENT JOHNSON'S CRAB CASSEROLE

1-1/2 cups grated Cheddar   3 egg yolks, beaten
   cheese   2 cups crab meat
2-1/2 cups Basic White Sauce   3 tablespoons melted butter
   (see Index)   1/3 cup cracker crumbs

Stir cheese into hot white sauce until melted. Take off stove. Gradually incorporate egg yolks; then gently fold in the crab meat. Mix butter and cracker crumbs, and sprinkle over all. Bake at 350° about 30 minutes. Serves 4 to 6.

Strangely enough, spinach was one of President Lyndon Johnson's favorite vegetables. But that was because his wife had two marvelous recipes for it—one with cheese and the other cheese and eggs:

LADY BIRD'S SPINACH PARMESAN

3 pounds spinach, cleaned   6 tablespoons heavy cream
6 tablespoons grated Parmesan   5 tablespoons melted butter
   cheese   1/2 cup cracker crumbs
6 tablespoons minced onion

Cook the spinach until tender. Drain thoroughly. Chop coarsely, and add the cheese, onion, cream and 4 tablespoons of the butter. Arrange in a shallow baking dish, and sprinkle with the crumbs mixed with the remaining butter. Bake for 10 to 15 minutes. Serves 8 to 10.

LADY BIRD'S SPINACH SOUFFLÉ

1/4 cup chopped onions
2 tablespoons butter
2 tablespoons flour
1 cup milk (or light cream)
1/2 teaspoon salt

1/8 teaspoon pepper
3 eggs, separated
1 cup chopped cooked spinach
1/2 cup grated Cheddar cheese

Sauté onions in small amount of butter. Make white sauce of 2 tablespoons butter, flour, milk or light cream, salt, and pepper. Beat egg yolks until thick and lemon-colored. Stir into white sauce, and add spinach and cheese. Fold in stiffly beaten egg whites, and turn into greased casserole. Set in pan of hot water, and bake in moderate oven (350°) for about 50 minutes. Serve at once. Serves 6.

A vegetable family favorite of the Johnsons was lima beans combined with mushrooms. Mrs. Johnson varied this recipe according to the ingredients on hand at the time of preparation:

JOHNSON FAMILY LIMA AND MUSHROOM CASSEROLE

1 pound baby lima beans
2 tablespoons butter
1 cup mushrooms
1 cup Basic White Sauce (see
    Index)

1/2 cup grated Cheddar cheese
Salt, chili powder, and pepper to
    taste

Cook lima beans in salted water. Drain thoroughly. Put butter in saucepan, and melt. Add mushrooms, and sauté for 5 minutes. To Basic White Sauce add the cheese, and let melt. Combine beans, mushrooms, and sauce. Season with salt, chili powder, and pepper. Bake in casserole for 30 minutes in moderate oven. Serves 4 to 6.

Lady Bird Johnson brought back old-fashioned home cooking to a greater degree than any recent First Lady. For example, she believed in serving homemade bread even if she was in the White House, and it was greatly appreciated by the President. Zephyr, the family cook, who had accompanied them to Washington, made this bread two loaves at a time:

LADY BIRD'S WHITE BREAD

3 tablespoons shortening	1/4 cup warm water
1/2 cup sugar	1 teaspoon salt
1 cup scalded milk	1 egg
2 yeast cakes	4-1/2 to 5 cups flour

Cream shortening and sugar, and pour milk over mixture. Dissolve yeast in warm water; allow to cool. Combine both mixtures, and using egg beater, add salt and egg, beaten till light. Add flour, one cup at a time, just enough so that the dough can be worked by hand. Put dough in a greased large bowl. Grease the top part of the dough, and allow to rise until double in bulk. Cover with hot damp cloth several times—it takes about 2 hours for it to rise in a warm spot, not too near the stove. Toss on board with enough flour to keep it from sticking to the board. Knead bread for 5 minutes, working outside edges in, kneading with the ball of the hand, repeating until dough no longer sticks to the board, is "bubbly," and puffs right back up. Divide into two equal loaves, and place in greased Pyrex baking dishes. Let dough rise again until double in bulk. Bake at 450° for 10 minutes; then reduce to 350° and bake for 30 minutes more. Bake until bread is brown and shrinks from the sides of dish. Remove and turn out to cool on wire tray. Slice when bread is cold. Can be baked a day or two before and wrapped in waxed paper. It is delicious sliced, buttered, and reheated. Makes 2 loaves.

The Johnson family liked all kinds of hot breads and rolls. One of the family favorites at the White House was Lady Bird's Popovers:

LADY BIRD'S POPOVERS

1 cup sifted flour	1 cup milk
1/4 teaspoon salt	2 tablespoons shortening, melted
2 eggs, beaten	

Mix and sift flour and salt. Combine eggs, milk, and shortening; gradually add to flour mixture, beating about 1 minute, or until batter is smooth. Fill sizzling-hot greased muffin pans three-fourths full, and bake in very hot oven (450°) about 20 minutes. Reduce heat to moderate (350°) and continue baking for 15 or 20 minutes. Makes 8 to 10.

Another favorite was hot garlic bread:

LADY BIRD'S GARLIC BREAD

Use French bread, and slice the loaf almost through, making thick slices. Insert butter generously between slices and, spread apart to sprinkle in chopped garlic and a dash of onion salt. Put in oven to heat.

The Johnson family liked reminders of Texas in their family dining. Including corn delicacies like spoon bread:

LBJ'S TEXAS SPOON BREAD

1 scant cup cornmeal	1 level teaspoon salt
3 cups milk	3 level teaspoons baking powder
3 eggs, well beaten	Butter the size of a walnut

Stir cornmeal into 2 cups of the milk, and let mixture come to a boil, making a mush. Add balance of milk, and add eggs. Stir in salt, baking powder, and butter. Bake in casserole 30 minutes in oven at 350°. Serves 6.

One of the prize possessions in the Johnson family is a recipe for Lady Bird's Winesap Apple Pie, which has a lovely tart flavor. Before moving to the White House, in fact, when Lyndon was still a Senator, she used to send these pies to her next-door neighbors on Thirtieth Place, NW, Washington, D.C., the Reeds, and receive in return huge bouquets of roses.

LADY BIRD'S WINESAP APPLE PIE

6 Winesap apples, peeled	Juice of 1 lemon
1 cup sugar	1/4 pound butter
2 tablespoons flour	Additional sugar
1 9-inch Pastry Shell	

Dice apples in pastry shell. Sprinkle with sugar and flour, which have been mixed. Add lemon juice, and dot with three-fourths of the butter. Sprinkle with sugar, and dot with remaining butter. Bake in 350° oven about 1 hour, or until brown.

PASTRY SHELL

1 cup flour	2 tablespoons shortening
1 teaspoon salt	3 tablespoons cold water
1 tablespoon sugar	

Cut dry ingredients into shortening with pastry blender. Add water, and stir with fork until small lumps the size of peas appear. Form into a ball, and roll on floured board. Line 9-inch pie pan, and trim.

Lyndon Johnson liked unusual flavors—dill and the biting taste of jalapeno peppers and, for an abrupt change, the bland sweetness of bananas. Unfortunately, his doctor put him on a diet that excluded them.
So whenever the family had banana pudding, Zephyr made a substitute low-calorie pudding instead. Perhaps even more than banana pudding, the President liked banana bread made from his wife's recipe:

LADY BIRD JOHNSON'S BANANA BREAD

1/2 cup butter	2 cups flour
1 cup sugar	1 teaspoon baking soda
2 eggs, well beaten	1/4 teaspoon salt
3 ripe medium bananas, mashed	1 cup sour milk

Blend butter and sugar. Add eggs. Beat in bananas. Sift flour, soda and salt together, and add to above mixture, alternating with sour milk. Bake in 9-by-5 loaf pan in moderate oven for 1 hour.

Like Eleanor Roosevelt, Lady Bird Johnson liked to serve things that were healthful, as well as sweet. One of her favorite desserts along this line was Prune Cake, and she served it frequently:

LADY BIRD'S PRUNE CAKE

1/2 cup shortening	1/2 teaspoon nutmeg
1 cup granulated sugar	1/2 teaspoon allspice
2 eggs	1/2 teaspoon baking powder
1-1/3 cups flour	1/2 teaspoon baking soda
1/2 teaspoon salt	2/3 cup sour milk or buttermi
1/2 teaspoon cinnamon	2/3 cup chopped prunes

Cream shortening; add sugar and eggs; beat well. Mix dry ingredients, and add alternately with sour milk to creamed mixture. Add prunes. Bake in two waxed-paper-lined cake pans for 25 minutes at 350°.

FROSTING FOR PRUNE CAKE

2 tablespoons butter
2 tablespoons prune juice
1 tablespoon lemon juice

1/2 teaspoon salt
1/2 teaspoon cinnamon
1-1/2 cups powdered sugar

Cream butter; then add prune and lemon juices, salt, and cinnamon. Beat in sugar gradually.

Here is another Lady Bird health special—Strawberry Icebox Pie:

LADY BIRD'S STRAWBERRY ICEBOX PIE

1 17-ounce package
  marshmallows
1 package frozen strawberries or
  2 cups fresh, sweetened to
  taste (let stand 30 minutes
  to make juice)

1 cup heavy cream, whipped
1 cool baked pastry shell

Put marshmallows in double boiler. Add 2 tablespoons of the strawberry juice. Cook until marshmallows are dissolved. Mix strawberries and marshmallows thoroughly. Chill about 2 hours. Fold in cream to marshmallow mixture, and pour into 9-inch pastry shell. Chill until firm. (You may use the same recipe for the pastry shell that the Johnson cook, Zephyr, used in the President's favorite Winesap Apple Pie. See Index.)

When Chef Henry Haller came to the White House in 1966 to cook for President Johnson, one of the recipes he brought with him was the famous Sacher torte from Austria. Here is his version as enjoyed by the President:

CHEF HALLER'S SACHER TORTE

3/4 cup butter
3/4 cup sugar
6 eggs, separated
12 squares semisweet chocolate,
    melted and cooled

2 cups sifted flour
2 teaspoons baking powder
1 cup apricot jam

Cream butter until fluffy. Add sugar gradually while continuing to cream. Add one egg yolk at a time, beating after each. Add cooled chocolate to this mixture, and blend thoroughly.

In another bowl beat the egg whites until stiff, and fold into the first mixture. Fold in flour, which has been sifted with baking powder. Pour batter into 2 well-greased and floured 9-inch round layer pans which have removable rims, or line pan with buttered waxed paper. Bake at 325° for 30 minutes. Remove layers from pans and cool on racks.

Spread layers generously with apricot jam. Cover the assembled cake with Chocolate Glaze (below). Serves 12 to 16.

CHOCOLATE GLAZE

1 6-ounce package semisweet
    chocolate bits

3 tablespoons light corn syrup
2 tablespoons coffee

Heat ingredients in top of double boiler, stirring until well combined.

The next recipe I want to give you has historic and tragic significance. It is the recipe for the pie that President John F. Kennedy would have eaten had he been able to visit the LBJ Ranch as was scheduled that day of his assassination. The pies—pecan pie made with pecans grown on the then Vice President's ranch—were made from Lady Bird's own recipe and were already cooling on the sideboard of the ranch kitchen when the tragedy occurred.

LADY BIRD'S PECAN PIE

1/4 pound butter	3 eggs, beaten
1 cup sugar	2 cups pecans, coarsely chopped
1 cup dark corn syrup	1 9-inch pastry shell
1-1/2 teaspoons vanilla	8 whole pecans
1/2 teaspoon salt	

Let butter stand at room temperature in a covered mixing bowl until very soft. Add sugar, corn syrup, vanilla, and salt, and beat until thoroughly blended. Add eggs, and beat gently until blended. Add chopped pecans. Pour into pastry shell, place whole pecans in circle on top, and bake in moderate (375°) oven for 40 minutes, or until top is toasted brown and filling is set when the pie is gently rocked. Serves 8.

Now for that President Johnson favorite of favorites—coconut pudding. Here is a White House coconut pudding based on an old Thomas Jefferson recipe and still delicious, although admittedly loaded with calories:

LBJ'S JEFFERSONIAN COCONUT PUDDING

2 cups heavy cream	6 eggs, beaten
2 cups sugar	Rind of 1 lemon, grated
Milk of 1 coconut (from the same coconut which is grated)	1 coconut, grated fine

Combine the cream, sugar, and coconut milk, and then fold in the eggs and lemon rind. Finally sprinkle on the coconut, distributing evenly. Bake in slow oven until it sets—about 1 hour. Cover toward end if necessary, to prevent mixture from getting too brown. Pour over cake squares. Serves 8.

I I

❯❯❯-❯❯❯-❮❮❮-❮❮❮

AT HOME WITH THE KENNEDYS

The Kennedys were a fascinating family, foodwise. He liked New England chow—and chowder—and she liked everything French. As a chef that is the way I looked at them, but the nation was captivated for other reasons.

Some say it was the youth of the Kennedys that captured the imagination of the nation. Jackie, at thirty-one, was the youngest First Lady of the century. Surely they did usher in a whole new style of entertaining. Informality was the key word. So anxious were the President and Jacqueline to make everyone feel at home that they even did away with the formal receiving line.

Guests would arrive and be served a cocktail and wander around the rooms getting acquainted if they did not already know each other. Then at the appropriate time the Presidential couple would come down the stairs and mingle with the guests.

The President and Jacqueline surrounded themselves with creative people and avant-garde intellectuals. Witty people were especially welcomed.

President Kennedy was a light eater who had to be enticed into eating a full meal. The Kennedys were one of the few First Families to use a French chef on a daily basis. Of French descent, Jackie liked French cooking. To keep her husband happy, however, she would serve him some of the New England dishes which he preferred.

Though I was a French chef, cooking for the Eisenhowers, I saved the French cooking for formal dinners and tried to cook in the American tradition for their at-home meals.

Like the Nixons, the Kennedys talked over each of their formal dinners together, and the President even took the time to taste the wines in advance to be sure that only the best would be served his guests.

Not since President Cleveland took a young bride has the nation so copied a First Lady. Jacqueline was indeed beautiful and brought new glamor to the image of the First Lady. But she remained a mystery to the public, avoiding the press, living her own life and only taking the public into it on rare occasions involving projects she had chosen—for example the refurbishing of the White House with more authentic and historic furnishings.

Naturally, I was interested when the Kennedys came to the White House to learn how they dined when not entertaining guests—and especially how Mrs. Kennedy kept so slim. The secret, I concluded, was that she only ate one substantial meal a day.

For breakfast: dry toast, orange juice, and coffee. For lunch: a grilled cheese sandwich or a soufflé or a hamburger with salad and a glass of milk. She was careful not to eat many starches and merely to nibble at fattening dishes.

President Kennedy was a "soup, sandwich and fruit" man for lunch. His luncheon was almost bound to be soup.

On summer days, instead of hot soup, he would have a chilled soup or tuna fish salad. He might also have, with his luncheon milk, a piece of angel food cake generously covered with his favorite topping—whipped cream. Whipped cream was also often served with baked apple at noon.

PRESIDENT KENNEDY'S ICED TOMATO SOUP

1 onion, chopped	2 tablespoons flour
6 large tomatoes, chopped coarsely	2 cups chicken consommé, or 2 chicken bouillon cubes
1/2 teaspoon salt	dissolved in 2 cups boiling
Pepper to taste	water
1/4 cup water	1 cup heavy cream
2 tablespoons tomato paste	

Mix the onion, tomatoes, salt, pepper, and water, and cook over moderate heat for 5 minutes. Mix the tomato paste and flour, and add to the tomatoes, to which you have added the consommé or bouillon. Simmer for 3 minutes. Put the mixture through a fine sieve, and chill for 2 or 3 hours. Before serving, add the cream. Serves 6.

Unlike the Nixons, the Kennedys were very fond of lamb. Here is one favorite:

SELLE D'AGNEAU CLAMART

1 saddle of lamb   Buttered artichokes bottoms
Potatoes Château (see Index)   Buttered green peas

Roast the saddle of lamb in a 300° oven for 13 minutes per pound. Garnish the lamb with Potatoes Château and the artichoke bottoms filled with the peas. Serves 6.

President Kennedy was fond of broiled lamb chops. Chef Andraeas, who has cooked for President Kennedy, as well as for President Nixon in Florida, maintains that JFK's favorite dinner was lamb chops, mashed potatoes, tossed salad with Andraeas' special bleu cheese dressing, strawberry tarts, and coffee. Here is the salad dressing Kennedy enjoyed:

JFK'S FAVORITE BLEU CHEESE DRESSING

1 cup mayonnaise   6 ounces bleu cheese
3-1/2 tablespoons vinegar   3/4 cup milk
1/2 cup sour cream   1/2 teaspoon salt

Beat all ingredients together until thoroughly blended, or place everything in a blender and blend until smooth and creamy. Makes a little more than 1 pint.

President Kennedy was particularly fond of seafood. Here is his top favorite along with the seafood casserole you have seen in Chapter 3. The chowder is the one he took along in a thermos when he was campaigning for the Presidency:

PRESIDENT KENNEDY'S NEW ENGLAND FISH CHOWDER

2 pounds haddock   1 bay leaf, crumbled
2 cups water   1 teaspoon salt
2 ounces salt pork, diced   Freshly ground black pepper
2 onions, sliced   1 quart milk
4 large potatoes, diced   2 tablespoons butter
1 cup chopped celery

Simmer the haddock in the water for 15 minutes. Drain. Reserve the broth. Remove the bones from the fish. Sauté the pork until crisp, remove from pan, and set aside. Sauté the onions in the pork fat until golden brown. Add the fish, potatoes, celery, bay leaf, salt, and pepper. Pour in fish broth, plus enough boiling water to make 3 cups liquid. Simmer for 30 minutes. Add the milk and butter, and simmer for 5 minutes. Serve the chowder sprinkled with pork dice. Serves 6.

This is how the Kennedys liked lobster prepared:

KENNEDYS' LOBSTER CARDINALE

Boiling water
6 1-1/2-pound lobsters
3/4 cup butter
4 tablespoons flour
1-1/2 teaspoons salt

4 tablespoons chopped canned mushrooms
2 tablespoons dry white wine
2 tablespoons grated Parmesan cheese

Into the boiling water, place the lobsters, and when the water comes to a boil again, cook them 15 minutes. Take lobsters from the water, and cool. Then continue boiling the water, very rapidly, until it boils down to about 2 cups.

With the lobsters turned on their backs, cut down the entire length of the membrane on the other side, using a very sharp knife. Cut out the stomach portion (just below the head of the lobster), and discard it. Take out the meat from the rest of the body and the claws, and cut into chunk-size pieces.

In a saucepan, melt 4 tablespoons of the butter; add the flour and salt. To this, add the 2 cups of reduced liquid, very gradually, and stir constantly until the sauce is smooth and thickened. Cook 15 minutes, stirring often. Then add the mushrooms, wine, and the remaining butter.

Spread a little of this sauce in each lobster shell. Add the lobster meat. Pour the rest of the sauce over the lobsters, and sprinkle with the cheese. Have your broiler preheated, and place the baking pan with the lobsters close to the heat until golden brown. Serves 6.

Like FDR, President Kennedy was fond of salmon, especially this way:

MEDALLIONS OF SALMON (COLD)

1-inch-thick salmon slices   Court Bouillon (see Index)

Cook salmon in court bouillon. Let cool; then glaze with Green Sauce
(below). Use 1 slice of salmon per person.

(Check the Index for La Sauce Verte, the French version of the
following recipe, which contains wine.)

GREEN SAUCE

1-1/3 cups fresh spinach leaves   Fresh tarragon leaves or pinch of
1-1/3 cups watercress   dried tarragon
1-1/3 cups parsley   1 quart mayonnaise
Fresh chervil leaves or pinch of   Green vegetable coloring
    dried chervil   (optional)

Drop the spinach, watercress, parsley, chervil, and tarragon into boiling
water, and blanch for 5 minutes. Strain off the water. Cool quickly, and
mix in the blender until it is smooth and green. Then add the mayonnaise.
If desired, add a touch of vegetable coloring.

Jackie was also partial to fish—especially sole combined with other
seafood in a sumptuous way:

FILETS DE SOLE NORMANDE

2 large filets of sole   1-1/2 tablespoons flour
Court Bouillon (see Index) or fish   1 cup milk
    stock   1 cup reserved fish stock
A few mussels, poached and   Salt and pepper to taste
    trimmed   1/2 cup heavy cream
A few shrimps, poached and   3 egg yolks
    trimmed   For the garnish:
6 oysters, poached   A few sliced truffles
4 mushroom caps, cooked   6 small fried smelts
For the sauce: Small Puff Paste crescents
3 tablespoons butter

Poach the filets of sole in court bouillon or fish stock. Drain well, reserving 1 cup of the stock, and surround the filets with mussels and shrimps. Make a line down the middle of the platter of filets with the oysters and mushrooms. Let the platter of filets dry in the oven for a few minutes; then cover both filets and their garnish with a sauce.

To make the sauce, first make a *roux* with the butter and flour, into which you slowly stir the milk and reserved fish stock. Cook until thickened, season with salt and pepper, and then add the cream and egg yolks. Stir the sauce, and remove from fire. The sauce should cook no longer.

Complete the garnish with truffles, the smelts, and little crescents made of Puff Paste dough (see Index). Serves 4.

Jackie liked everything cooked the French way, but for state dinners she took off the French name so that guests would understand what the dish was. She loved Poulet au Vin, which she called Chicken in Wine on her menus. Here is the rest of the menu she served it with on one state occasion honoring Nationalist China.

Melon and Ham

Chicken in Wine
Green Peas
Potatoes Rissolé

Mixed Green Salad
Cheese and Crackers

Baked Alaska

Demitasse

MELON AND HAM

1/2 pound prosciutto ham	Freshly ground pepper
1/2 ripe honeydew melon	

Use very thin slices of ham. Peel the melon, remove the seeds, and cut into thin crescent-shaped strips. Chill the ham and melon. Alternate slices

of ham and melon on cold serving plate, sprinkle with pepper, and serve.
Serves 4.

CHICKEN IN WINE

4 tablespoons butter	2 tablespoons chopped parsley
1/4 pound minced salt pork	1 teaspoon marjoram
3/4 cup chopped onion	1/2 bay leaf
1 carrot, sliced	1/2 teaspoon thyme
1 clove garlic	1 teaspoon salt
2 shallots, minced	Pinch of pepper
1 3- to 4-pound fryer, disjointed	2 cups dry white wine
2 tablespoons flour	3/4 pound mushrooms, sliced

Melt the butter; add to it and brown lightly the salt pork, onions, carrot, garlic, and shallots. Put the vegetables aside, and brown the pieces of chicken in the fat. Add and mix in the flour, parsley, marjoram, bay leaf, thyme, salt, and pepper. Stir in the wine. Simmer the chicken over low heat about 1 hour. For the last 10 minutes of cooking add the mushrooms. Season to taste. Serve the chicken on a hot platter with the sauce and vegetables poured over it. Serves 3 or 4.

GREEN PEAS

See Index for recipe for Thyme Peas.

POTATOES RISSOLÉ

Potatoes	Chopped parsley
Butter	

With a ball vegetable cutter, scoop out pieces of potato about the size of a hazel nut; cook them in butter until they are golden brown. Sprinkle with parsley, and serve.

BAKED ALASKA

1 layer Genoese Cake (see Index)	1-1/2 pints chocolate or vanilla
4 egg whites	ice cream, frozen in a mold
7 tablespoons powdered sugar	Meringue
1 teaspoon vanilla	

Take a layer of Genoese Cake, which is cut a little larger than the mold of the ice cream. Put it on a board covered with heavy paper. Beat the egg whites until stiff; add the sugar gradually, and continue beating. Add the vanilla. Unmold the ice cream onto the cake. Cover thickly with meringue, place on a baking sheet, and brown in a very hot oven (450°) for about 5 minutes. Serve immediately. Serves 6 to 8.

One of Jackie's favorite main courses for a family dinner was Beef Stroganoff:

JACKIE KENNEDY'S BEEF STROGANOFF

About 2 pounds beef sirloin, cut into thin strips
Salt and pepper to taste
3 tablespoons flour
3 tablespoons butter
2 cups beef stock
1/2 cup sour cream
3 tablespoons tomato juice or paste
1/4 cup grated onion

Season beef strips generously with salt and pepper. Cover and let stand for 2 hours in cool place.

Blend flour and butter over low heat until mixture bubbles and forms a smooth paste. Slowly add the beef stock, stirring constantly until mixture thickens. Let boil for 2 minutes.

Add sour cream alternately with tomato juice or paste, still stirring. Simmer slightly without boiling for 1 minute.

Brown beef and onion in butter; then add contents of meat pan to the prepared sauce, seasoning with salt and pepper. Simmer very gently or cook over hot water in double boiler for 20 minutes. Serves 6.

Another dish that Jackie liked was Foie Gras en Gelée, which she called Chicken in Aspic in formal menus:

FOIE GRAS EN GELÉE

1 can chicken consommé
1 can beef consommé
1 cup port wine
2-1/2 tablespoons unflavored gelatin
1/2 cup water
1 pound good foie gras in a block with truffles in the center

Prepare the aspic: Mix the chicken consommé, beef consommé, and port, and heat. Soak the gelatin in the water, and add to the consommé and wine mixture, stirring until the gelatin is completely dissolved. Let cool until the aspic *starts* setting. Make 1/2-inch slices of the foie gras, using a hot thin, sharp knife. Arrange these slices on a platter, glaze them with some of the aspic, and keep in a cool place. Let the remaining aspic set completely, cut into cubes, and place around the glacéed foie gras and keep cool. Serves 5 or 6.

Now for a typical family menu of the Kennedys.

Jellied Consommé Paysanne

Roast Veal Filet
Potatoes Suzette
Savory Mushrooms
Fresh Asparagus
With Butter and Parmesan Cheese

Crème Brûlée

Demitasse

JELLIED CONSOMMÉ PAYSANNE

2 pounds lean beef, cut into 1-inch cubes
1 pound knuckle of veal, chopped in pieces
1 pound chicken bones
1 quart cold water
2 small carrots, cut into pieces
2 stalks celery, cut into pieces
1 medium onion, quartered
1 medium leek, cut into pieces
1 small bunch parsley
1/2 tablespoon salt
5 peppercorns
Another 1 quart water
2 tablespoons unflavored gelatin

Put into a kettle the beef, veal, chicken bones, and first quart water. Then add the carrots, celery, onion, leek, parsley, salt, peppercorns, and additional water. Let simmer 2-1/2 hours. Then strain, cool, and skim off the fat. This makes about 1-1/2 quarts.

To the clear consommé add gelatin and chill, and put a garnish of cooked vegetables on top of the jelly (see below). Slice the cooked vegetables very thin—julienne. Serves 6.

GARNISH FOR CONSOMMÉ PAYSANNE

1/2 cup carrots, cut in 1/3-inch cubes
1/4 cup potatoes, cut same as carrots

1/4 cup green beans, cut 1/3 inch long
1/4 cup celery, cut 1/3 inch long

All the vegetables should be cooked separately in water and added to the consommé just before serving.

ROAST VEAL FILET

See Index for Jacqueline Kennedy's Veal Filet.

Here's how to make the Potatoes Suzette, a way of having a baked potato without ignoring President Kennedy's preference for mashed potatoes:

POTATOES SUZETTE

3 large baking potatoes
3 tablespoons butter
3 tablespoons heavy cream
2 egg yolks, well beaten

Salt and pepper to taste
3 tablespoons grated Parmesan cheese

Bake the potatoes in a hot oven until done, and cut in half lengthwise. Scoop out the insides, and mash with the butter, cream, and egg yolks. Season with salt and pepper. Beat the mixture until fluffy, and repack in the potato shells. Top with grated Parmesan cheese, and place in oven until the cheese is golden brown. Serves 6.

SAVORY MUSHROOMS

1 pound mushrooms	Salt and pepper to taste
3 tablespoons butter	Chopped chives
1 tablespoon finely chopped onion	Buttered toast
3/4 cup heavy cream	Chives

Wash the mushrooms well, and slice very thin. Sauté them in the butter and onion about 10 minutes. Then add the cream, and season with salt and pepper. Serve on buttered toast with chives sprinkled on top. Serves 6.

The mushrooms may also be served as canapés, either on toast or in small puff paste turnovers with the chives sprinkled on top, and as canapés this amount will serve 10. My recipe for puff paste turnovers, or appetizers, is listed in the Index.

JACQUELINE KENNEDY'S CRÈME BRÛLÉE

1-inch piece vanilla bean or 1/4	6 egg yolks
teaspoon vanilla extract	6 tablespoons granulated sugar
3 cups heavy cream	1/2 cup light brown sugar

If you are using the vanilla bean, heat it with the cream in a double boiler.

In a large bowl, beat the egg yolks and granulated sugar until the mixture is light and creamy. If you have used vanilla bean, remove it from the cream now. Stir the warm cream into the egg yolk mixture very slowly.

Return the mixture to the double boiler, and cook until the custard coats the spoon, stirring constantly. If you are using the vanilla extract, add it now. Pour into a 2-quart heatproof casserole. Put in the refrigerator, and chill for several hours. When ready to serve, sprinkle the brown sugar evenly over the top.

Have your broiler preheated. Place the casserole in a pan of crushed ice, and place under the broiler until the sugar melts and caramelizes. It must be watched very carefully, so that the sugar will not burn. Serve immediately. Serves 6.

Mrs. Kennedy varied the menu of this favorite family meal at a typical small private White House dinner. On this occasion, the menu again had Crème Brûlée for dessert, but this time it was served with Strawberry Sauce.

Consommé Julienne

Filet of Beef with Sautéed Mushrooms and
Potato Balls
Green Mixed Salad

Assorted Cheese and Crackers

Crème Brûlée with Strawberry Sauce

Coffee

With President Kennedy—like Lincoln—politics always took precedence over food. Lincoln also had to be reminded of dinnertime. Stories have been handed down among the White House help of how disappointed Mary Todd Lincoln would be after supervising a fine meal, to have the President eat practically nothing. Lincoln still holds the title of the smallest eater in Presidential history, but Kennedy ran him a close second.

When all else failed to lure President Kennedy to the table, fish chowder was produced. The recipe for this is given elsewhere in this book.

For dinner a favorite menu consisted of lamb chops, mashed potatoes, string beans, tossed salad with Roquefort dressing, and his favorite dessert of baked apple topped with whipped cream.

Substitute medium rare steak for the chops and the President would be just as happy. He liked the potatoes best with just a pat of butter. The same applies to the string beans. Adding slivers of almonds to make String Beans Amandine was a waste of time.

The President also liked baked chicken and turkey—white meat, please— but seldom ate pork roast or pork chops.

He was very fond of Boston baked beans. Try baking them according to the Kennedy recipe:

KENNEDY BAKED BEANS

4 cups dry pea beans	2 teaspoons salt
1 small onion, chopped	1 tablespoon Worcestershire
1/4 pound salt pork, diced	sauce
3/4 cup brown sugar or molasses	1 cup boiling water
1/2 cup catsup	1/4 pound salt pork, cut into
1 teaspoon dry mustard	strips

Cover the pea beans with water. Bring slowly to a boil, or soak overnight. Drain. Cover with fresh water, and simmer slowly. When the skins of the beans start to burst open, the beans are sufficiently cooked. Drain and add onion, diced salt pork, sugar or molasses, catsup, mustard, salt, Worcestershire sauce, and boiling water.

Place in a greased casserole dish, and decorate top with salt pork strips.

Bake, covered, in a very slow oven 6 to 8 hours. Uncover for the last hour of cooking. Add more water or stock if the beans become dry. Serves 12 to 16.

Of course, when the Kennedys entertained more formally, even for members of the family, the menu was more elaborate. Let's take a look now at what was served Mrs. Kennedy's sister and brother-in-law:

DINNER AT THE WHITE HOUSE
IN HONOR OF PRINCE AND PRINCESS RADZIWILL

March 15, 1961

Salmon Mousse with Cucumbers

Poulet à l'Estragon
Grilled Tomatoes
Mushrooms in Herbs
Casserole Marie-Blanche

Baba aux Fraises

Demitasse

SALMON MOUSSE WITH CUCUMBERS

For Salmon Mousse see Index. Then serve with Cucumber Sauce (below), and decorate with sliced unpeeled cucumbers.

CUCUMBER SAUCE

1 cup heavy cream	1/4 teaspoon paprika
2 tablespoons lemon juice	1 large cucumber
1/4 teaspoon salt	

Beat the cream, and add the lemon juice. Season with salt and paprika. Pare, seed, and finely chop the cucumber. Add to the cream mixture. Serve with the Salmon Mousse. Makes about 2 cups.

POULET À L'ESTRAGON

See Index for recipe for Chicken Tarragon.

GRILLED TOMATOES

Tomatoes, 1 per person
Salt and pepper to taste

Melted butter

Cut nice large tomatoes in halves; sprinkle salt, pepper, and a few drops of butter over them; broil under medium heat for about 10 minutes. Serve 2 halves for each person.

MUSHROOMS IN HERBS

1 pound mushrooms
3 tablespoons butter
Salt and pepper to taste
1-1/2 tablespoons chopped
parsley

1-1/2 tablespoons chopped
chives
1 teaspoon tarragon

Slice the mushrooms, and sauté them in a skillet with the butter. When the mushrooms are well coated with butter, reduce the heat to a moderate flame; season with salt and pepper. Just 1 minute before serving, add the parsley, chives, and tarragon, sprinkled on top. Serves 4.

CASSEROLE MARIE-BLANCHE

1-1/2 pounds narrow noodles or
fettucini
1 cup sour cream
1 cup creamed cottage cheese

1/3 cup chopped chives
1/8 teaspoon pepper
1/2 teaspoon salt
1 tablespoon butter

Cook and drain the noodles. Combine the sour cream, cottage cheese, chives, pepper, and salt with the noodles, and pour the mixture into a buttered casserole. Put small dabs of butter on top, and bake at 350° until it starts to brown—about 30 minutes. Serves 6.

From the very first, it was clear that the Kennedys were going to be different. Their first party was held on a Sunday—no one could recall when that had happened before—in honor of the new Presidential appointees. The President and First Lady made their appearance in the East Room unannounced and without the musical fanfare of the Marine Band.

It was the first time in many years that more than the usual cookies, small cakes, and tiny sandwiches were served. On the buffet there were serving dishes of hot cheese patties, fresh shrimp and cauliflower with a mustard dip, celery, cocktail canapes and drinks.

The Kennedys' first formal luncheon showed that their menus would be excellent and in the French tradition:

LUNCHEON
IN HONOR OF THE PRIME MINISTER OF GREECE
AND MRS. CARAMANLIS

April 17, 1961

Consommé Ambassadeur

Chicken Lafayette
White House Terrine

Dame Blanche
Pastry

Demitasse

CONSOMMÉ AMBASSADEUR

Chicken consommé for 6   3 egg yolks
2 pinches chervil   4 ounces very black truffles,
1 egg   finely chopped

This is clear consommé with Truffles Royale. To make the royale, steep the chervil in 3 tablespoons of the boiling consommé. Beat together, as if for an omelet, the egg and the egg yolks. Add the consommé and chervil, slowly, a bit at a time. Strain through a cloth. Then add the truffles, and pour into buttered molds. Set the molds in a casserole in hot water, and poach, taking great care that the water does not boil. The strict rule is that the royale must not be sliced until it is completely cold and the inside has definitely hardened. Then slice in strips, and serve in the consommé. Serves 6.

CHICKEN LAFAYETTE

1 roasting chicken	1/2 cup bacon drippings
Salt and pepper to taste	1-1/2 cups chicken consommé
Flour	1 cup sour cream
1 cup butter	1 tablespoon grated onion

Cut the chicken into pieces proper for serving, dredge the pieces with seasoned flour, and fry in the butter and bacon drippings to a golden brown color. Remove the chicken, and drain the drippings, leaving only about 3 tablespoons of the drippings in the pan. To this add 1 tablespoon flour, the consommé, sour cream, and onion. Return the chicken to the sauce, and let simmer until the chicken is done. Serve with rice. Serves 6.

DAME BLANCHE

1 pint milk	4 egg yolks, slightly beaten
1/3 cup sugar	1 teaspoon vanilla

To make this custard sauce, let the milk and sugar heat until they reach the boiling point. Beat together the yolks and vanilla. Pour in the hot milk mixture gradually, and beat vigorously. Place over a very slow fire, stirring constantly. The mixture should not boil. When it starts to thicken, strain and cool. Serves 5.

Strangely enough, one of President Kennedy's favorite desserts was hot fruit:

PRESIDENT KENNEDY'S HOT FRUIT DESSERT

3 oranges	3 No. 1 cans pineapple pieces
3 lemons	3 No. 1 cans peaches
1-1/2 cups light brown sugar	3 No. 2 cans pitted Bing cherries
3 No. 1 cans apricots	Sour cream

Grate the rinds of the oranges and lemons into the sugar. Drain the liquid from the canned fruit. Slice the oranges and lemons very thin. Spread fruits, layer by layer, including the oranges and lemons, in a baking dish, sprinkling each layer with the sugar mixture. Heat until very hot, and serve topped with some sour cream. Serves 12 to 15.

All the Kennedys liked chocolate. The President teased his brother Robert, however, about his favorite dessert: chocolate ice cream with chocolate sauce, served with chocolate cake with chocolate frosting.

Here is one of the Kennedys' chocolate desserts, which delighted all members of the family when they dined together, particularly Mrs. Kennedy who adored all soufflés:

JACQUELINE KENNEDY'S
SOUFFLÉ FROID AU CHOCOLAT

2 1-ounce squares of unsweetened chocolate	3 tablespoons cold water
	3/4 cup granulated sugar
1/2 cup powdered sugar	1 teaspoon vanilla extract
1 cup milk	1/4 teaspoon salt
1 envelope unflavored gelatin	2 cups heavy cream, whipped

Melt the chocolate, and add the powdered sugar. Add the milk, which you have heated, to the chocolate and sugar mixture, very gradually, stirring constantly. Place over low heat, and continue stirring until the mixture reaches the boiling point, but do not let it boil. Remove from stove, and stir in the gelatin which you have softened in the cold water. Then add the granulated sugar, vanilla, and salt. Place in refrigerator, and chill until it is slightly thickened. Then remove and beat until it is light and fluffy. Fold in the whipped cream. Pour into a serving dish, and chill thoroughly, about 3 hours. Serves 6 to 8.

Like many of their predecessors at the White House, including the

Franklin Roosevelts, the Kennedys liked everything that had strawberries. Jacqueline served this on occasion:

COURONNE GLACÉE IMPÉRIALE
(Vanilla and Strawberry Mold)

Vanilla ice cream   Whipped cream
Strawberry ice cream   Fresh strawberries

Line a ring mold with vanilla ice cream, about 1/2 inch thick, fill the center of the mold with strawberry ice cream, and let it freeze. Then unmold and decorate with whipped cream and fresh strawberries. A medium ring mold serves 6 to 8.

Would you like to serve the same menu—at some special party of your own—with which the Kennedys regaled Prince Rainier and Princess Grace? And for your centerpiece, copy that of Mrs. Kennedy's? It was a silver bowl filled with lilies of the valley.

Luncheon was served in the family dining room of the White House, and the small guest list included Mr. and Mrs. Franklin Roosevelt, Jr., and the Washington artist William Walton, who helped Mrs. Kennedy select the paintings to be hung in the President's study.

LUNCHEON
IN HONOR OF THE PRINCE AND PRINCESS OF MONACO

May 24, 1961

Soft-Shell Crabs Amandine

Spring Lamb à la Broche aux Primeurs

Salade Mimosa

Strawberries Romanoff
Petits Fours

Demitasse

SOFT-SHELL CRABS AMANDINE

12 soft-shell crabs
1 teaspoon salt
1/4 teaspoon pepper
1-1/2 teaspoons lemon juice

Flour
1/2 cup butter
1/3 cup slivered almonds

Wash and dry the crabs, and sprinkle with salt, pepper, and lemon juice. Dust lightly with flour. Sauté in butter for about 6 minutes, turning once. Do not overcook. Remove to a serving platter. Pour the almonds into the drippings, let them brown to a golden color, and pour over the crabs. Serves 3 or 4.

SPRING LAMB À LA BROCHE AUX PRIMEURS

1 4- or 5-pound leg of spring
    lamb, boned
1/2 pound onions, peeled and
    sliced thin
1 tablespoon salt
1/2 teaspoon pepper
1/2 cup sherry
2 tablespoons salad oil
Salt and pepper to taste

Garlic
Cooked mixed vegetables, diced
    about 1/2 inch in diameter
    and sautéed in butter
1 cup carrots
1 cup green peas
1 cup green beans
1 cup celery
1 cup potatoes

The night before you plan to barbecue the meat, trim the fat and gristle from the lamb, put it in a large bowl, and soak in a marinade made of the onions, 1 tablespoon salt, 1/2 teaspoon pepper, sherry, and oil. The next day, before placing the lamb on the spit, season it with salt and pepper and rub with garlic. Barbecue about 2 hours at 250° or 300°. Check temperature with thermometer.

Garnish with the vegetables. Serves 5 or 6.

SALADE MIMOSA

1 head Boston lettuce
1 head romaine lettuce
1 head escarole lettuce
1 bunch watercress

French Dressing Rysavy (see
    Index)
2 hard-cooked eggs, chopped
1 teaspoon chopped parsley

Clean the lettuce and watercress, and dry. Mix with French Dressing Rysavy, and then sprinkle the eggs and parsley over the salad. Serves 12.

STRAWBERRIES ROMANOFF

2 pounds strawberries
Powdered sugar
1/2 cup kirsch or maraschino
   liqueur

Whipped cream

Place the washed strawberries in a serving bowl, sprinkle with powdered sugar, flavor with kirsch or maraschino, and decorate with whipped cream. Serves 4.

FDR, who counted Strawberries Romanoff as his favorite dessert, preferred the berries flavored with port wine instead of liqueur.

I 2

➤➤➤➤➤➤◄◄◄◄◄◄

AT HOME WITH THE EISENHOWERS

The Eisenhowers truly enjoyed living at the White House. Because they enjoyed the White House so much, I did too. I would enjoy seeing Ike chasing his golf ball around the putting green. Mrs. Eisenhower enjoyed being surrounded by her female friends, and sometimes days in a row there would be canasta games or bridge. Washington female society vied to be a part of "Mamie's Bridge Cabinet."

Mamie Eisenhower's health was not too good. She suffered an inner ear ailment that affected her sense of balance. Many times Pat Nixon, as the wife of the Vice President, would substitute for her at functions.

But Mrs. Eisenhower did contribute something of great value to the social history of the White House. She made a project of collecting the china of past administrations and had it catalogued and displayed in the marvelous China Room of the White House. Most of the dishes were found in storage around the White House, but some were tracked down in the far corners of the country.

As a military man the President was used to good food and precision service, but he was easy to get along with, had a great sense of humor, and made my work at the White House very agreeable.

No outsider can know the thrill of realizing I was actually at the White House. I, François Rysavy, would cook for the President of the United States.

I remember my first meal, my first surprise. I looked at the menu. I gasped.

I had cooked, for many gourmets, many fancy dishes—but what was this! President Eisenhower had ordered the plainest of foods. Suddenly I knew why he was so popular. Here was truly a man of the people. A man of simple tastes.

I could see why he wanted a French chef. The fancy, the elegant, the sophisticated was for affairs of state. In the privacy of his "home" he would be just an average American. I determined that I would fulfill the task he had set for me. If he wanted plain American cooking, I'd deliver. I studied the menu for the umpteenth time:

Chicken Noodle Soup

Toasted Points

Broiled Sirloin Steak
Horseradish Sauce
Baked Acorn Squash
String Beans

Peaches
Caramel Cake

I would not have to make the Caramel Cake, I was told by one of my assistants, because the First Lady was having a tea for 150 ladies at four thirty. Caramel Cake was one of the refreshments being served. We would have some of the leftover cake.

Sirloin steak is broiled at the last minute; acorn squash was a moment's work of splitting and putting in the oven with brown sugar and butter. String beans are string beans. The only thing I could let loose on was the chicken noodle soup.

When friends ask me facetiously if I ever made "Mother's chicken soup" at the White House, I tell them, "Of course!" and I give them this recipe, as the chicken soup was made that day for the Eisenhowers:

WHITE HOUSE "MOTHER'S CHICKEN SOUP"

1 4-pound stewing chicken, cut up	Salt and white pepper to taste
3 carrots, sliced	6 cups cold water
3 stalks celery, sliced	1-1/2 cups cooked fine noodles
1 onion, sliced	Chopped parsley

Boil the chicken with the carrots, celery, onion, salt and pepper in the water.

When the chicken is done, take it out, strain the stock, and add the noodles. Serve the soup with a sprinkling of parsley on top. The chicken, of course, is then used for sandwiches and creamed chicken.

Take the chicken liver, which you have boiled, slice it julienne, and just before serving, stir it in gently with a wooden spoon so as not to break the slivers too much. Serves 6.

I looked over the menus for several days in advance and noticed that I would have a few things that would be more challenging than the first day's meal. But I determined to introduce a few of my favorite foods. If the President wanted a French chef with a flair for American cooking, I would be the best American-French chef he ever saw. But I would try to please the Presidential palate with a few food tricks I'd learned around the world. After all, that's what he was paying me for.

As I walked around inspecting my new domain, I thought of all the Presidents who had trod the boards of the White House—I smiled at the aptness of the phrase, when is a President not onstage? I had just recently got well acquainted with the Presidents of the United States while studying for my citizenship test. There was one President with whom I felt a special kinship. He, too, had been an apprentice. He, too, had risen from the bottom to the top of the field he chose. That was Millard Fillmore, who had been a mere wool carder's apprentice before going into law and politics. A woman had helped him—Abigail, a schoolteacher who first taught him for eight years and then became his wife. Even after Fillmore was a lawyer, she had continued to teach, as well as rear a child, until he could support the family.

Come to think of it, the wife of the thirty-fourth President had not exactly had an easy time of it, either. Mamie had been shuffled from place to place around the world, preferring to stay near her husband.

I knew I was up against an unusual situation—a First Lady who did not particularly like to cook and a President who did. In fact, I was to learn that Ike considered cooking a great hobby and used it as therapy.

On the other hand, Mamie Eisenhower, I had been told, actually had been advised by her mother not to learn to cook because if she ever learned, she'd have to keep doing it.

I wondered when I would meet the First Lady. With 150 women for tea, surely she would not have time for me this day.

Then it happened. The First Lady whisked through my kitchen, made directly for me.

"How do you do, Mr. Rysavy," she was saying, and her hand was outstretched. "I hope that you will be happy with us."

Then there was some momentary talk about the kitchen, its equipment, and she was gone.

Several days later I was busying myself about the stove when I looked up and there was President Eisenhower with General Alfred Gruenther, who later became the president of the Red Cross. The President was proudly showing him a machine which had been installed to cut frozen meats, showing off a new gadget just like any other husband.

On my second day at the White House, February 18, 1955, I had served the President's favorite fish—Broiled Filet of Trout. I had fixed it with a strip of bacon across each filet and with lemon butter sauce.

The menu had begun with Cream of Pea Soup and Croutons. With the trout, I had served Coleslaw, Parsleyed Potatoes, Smothered Romaine, and a French dessert, Tartlet of Pears.

In French it would be called *Tartelettes aux Poires*. The French do not bake pies, American style. They make individual-size pies, using a sweet dough rather than American pie dough.

For my pear tartlets, I used the famous French 1-2-3 dough made using the proportion of 1, 2, 3 for sugar, butter, and flour. Because I was making enough to put in the freezer for future use, I used 1/2 pound sugar, 1 pound butter, and 1-1/2 pounds flour. In France we use ingredients by weight instead of cup, and no housewife could cook for a minute without a small scale in her kitchen.

Since sugar is just twice as heavy as flour, this throws the 1, 2, 3 measurements off, so I will give you the proportions for a family meal, American style:

TARTLETS OF PEARS

1 cup flour	1/2 package instant vanilla
1/2 cup butter	pudding mix
1/4 cup sugar	1/2 cup milk
1 egg yolk	1 tablespoon Cointreau
1 tablespoon cream	1 cup whipped cream
Dash of cinnamon	8 pear halves
Pink or red marmalade or jam	1/2 cup sliced browned almonds

To the flour, butter, and sugar, add the egg yolk, cream, and cinnamon. Blend the dough thoroughly instead of lightly as in your pie dough.

Roll the dough to the thickness of pie dough, and cut 3-inch-diameter circles, using a cookie cutter. Place each little circle—you will have about eight—in individual forms 2 inches across, 1 inch deep. I placed an empty cupcake paper in each empty tartlet to keep the dough from rising, and baked in a 375° oven for 15 minutes or until done.

Take off the paper cups, cool, and pour a thin film of marmalade or jam in the bottom of each.

Make the creamy filling: To the pudding mix add the milk and Cointreau. As soon as it begins to set, fold in the whipped cream.

Pour this filling into the tartlets, placing one pear half, rounded side up, on top of each. Brush marmalade or jam over each pear and sprinkle with almonds. Serves 8.

You might like to know the recipe for the pea soup I served at the White House, since I start with fresh or frozen peas.

I have found your wonderful American invention, the electric blender, indispensable for making perfect cream soups. And also for gravies.

CREAM OF PEA SOUP

2 cups fresh green peas   Salt and pepper to taste
1 quart chicken consommé   Croutons fried in butter
1/2 cup light cream
1 tablespoon chopped dry fried
   bacon

Cook the peas in the consommé. When the peas are done, pass them through the blender for 3 minutes at high speed, adding the cream and the bacon just before taking it off.

Use only salt and pepper seasoning. Reheat and serve with a separate serving dish of croutons. Serves 6.

The third day in the White House, I fried chicken Southern style. I have seen many Southern fried chicken recipes. But here is how Mrs. Eisenhower liked it prepared:

MRS. EISENHOWER'S SOUTHERN FRIED CHICKEN

1 fryer   Vegetable shortening
Salt and pepper to taste   Lemon juice
Flour   Lemon wedges
1 egg, beaten

Split the chicken into halves and season with salt and pepper. Dip first in flour, then in egg, and back in the flour. Fry in deep fat, using a vegetable shortening, about 10 minutes. Then take it out of the fat, and place on a rack in a casserole with a little water at the bottom to produce steam. Bake, covered, for 45 minutes in 375° oven. Uncover to dry for an additional 10 minutes' baking at the same temperature. Serve with a bit of lemon juice sprinkled on top and a wedge of lemon on the side. Serves 2.

My menu for the full dinner was:

Hot Tomato Juice
Melba Toast

Fried Chicken
Stuffed Baked Potatoes with Cheese Tops
Brown Gravy
French String Beans
Cloverleaf Rolls

Tossed Salad
Herb Dressing
Triscuits

Apple Strudel
Foamy Sauce

When there were rolls on the menu, company was coming. The President and the First Lady did not eat breads with their main course at dinner. But I kept a supply of yeast dough on hand ready to use on short notice.

I use the same basic recipe as for the cloverleaf rolls, which follows, for rolls of other shapes:

CLOVERLEAF ROLLS

1 fresh yeast cake
1/2 cup lukewarm milk
1-2/3 cups scalded milk
6 tablespoons melted butter

4 egg yolks
2 teaspoons salt
6-1/2 cups flour

Dissolve yeast in lukewarm milk, scalded milk, butter, egg yolks, and salt. Mix all these together after your yeast has risen to the top. Then add the flour, beating vigorously. Let rise about 20 minutes. When the dough has risen to about double size, beat it a second time. The more you beat, the lighter it is. When I made these for my own family, I beat with a wooden spoon, but in the White House I used an electric mixer. The second rising takes the same length of time as the first. Then put on a floured board, roll into strips, and cut into small pieces. Take each piece, and roll into a small ball in the hand.

Put three in each section of a muffin tin, greasing them with butter where the three balls touch so that they come apart easily when pulled apart at the table. Let rise an additional 30 minutes in a warm place, or until they rise to the top of the muffin tin. They will rise a bit more in the oven. Bake at 400° about 20 minutes or until browned.

The baked potato gave me a chance to show what a pastry tube can do to improve the appearance of that old American favorite:

STUFFED BAKED POTATO

Potatoes	Butter
Salt and white pepper to taste	Grated American cheese
Egg yolks	Chopped parsley
Cream	

Make a large circular hole in the top of each potato, and take out the insides. Mash the potatoes in the electric mixer, adding salt, pepper, egg yolks, cream, butter, and cheese to make a medium consistency. My proportion is 1/2 egg yolk and 1 teaspoon cheese per potato.

Next, using a pastry tube with a star point, fill the baked potato shells, and make a fancy design across the top, building up each potato as high as possible. It is necessary that the stuffing not be too liquid for this reason. The egg in the stuffing helps hold it together and makes it puff up even more. For final decoration, sprinkle butter and cheese on top. Before serving, put just a pinch of parsley on the center.

You can, with hardly any practice, turn out a very decorative baked potato. I wish that American housewives would experiment with their pastry tubes in making plain dishes more attractive. Even when you serve a platter of meat, you can make it so decorative with a nice design around the platter made with mashed potatoes passed through the pastry tube. A sprinkling of parsley or paprika spaced a few inches apart along your potato ring will make any guest sit up and take notice.

The Tossed Salad with Herb Dressing was made of Boston lettuce leaves:

HERB DRESSING

Use 1-1/2 cups basic French dressing, but add 1 tablespoon chopped parsley, 1 tablespoon chopped fresh herbs consisting of basil, chervil, chives, mint, and tarragon. You can use my French Dressing recipe (see Index).

The apple strudel was the very one that I had been tested on so long ago in Paris for my job with George Sebastian in North Africa. It was a thrill to be making it now again in such different surroundings. Then it had been at the home of Sebastian's friend in the Parisian suburbs, and I had bribed the kitchen helper to clean my vegetables for that meal which meant so much to me.

Now in the White House, as head chef, I no longer had to bribe anyone for help. I had a staff of four women cooks and helpers and two men. One of the men was the second chef, in charge of cooking for the thirty-four persons of the household staff.

When the First Family had company for lunch, I came early. If it was a family-type luncheon, I came at eleven, but if it was to be a formal luncheon, then I arrived at seven thirty and stayed until nine thirty at night or as long as necessary. I wanted to make sure of every detail.

Getting back to the menu, apple strudel is great with a foamy sauce which I served. Again it was made with one of your wonderful American inventions—instant pudding.

FOAMY SAUCE FOR APPLE STRUDEL

1/2 cup milk
1/2 package vanilla instant
    pudding

1 cup whipped cream

Add milk to the instant pudding. As soon as it starts to set, fold in the whipped cream. If it's a bit too stiff for a topping, add a little extra milk.

Menus at the White House were made in quadruplicate. I had one. Mrs.

Eisenhower had one, the pantry had one and the fourth went to the housekeeper. I worked out the menus with Charles, the first butler, one or two days ahead. For a big party it was three or four days ahead so that I could prepare the many cakes and things necessary. But for a state dinner, it was sometimes done a week in advance. Charles would take the menu to Mrs. Eisenhower to check over at breakfast.

Once, in the first week, I made Crêpes Suzettes with strawberries for a luncheon treat, but this flaming dessert was not a hit with the First Lady, and I did not have Crêpes Suzettes on the menu again.

But the Veal Périgueux, which I had served Somerset Maugham many years before, became a White House favorite.

My first Sunday at the White House the menu was:

Oyster Bisque
Sea Biscuit

Broiled Sirloin Steak
Horseradish Sauce
Corn Pudding
Broccoli
Mock Hollandaise
Orange Roquefort Salad
French Dressing
Club Crackers

French Vanilla Ice Cream
Tutti Frutti
Hot Maple Syrup
Cakes

Let me tell you how to make the Oyster Bisque:

OYSTER BISQUE

2 cups oysters	2 stalks celery, chopped
1/4 cup butter	1 bay leaf
1 small onion	1 teaspoon parsley, chopped
2 tablespoons flour	Salt and pepper to taste
2 cups milk	Chopped parsley for garnish

Simmer the oysters in their own liquor or juice for 15 minutes, or until they start to curl. While they are simmering, make a sauce with the butter, onion, flour, and milk. Then drain the oysters, and put the liquor into the mixture. Add the celery, bay leaf, 1 teaspoon parsley, salt, and pepper to the sauce, and simmer about 30 minutes. Then pour the sauce into the blender (or strain it if you have no blender). At the last minute, add the oysters, coarsely chopped, and serve in small cups with a sprinkling of parsley on top. Serves 4.

The Broiled Sirloin Steak, à la Eisenhower is served rare and with a basting of butter and smoked salt and pepper fresh from the pepper mill. For a 1-1/2-inch steak, I broiled it 3 minutes on each side. Just before serving, the pantry boys squeezed just a few drops of lemon on top of the steak.

HORSERADISH SAUCE

1 3-ounce jar horseradish   1 cup whipped cream
1 sour apple, grated

Strain horseradish. Add sour apple. Fold in whipped cream. This makes a delightful sauce for steak or roast beef.

See Index for President Eisenhower's Corn Pudding.

On the boiled broccoli we served mock hollandaise. It is less expensive and much less fattening than hollandaise:

MOCK HOLLANDAISE

3 egg yolks, beaten until thick   5 tablespoons butter
1 cup Basic White Sauce (see   1 tablespoon lemon juice
    Index)

Add the egg yolks to the white sauce gradually, beating continually, and then add the butter, one tablespoon at a time, and the lemon juice.
Put into top of double boiler, and stir constantly as it thickens to the right consistency. Makes a little more than 1 cup.

For the Orange Roquefort Salad, orange sections topped with finely chopped mint are placed on a bed of lettuce and served with Roquefort dressing.

The dessert reminded me of my old days in Rumpelmayer's in Paris. It was a fancy ice-cream dessert which is a nice treat on a summer's day on the patio:

TUTTI FRUTTI

In a champagne glass, put a large scoop of vanilla ice cream topped with different colored candied fruit—otherwise known as tutti frutti, which is Italian for "all fruit." At the table the butler passed hot maple syrup to top it.

With the Sunday dinner dessert I served petits fours. I kept a good supply of them in the freezer, and when company came to the White House there were always some at hand. They could be defrosted in less than a half hour. Those with caramel frosting were the favorites of the First Lady.

If I were going to make a composite meal that would have pleased the Eisenhowers equally and yet include President Eisenhower's favorite dessert, meat, and soup, it would be:

Chicken Noodle Soup

Broiled Steak (rare)

String Beans   Stuffed Baked Potatoes

Tossed Salad
Green Goddess Dressing

English Rice Pudding

Recipes for preparing the chicken soup and steak appeared earlier in this chapter. Now try Ike's favorite pudding:

IKE'S ENGLISH RICE PUDDING

1/2 cup rice
3 cups milk
1/2 teaspoon lemon rind, very
    finely grated

3 egg yolks
1/2 cup granulated sugar
Seedless raisins
Powdered sugar

Cook the rice in the milk, adding the lemon rind so that the rice is lightly flavored.

After the rice is cooked, combine it unstrained with the egg yolks and granulated sugar, adding a very generous quantity of raisins and pouring the mixture into a buttered Pyrex dish. Let it bake for 35 minutes at 300°; at this low temperature you don't have to set it in a pan of water. Just before removing it from the oven, cover the top heavily with powdered sugar, and place it under the broiler for a few minutes to caramelize. Be careful not to let it burn.

Serve with a pitcher of cream. Serves 6.

Now let's reconstruct a few more Eisenhower family meals:

EISENHOWER FAMILY DINNER

Tuesday, March 1, 1955

Cream of Spinach Soup
Toasted Points

Roast Leg of Lamb
Fresh Mint Sauce
Baked Acorn Squash   Chinese Cabbage

Raisin Rice Pudding
Cream

CREAM OF SPINACH SOUP

1 pound fresh spinach
2 No. 2 cans (5 cups) chicken
    consommé

Salt and pepper to taste
1 cup half-and-half

Boil the spinach 15 to 20 minutes in the chicken consommé, adding a bit of salt and pepper. Run it through the electric blender after it is cooked until it's smooth. Just before it comes off the blender, add the half-and-half. Serves 8 to 10.

TOASTED POINTS

With the cream soup I served toasted points, which were a favorite at the White House. Just take slices of white bread and cut them into three strips with a little point at the crust. Using a scissors, cut off all the crust. Let the strips dry about 1 hour. Then put them under the broiler for a few seconds to give them a nice color, and turn them over to brown the backs.

ROAST LEG OF LAMB

1 6- or 7-pound leg of lamb	Slivered garlic
Salt: 1 teaspoon per pound	4 tablespoons flour
Pepper	1-1/2 cups water
1 medium onion, sliced	Salt and pepper to taste

Trim all the fat off the leg of lamb. Season it with salt and pepper, and put it in the roaster with some water in the bottom. In the water put the onion and insert slivers of garlic in slashes cut near the bone. Of course I did not use onion or garlic if Mrs. Eisenhower was going to be home. But it is much more flavorful if you use onion and garlic.

Roast at 300° until well done, 30 to 35 minutes per pound, basting frequently with the drippings. The President liked the end of the roast best—the narrow part of the leg.

To save time and your patience I am giving you recipes the way they are made ideally so that in cases where onion and garlic improve the flavor you will be able to add these ingredients, even though I seldom got to use them at the White House.

To make gravy for the roast, skim 4 tablespoons grease from top of liquid in the bottom of the pan after removing the lamb. Sprinkle in the flour, stirring constantly to make a brown paste; then pour the water over it. Continue stirring until gravy is smooth, about 5 minutes. Add salt and pepper to taste. Pass through the blender.

The gravy is served separately at the table. Serves 8 to 10.

FRESH MINT SAUCE

Leaves from 1 bunch fresh mint   3/4 cup apple-mint jelly

Wash, dry, and chop the mint leaves. Add them to apple-mint jelly, and simmer over low heat about 10 minutes. Serve warm. If you do not have fresh mint leaves, use apple-mint jelly, and add 3 or 4 drops mint extract to heighten the flavor.

RAISIN RICE PUDDING

See Index for recipe for Ike's English Rice Pudding.

And here is another favorite Eisenhower family menu:

EISENHOWER FAMILY DINNER

Sunday, March 20, 1955

Clam Chowder Manhattan
Sea Biscuits

Roasted Turkey
Whole Cranberry Sauce
Gravy
Cauliflower
String Beans
Rolls

Tossed Salad

Lemon Sherbet
Napoleons

CLAM CHOWDER MANHATTAN

1/4 pound salt pork, cubed
2 medium onions, thinly sliced
1-1/3 cups cubed raw potatoes
3 cups hard-shelled clams,
  chopped
2-1/2 cups fish stock or chicken
  consommé

Salt and white pepper to taste
Pinch of thyme
1 bay leaf
1-1/2 cups peeled cubed
  tomatoes

Put pork into a frying pan, and melt fat a little in order to sauté the onions. Cook the onions and pork about 8 minutes. Add potatoes, stock or consommé, and seasonings. When the potatoes are almost done, add the clams and tomatoes, and boil about 10 minutes. Serves 6 to 8.

NAPOLEONS

I used Puff Paste told about earlier (see Index), rolled out as thin as I could on a floured board. Marble makes the best rolling surface, because it keeps cool and because the surface is without grain. At the White House I converted a marble windowsill into my marble tabletop. I cut my rolled dough to the size of the baking sheet, and I saved the cut-off pieces for future use in other recipes. Bake the puff paste in a 400° oven until brown. When it comes out of the oven and is still on the tin, cut into 2-1/2-inch strips, leaving it on the tin.

Now spread a cream filling (see below) on two out of three of the strips, since you need every third strip for a top layer, and a napoleon is three layers high.

FILLING FOR NAPOLEONS

1 package instant vanilla pudding
  mix
1 cup milk

1/4 cup rum
1 pint heavy cream
1 tablespoon sugar

Mix the vanilla pudding mix and milk. Add the rum. Whip the cream with the sugar. As soon as the pudding starts to set, fold in the whipped cream very gently so that it stays stiff.

Then spread the mixture gently on the layers. About 1/2 inch is the most you can build it up.

On the third strip, which will be the top layer, use the Fondant Frosting with a bit of pink food coloring. This is the same fondant used as the frosting for the Petits Fours described earlier (see Index). As soon as you have spread the fondant on the third strip, cut the strip into 1-1/2-inch widths.

Now place one filled layer on top of another filled layer, and arrange the 1-1/2-inch widths across the top to make the third layer. It is important that the top layer be pre-cut, because it would crush the napoleons if you did not do so. The napoleons are now ready to be separated by cutting the bottom two layers as indicated. Serves about 12.

Vegetables that I often served the Eisenhowers were Eggplant Casserole and Tomatoes Provençale:

EGGPLANT CASSEROLE

1 medium eggplant	Bread crumbs
Chicken stock or consommé	1/4 cup grated sharp Cheddar
Salt and pepper, if desired	cheese

I made this the French way, *Aubergine en Casserole*. Peel the eggplant, cut into small cubes, and precook submerged in chicken stock or consommé. Drain. Make 1 cup cream sauce from the stock (see Index for Basic White Sauce), adding salt and pepper if necessary. Consommé is salty, remember. Put the precooked eggplant in a buttered casserole, cover with the cream sauce, and top with bread crumbs and cheese. Bake about 20 minutes in a 375° oven. Serves 6.

TOMATOES PROVENÇALE

6 ripe large tomatoes	1 tablespoon finely chopped
1 onion, chopped	parsley
4 tablespoons butter	Salt and freshly ground pepper to
2/3 cup bread crumbs	taste
1 clove garlic, crushed and	Dash of celery salt
chopped	

Wash the tomatoes, and cut them in half so that you have a top and bottom. Carefully scoop out the seeds, and take out the meat from the center—about a teaspoon from each half.

Arrange the tomatoes in the casserole, and fill them with a bread crumb and onion mixture as below.

Chop the onion and brown in butter. Then add bread crumbs, garlic, and parsley. To this add the bits of tomatoes which have been scooped from each tomato half, and if necessary, chop more finely. Season with salt, pepper, and celery salt, and pile the mixture into the centers. Bake at 375° from 25 to 30 minutes. Serves 6

I am very proud that one White House specialty has been named for me and is a part of the White House files. In my small way, I have added to the culinary history of the White House.

It is really a simple little thing, a soup which I concocted in France and used first at the White House during my second month. First Lady Mamie liked it, and since there was no name for it, she and Charles, the head butler, named it Cream of Celery-Clam Soup Rysavy and promised to leave it behind for future Presidents:

CREAM OF CELERY-CLAM SOUP RYSAVY

Clam juice	Chicken consommé
Homemade or canned celery soup	Chopped chives

Use twice as much clam juice, which you can buy at any grocery store, as celery soup and half as much chicken consommé as celery soup.

Run this through the electric blender until it is creamy. Serve with a sprinkling of chives.

But I must admit I made my share of mistakes too—though one does not permit oneself too many mistakes in the White House. The funniest one came about because of the language barrier. The menu said Scalloped Potatoes, which my mind, used to thinking in French, thought meant "sautéed," so I made fried boiled potatoes with onions and sprinkled with parsley.

Now I finally know that in America scalloped potatoes are baked in the oven in layers. Mrs. Eisenhower was very sweet about it—even about the onions—but I never tried to guess again when a dictionary was handy.

It was a delightful coincidence that for the last family dinner I prepared for the Eisenhowers, I served my favorite meat, roast loin of pork. For sentimental reasons, I would like to include the rest of that menu—Beef Consommé, Toasted Points, Apple Sauce, Scalloped Potatoes, Broccoli (which had come from the President's farm in Gettysburg), Lettuce and Tomato Salad with French Dressing, Sliced Mangos, and Coconut Cupcakes.

Let me tell you the recipe the First Lady preferred:

MAMIE'S SCALLOPED POTATOES

6 medium potatoes, peeled and cut into 1/4-inch slices
Salt
6 tablespoons butter
2 tablespoons flour
3/4 cup milk

3/4 cup chicken consommé
White pepper to taste
1 cup grated American cheese
1/4 cup buttered bread crumbs
1/2 cup finely chopped onions, if desired

Parboil the potatoes in salted water, being careful not to overcook. Have a greased Pyrex dish ready. Lay the slices in the baking dish in layers with the cream sauce that follows in between.

Use 1-1/2 cups of cream sauce made with the butter, flour, milk and consommé, salt, and white pepper paste.

The top layer is potatoes. Cover this heavily with the cheese and bread crumbs.

Adding onions when making the cream sauce gives more flavor. Serves 4 to 6.

Let me tell you now how I made the Roast Pork on my last day at the White House. Of course, I did not use the onion and garlic clove which are in my favorite pork recipe because the First Lady found they did not agree with her.

ROAST PORK

1 3-pound loin of pork
1/2 teaspoon salt per pound of meat
Pepper to taste
1 large onion, chopped
1 large clove garlic, chopped

1/2 teaspoon caraway seed
1 tablespoon horseradish mustard
1 cup chicken consommé
Bit of flour and additional consommé for gravy

Season pork with salt and pepper, and place in a hot oven to brown. While it is browning, make the following mixture for basting:

To the onion and garlic add the caraway seed, horseradish mustard, and chicken consommé. Pass this through the blender. Baste the roast with it frequently, lowering the oven temperature to 300° after it is browned. Allow 40 minutes per pound.

The liquid at the bottom of the roaster makes a wonderful gravy with the addition of only a bit of flour and a little more consommé, if necessary. Serves 4 or 5.

When blueberry pies were blamed for the President's indigestion attack in early June, everyone became very blueberry-pie-conscious. My friends all wanted to know the recipe for the blueberry pie that was so good that the President overate it to the extent he suffered an economy-shaking stomachache. What kind of pie can influence the stock market, they wanted to know?

Of course, I did not make those particular pies because my resignation was effective the end of May. But it had to be the same recipe that I used at the White House.

MAMIE'S "BILLION DOLLAR" BLUEBERRY PIE

Piecrust for 1 9-inch pie   1/3 cup granulated sugar
2-2/3 cups fresh blueberries   Pinch of salt
1/2 tablespoon flour   1/2 teaspoon cinnamon
1/2 teaspoon grated lemon rind   1 teaspoon melted butter
1/3 cup light brown sugar

We made double-crusted blueberry pies. Mix the blueberries lightly with the flour, lemon rind, light brown sugar, granulated sugar, salt, and cinnamon. Fill the pie, and sprinkle the butter over it before covering with the top crust. Bake in hot (450°) oven for 10 minutes, and reduce to 350° for another 40 minutes, or until pie is done.

I spoke before of Mamie Eisenhower's and Dolley Madison's love of caramel. Here are some of Mamie's recipes. (For Dolley's Caramel Icing, see the Index.)

MAMIE EISENHOWER'S APPLE CARAMEL

5 tablespoons sugar   1/2 teaspoon vanilla
4 tablespoons butter
5 apples, peeled and cut into
  wedges

Melt the sugar in an iron skillet over a low flame until it is golden brown to caramelize the sugar. Add the butter, and blend. Then add the apples. Cover and let simmer until apples are soft, adding the vanilla a little before taking off heat. I served the apples in a silver dish, warm, with a pitcher of cream to be passed. Serves 4.

MAMIE EISENHOWER'S CREAM CARAMEL CUSTARD

1 pint milk   2 egg yolks
1/2 cup sugar   Additional 2/3 cup sugar
1 egg

I make this the French way. It is called *Crème Renversée au Caramel*. Bring the milk to a boil. Add the 1/2 cup sugar. While waiting for it to boil, beat the egg and the egg yolks with a wire beater. When the milk boils, pour it slowly over the eggs, and continue beating to keep the eggs from cooking. Strain and pour the mixture into a buttered Pyrex dish on the bottom of which there is a layer of caramelized sugar, which is made as follows:

Melt the 2/3 cup sugar in a heavy pan without water or butter until it is light brown. When caramelized, pour it into the bottom of a heated Pyrex dish to make an even film on the bottom.

Let the caramel cool before the milk mixture is poured into it, so that it will stay separated. Put the baking dish in a pan of warm water, and bake in a 350° oven for 30 minutes, or until a toothpick comes out dry. Let cool and put in refrigerator.

Serve upside down so that the caramel sits on top. Serves 4.

Now let's look at some of Mrs. Eisenhower's mint desserts:

MINTED APRICOTS

1 can apricot halves, drained, or   1 cup melted apple-mint jelly
    fresh peeled apricots, halved   Several drops mint extract

Arrange apricots in the bottom of a stewing pot. Pour over it a hot mixture of apple-mint jelly and mint extract. Cook slowly for 5 minutes. Serve 2 or 3 halves per person.

HALF-AND-HALF MINT-CHOCOLATE PIE

1-1/2 cups graham cracker   Additional 3/4 cup sugar
    crumbs   3 egg yolks
1/4 cup sugar   3 squares unsweetened chocolate,
4 tablespoons melted butter   melted
1 envelope unflavored gelatin   1/2 cup heavy cream
2 tablespoons water   4 drops mint extract
1 cup scalded milk   3 egg whites, stiffly beaten

This requires a graham cracker crust which is made in the usual way by combining the graham crumbs, 1/4 cup sugar, and melted butter. Pack firmly as you spread it over the pie tin to form a lower crust. Bake at 375° for 5 minutes.

The filling is not too hard. First dissolve the gelatin in cold water. While it is softening, pour the milk, bit by bit into a mixture of the 3/4 cup sugar and egg yolks.

In a double boiler cook the milk and egg mixture, stirring constantly until it starts to thicken. Then take off stove, and stir in softened gelatin.

Now take half the custard mixture, add the chocolate to it, and put in the refrigerator until partially set. Then whip the cream, fold into the chocolate mixture, and pour into the crumb crust.

With the other half of the custard which you did not put in the refrigerator, add the mint extract and the egg whites, and pour over the chocolate layer. Serve when it is cold. To keep the two layers separate, make sure the bottom chocolate layer is firm and cold before pouring in the warmer topping. Serves 6 to 8.

You can find the Frosted Mint Delight recipe in the Index, but meanwhile I have thought of two other mint-brightened recipes. These are

Minted Meringue Peaches served with lamb, and Lime Sherbet Melon Mold, a favorite Eisenhower dessert:

LIME SHERBET MELON MOLD WITH STRAWBERRIES

Put the lime sherbet in a melon mold—which is simply a mold indented in sections like a melon—the day before you are going to use it. Put it in the freezer overnight. When you are getting it ready for serving, unmold it with a bit of hot water against the mold, and decorate it with fresh mint leaves and strawberries. Be very generous with the mint, and place the strawberries so that they are little hearts in the clusters of green.

MAMIE'S MINTED MERINGUE PEACHES

These are made almost like the minted apricots—that is, canned peach halves cooked in jelly, but this time using plain mint jelly: Cook about 10 minutes until the flavor and color penetrate the peaches. Then strain; lay in a baking pan; put a rosette of meringue (see Index for Meringue) in each peach indentation. Put in a warm oven (about 200°) to dry for 10 minutes.

Another of Mamie's favorite desserts was Strawberry Shortcake:

MAMIE'S STRAWBERRY SHORTCAKE

1 cup flour	1 tablespoon sugar
1/2 teaspoon salt	Butter
2 tablespoons shortening	2 cups sliced, sweetened
2 teaspoons baking powder	strawberries
1/3 cup milk	1 cup light cream

Combine the flour, salt, shortening, baking powder, milk, and sugar to make the dough as for regular biscuits, rolling 1 inch thick on the board and making large cakes for individual servings.

When they come out of the oven, cut each cake in half and butter inside. I usually baked these when the First Family started to eat dinner so that the shortcake would be nice and warm when served. Use part of the berries between the halves, and pour the rest over the top. Serve with cream. Serves 4.

13

❧❧❧❧❧❧❧❧

AT HOME WITH THE WASHINGTONS, LINCOLNS, AND OTHER FIRST FAMILIES THROUGH HISTORY

Had you visited every President at dinnertime, you would learn how unique each one was. Few seem to agree on anything from the liquor they drank—or didn't drink—to the food they ate.

The earlier Presidents indulged in feasts. If you had dined with President Washington at the Presidential house when it was in Philadelphia, you would literally have had a meal that ranged from soup to nuts. After the soup would come fish in some form, then a fowl of some kind, followed by a main course of meat and vegetables galore, especially root vegetables. Dessert would be an endurance contest of its own with pies and puddings and little cakes and fruits in season. Even watermelon was served both for at-home occasions and formal dining.

Abraham Lincoln dined in a Spartan fashion by comparison. He would rather nibble fruit. His wife Mary tried everything to make Abe eat but was frustrated time and again to see the finest foods left all but untouched on his plate. One of the few entrees that would tempt Lincoln was Chicken Fricassee. He liked the chicken cut up in small pieces, fried with seasonings of nutmeg and mace and served with a gravy made of the chicken drippings, flour, and rich cream.

Mary Lincoln set a table at the White House, which included such food as Aspic of Tongue, Pâté de Foie Gras, Turkey Stuffed with Truffles, and all sorts of wild game, such as venison, pheasant, or canvasback duck. But all too often the President merely picked at his food.

But no one had to tempt William Howard Taft, who stands in history as the biggest eater to occupy the White House. Of course, Helen Taft, his wife, tried to restrict him, but he would slip away and eat elsewhere. Here is one of the luncheons that helped keep his weight hovering around 320 pounds:

LUNCHEON FOR PRESIDENT WILLIAM HOWARD TAFT

The occasion was his dedication of the Pilgrim Memorial Monument in Provincetown, Massachusetts.

August 4, 1910

Lobster Stew

Salmon Cutlets with Peas

Cold Roast Tenderloin with Vegetable Salad

Roast Turkey with Potato Salad

Cold Tongue and Ham

Frozen Pudding
Cake, Fruit, and Coffee

President Theodore Roosevelt once got angry with the press when a reporter called him a gourmet. TR wanted it known he had very simple tastes. You can judge for yourself. One of his favorites was a suckling pig, roasted whole and stuffed with an apple-sage stuffing.

Now and then the food eaten by a President can become a national issue. Patrick Henry once accused Thomas Jefferson of "being so Frenchified when he came home from France that he abjured his native victuals."

True, Jefferson liked his foods, especially desserts, saturated with French wines and liqueurs, but so did many other Presidents.

A White House favorite throughout many administrations, including those of Thomas Jefferson and Zachary Taylor, was a dessert made with wine and brandy—Wine Jelly.

Wine Jelly is a delightful gelatin dessert in which a good dry sherry or Madeira and a teaspoon or so of brandy are substituted for one-fourth of the water used in making gelatin. It is served topped with whipped cream and berries or other fresh fruit.

Jefferson especially liked desserts that featured wine or brandy as an ingredient:

JEFFERSON'S FLOATING ISLAND

3 cups milk
Sugar and white wine to taste
Raspberry or strawberry
   marmalade

4 egg whites, very stiffly beaten
Slices of cake
Fruit slices (optional)

Mix milk, sugar, and wine. Add marmalade to egg whites. Lay egg white mixture in milk mixture, first putting in some slices of cake. Raise it in little mounds, and garnish with more marmalade or fruit slices. Serves 6.

JEFFERSON'S BRANDIED PEACHES

4 pounds peaches
1 pound sugar

Water to cover
1 pint brandy

Prick peaches in a half dozen places with a fork, and place in hot syrup made with sugar and water. Boil the syrup until it is thick enough to stick to a wooden spoon. Add the peaches after the syrup has cooled a little. Cover and let stand for 24 hours.

Now remove the peaches, and bring the syrup to a boil again. As soon as it starts to boil, take it off the fire and add brandy. Return the peaches to the liquid. Again let the peaches stand overnight. The following day simmer the peaches in the syrup until they are tender, adding brandy, if you desire. Strain, cool, and serve, storing the leftover peaches in jars for future use.

Here is a lovely wine dessert which has come down to us from President James K. Polk's family, handed down from generation to generation:

POLK FAMILY'S CHARLOTTE POLONAISE

7 egg yolks
3 cups milk
2 ounces sweet baking chocolate,
   grated
1/2 cup granulated sugar
4 macaroons, crumbled
3/4 teaspoon almond extract

3/4 cup almonds, ground
2/3 cup citron, diced
2/3 cup powdered sugar
2 large layers sponge cake
2 cups sweet white wine
Frosting or whipped cream

In saucepan stir egg yolks and milk for about 10 minutes until it boils and thickens into a custard. Remove half the custard to another saucepan, adding chocolate, granulated sugar, and macaroon crumbs to it. To remaining half add almond extract, almonds, citron, and powdered sugar. Bring the second mixture to a boil, stir to mix well, and cool both batches of custard.

Cut the sponge cake layers into 1/2-inch slices. Spread one slice heavily with the chocolate custard and another slice with the almond custard. Continue alternately until all ingredients are used. Layer the slices, alternating the type of filling as you pile them up. Pour the wine over all the layers before covering with frosting or whipped cream. Serves about 30.

More recently the Trumans had no particular liking for gourmet cooking and preferred plain, wholesome American food. If you had dined with that Presidential family, this is what you would have had on a typical day:

PRESIDENT TRUMAN'S FAMILY DINNER

Consommé

Broiled Steak   Mushrooms
Asparagus
French Fried Potatoes

Waldorf Salad

Chocolate Pudding

Coffee

Poor Franklin D. Roosevelt enjoyed gourmet food, but his wife was usually too busy with her myriad worthwhile projects to tend to kitchen details herself. Once, in disgust—but still with a bit of redeeming humor—Franklin Roosevelt sent First Lady Eleanor a letter saying that he had "bitten two foreign powers" because he was so hungry from having been served nothing but sweetbreads every day since his previous complaint that he had been given "chicken six times in a single week."

But then Mrs. Roosevelt had her troubles, too. Once no one had taken care of mailing out several hundred invitations and no one came to a White House party except the staff.

The Franklin Roosevelts had a Sunday night ritual that involved the First Lady and was greatly enjoyed by guests who were made to feel a part of the family because of it.

Mrs. Roosevelt made a chafing dish of scrambled eggs right at the table as guests and family sat talking. But there was a bit more to the menu than that:

ELEANOR ROOSEVELT'S SUNDAY SUPPERS

Scrambled Eggs
(Done at table in chafing dish)

Cold Cuts—Ham, Bologna, and Liverwurst
Shoestring Potatoes
Mixed Vegetable Salad

Fruit   Cheese   Crackers
Coffee

FDR liked to play bartender. He liked martinis and would whip them up for his guests on Sunday nights while his wife busied herself with the scrambled eggs.

Two decades later it caused a furor when the press reported that a bar had been set up in the White House State Dining Room to serve guests martinis at the first party the John F. Kennedys gave. Thereafter, the drinks were served by waiters carrying trays of ready-mixed drinks. You never know what the reaction will be when it comes to serving liquor at the White House, even in the family quarters.

Liquor has always presented a problem at the White House because so many Americans abstain from drinking. In order to avoid offending anyone, Presidents usually do not permit themselves to be photographed with a glass in their hands.

First Lady Lucy Hayes became "Lemonade Lucy" when she set a new standard of piety and propriety for the White House in 1877. The Blue Room of the White House became the scene of daily family prayers, and no alcoholic beverages were served to guests—not even wine for the toast at diplomatic dinners. Tea, the diplomats felt, was no substitute. But they drank it and smiled, as diplomats must.

What a far cry from the early Presidents. Washington liked a good claret, Madeira, and other spirits. Jefferson collected wines the way some people collect diamonds. And John and Abigail Adams, the first Presidential family to live in the White House, served the fancier spirits but liked a good glass of apple cider. At receptions, they liked to serve a punch made with Jamaica rum and brandy.

Jefferson is said to have spent $11,000 on imported wines during the time he was in the White House. That was a young fortune in those days. But Jefferson was as strongly against hard liquor as he was ardently in favor of wine. One of his comments on the subject was: "No nation is drunken where wine is cheap; and none sober, where the dearness of wine substitutes ardent spirits as the common beverage."

Jefferson's friends invariably consulted him about wines, and the record shows that he chose and ordered about sixty dozen bottles of wine in 1790 for President Washington.

But what is most amusing and certainly shows his preoccupation with the subject is that when Jefferson was writing a letter congratulating Monroe on being elected President in 1818, he wrote of nothing but advice on wines to be used for the White House and saved only a few lines for the congratulatory message.

In his own writings and ledgers, George Washington mentions all kinds of liquid refreshments—ale, beer, brandy, Canary wine, Lisbon wine, liquors, Madeira wine, porter, punch, rum, Rhenish wine, and just plain "whiskey and wine."

The record shows Washington bought claret and Madeira in great quantity. In the account of Washington's life written in 1798 by Niemcewicz, the author tells how Washington "likes to talk after dinner with a glass of Madeira wine by his side." Then, suitably mellowed, the account relates, the First President would read the newspapers and answer his mail.

John Adams fixed himself a concoction called a Berry Shrub. It was and still is great for holidays:

JOHN ADAMS' BERRY SHRUB

2 cups blackberry or raspberry
   juice
1/2 cup sugar, dissolved in a
   little hot water

1 cup brandy
1 cup rum

Shake all the ingredients in a shaker, and serve cold. Some guests preferred their Shrub made with rum alone and no brandy, and some with just a little brandy added to 2 cups of rum. Makes about 1 quart.

Early Presidents also had their servants make Mead or Honey Wine:

MEAD OR HONEY WINE

1 cup honey	1 teaspoon yeast
2 quarts water	1/2 cup brandy (optional)
A handful of whole spices made up of 3 or 4 buds each of: cloves, mace, ginger and cinnamon sticks	

Boil honey and water together for 30 minutes. Flavor with spices tied in a little bag and boiled with it. The brew is then fermented with the bag of spices still in it for at least 6 weeks, using yeast to speed the action. Brandy may be added to strengthen the flavor before serving. Makes about 2 quarts.

Syllabub was a popular alcoholic drink of the past of which one no longer hears. But Tom Jefferson liked it, as did Washington and Jackson.

SYLLABUB

Basically, a syllabub is a drink you make by mixing milk with sweetened wine and topping with whipped cream. Each President had his variation.

SYLLABUB JEFFERSON

Jefferson did not leave the exact measurements. He seasoned milk with sugar, then added white wine, being careful not to put so much in that it curdled the milk. He then poured the mixture in a glass and topped it with sweetened whipped cream.

SYLLABUB JAMES MONROE

President Monroe preferred a proportion of 4 to 1—2 cups milk to 1/2 cup wine. Making it his way, you mix the sugar and wine and then slowly add the milk, which is first warmed slightly. Instead of whipped cream, his topping was nutmeg.

SYLLABUB JACKSON

Jackson preferred his syllabub as a spooned dessert made with sherry which had been mixed with an equal amount of sugar. To make it, lightly beat 2 cups heavy cream, then gradually add 1/2 cup sherry which has been sweetened with 1/2 cup sugar, and pour into glasses.

During Van Buren's time no drinking was permitted in the White House and no refreshments of any sort were offered guests who came to the New Year's receptions or levees. All the guests could do was listen to the music of the Marine Band.

President Fillmore also barred alcohol at the White House door, and his successor, Franklin Pierce, was actually a leader in the temperance movement. And everyone knows about Rutherford and "Lemonade Lucy."

On the opposite end of the cork from the teetotaling Hayes was President Warren Harding, who was known for his hard-drinking poker parties. President Andrew Jackson, who gave parties for his military and frontier friends served a mad mixture called Daniel Webster Punch, which was made of brandy, champagne, rum, tea, lemon, sugar and arrack, an alcoholic drink distilled from rice or molasses. It was guaranteed to make a dancer out of someone who had never set foot on a dance floor.

Mary Todd Lincoln let it be known that she and Abraham did not touch liquor. She also did not serve it to guests, and once when a gift of wines arrived, she quickly sent it off to a military hospital.

Once, during the Civil War, a delegation of irate women called on President Lincoln to complain about General Ulysses S. Grant's drinking. President Lincoln suggested that the ladies find out what brand of liquor General Grant was drinking so that he could send it to all his generals.

Here is the recipe for the punch that was served by Grant after he became President. This is a very versatile drink which can be made with champagne, if it is for the ladies or with hard liquor for the men. It was served midway through a twenty- to thirty-course meal:

PRESIDENT GRANT'S ROMAN PUNCH

1 quart frozen lemonade, crushed   1/2 to 2/3 cup rum
1 bottle champagne

Place the frozen lemonade in a punch bowl, and pour the champagne and rum over it.

The stronger version is:

Brandy   Crushed frozen lemonade
Rum

Mix rum and brandy in equal portions, and pour over frozen lemonade in a punch bowl.

Many wondered what was in the glass that Winston Churchill, FDR's favorite guest, kept sipping around the White House. It was scotch and soda. He drank it at lunchtime, too. But for dinner he switched to champagne with a snifter of brandy to help his digestion at the end of the meal.

One day Churchill took it upon himself to explain why he drank. It was, he said, because in his youth he had gone to India and had been afraid to drink the water. He had continued to fear to drink it ever since, he added.

The Franklin D. Roosevelts, who came into the White House during Prohibition, were obliged to serve grape juice and fruit punch at their state receptions. However, FDR is credited with bringing about the repeal of Prohibition in his first term of office.

President Richard Nixon can nurse a single glass of scotch all evening. President Lyndon Johnson did not nurse his, nor did President Eisenhower.

President Harry Truman was a bourbon drinker.

John F. Kennedy drank Beefeater gin, preferably in a Tom Collins, but what he liked best with a meal, when he was relaxing at home, was a glass of Dutch beer, Heinekens. Jacqueline, on the other hand, liked daiquiris and was so particular about how they were made that she had the exact formula Scotch-taped to the various pantry walls wherever the butlers would be preparing them—at the White House, at Palm Beach, and at the Atoka, Virginia, Presidential hideaway.

Pat Nixon sips a glass of wine with her meal at formal dinners and joins in the champagne toast to the guest of honor when all assembled at the Nixon table raise their glasses.

Ironically, one President owed his life to the fact that he was drinking instead of watching a ceremony. That was John Tyler, and the date was February 29, 1844. The President was on board the USS *Princeton* to watch the firing of a new gun amusingly christened "The Peacemaker."

The President was supposed to be on deck, but he was belowdeck having a glass of champagne when the new gun was fired and exploded, killing several of the official party.

President McKinley could not have been as stuffy as some younger-generation members seem to believe—Andrew Carnegie once sent him a barrel of scotch.

Yes, sometimes guests even get a little tipsy at the White House.

In the Kennedy administration the guest of honor once drank a little too freely at a state dinner and could hardly make it from the table. President Kennedy slipped away with his guest to the White House library on the excuse of giving him a copy of the Kennedy book *Profiles in Courage*. Unfortunately, the guest of honor fell asleep looking at the book and had to be escorted out to his car without staying for the usual after-dinner entertainment.

But compared with some past occasions that was as nothing. When Andrew Jackson had his inaugural party at the White House, there was so much drinking that the lovely rooms were soon a shambles. In order to lure his most boisterous guests out of the White House, Andy Jackson ordered a big tub of heavily spiked punch taken out to the lawn. Only the most easily handled drunks were tricked into going out into the sobering winter air. The rest stayed inside, climbing on chairs and on tables and, in one case, crashing into a window and breaking it.

The amusing denouement is that Old Hickory stole away from his own inaugural party to have a quiet steak dinner with a few friends.

If you had visited Jackson at home at the White House, you would have been amazed at the company you found at every meal—and what meals! Guests would come away talking about the vast choice of victuals brought to table—things like wild turkey served with a dressing made with brains, roast canvasback duck, Virginia ham, pheasant, and partridges. The various fowl and meat dishes would be brought in to be admired by the President and his guests and then taken away to be carved.

Though Rachel Jackson did not live to preside over the White House, the

President continued to have his roast lamb fixed from her favorite recipe. And his continuing grief over her loss was obvious to all those around him.

MRS. JACKSON'S LEG OF LAMB WITH ROSEMARY

1 6-pound leg of lamb	2 teaspoons rosemary
3 strips bacon	2-1/2 teaspoons salt
3 lamb kidneys	1/2 teaspoon pepper
3 cloves garlic, crushed	

Preheat oven to 325°. Wrap bacon strips around kidneys, and skewer to underside hollow of the leg. Rub meat with a mixture of the garlic, rosemary, salt, and pepper. Place in shallow roasting pan and bake 2 to 2-1/2 hours (about 20 minutes per pound). Serve on hot platter. Serves 6 to 8.

When it came to drinks at the table, Jackson served Washington's favorite, Madeira, with turkey and duck and claret with dessert. Desserts, incidentally, were healthier than ours today because they always ended up with raw fruit. But how one could eat fruit after having cakes and tarts and ice cream is hard to say.

The Hoovers also loved a great deal of company. Once President Hoover invited a group of 200 to stop in for tea; but the invited guests brought friends, and the amount of tea sandwiches had to be doubled on the spot, with servants rushing out for more bread and sandwich spreads. Throughout the turmoil the President beamed happily, enjoying the sight of people having fun on the White House lawns.

First Lady Lou Hoover was an accomplished linguist; she spoke four foreign languages. She was also accomplished in the field of architecture. She designed the Hoovers' home in Palo Alto, California, to which they retired.

And she was a perfectionist about the food she served.

As a family guest, here is a soup you would undoubtedly have been served:

PRESIDENT HOOVER'S FAVORITE MUSHROOM SOUP

1 pound mushrooms, diced very
   small
2 cups cold water
2 cups chicken stock, seasoned to
   taste

2 cups light cream
1 tablespoon flour
Cold milk
3 tablespoons whipped cream
Paprika

Immerse mushrooms in cold water for 2 hours; then simmer over low heat about 30 minutes. Strain liquid, and add seasoned chicken stock. Blend cream and flour with a little cold milk until perfectly smooth. Add to mushrooms and chicken stock. Sieve through very fine strainer.

Immediately before serving add the whipped cream. Sprinkle with paprika. Serves 8 to 10.

And speaking of perfectionists about food, the Tafts had a special cook who was called in to do nothing but make turtle soup.

Incidentally, though the Tafts served a champagne punch for guests, the President did not drink. If he had, his six-foot-two frame would have probably had to support more than his 320 pounds.

If you dined with the William Howard Tafts at home, you might have been lucky enough to enjoy First Lady Helen's recipe for Turkey or Chicken Croquettes:

HELEN TAFT'S TURKEY OR CHICKEN CROQUETTES

2-1/2 cups leftover turkey or
   chicken, finely chopped
1 medium onion, chopped
Salt, pepper, and nutmeg to taste
2 tablespoons butter
3 tablespoons flour

About 1-1/2 cups heavy cream
2 eggs, beaten
Bread crumbs
Deep fat for frying

Combine the chopped turkey or chicken with the onion and seasonings. Melt the butter, stir in the flour, and add this to the cream over a low flame before combining the two mixtures. Chill, form into little croquette shapes, roll in egg and then bread crumbs, and fry in deep fat. Serves 4 to 6.

You will have to agree this is probably the kind of food that put poor President Taft in the 320-pound weight category. But the President was a good-natured host. And if you were at his table, you would undoubtedly have heard him play down his own importance and build up his wife, saying, "Helen is the politician in this family."

You might also have seen him bob his head and take a thirty-wink nap.

14
➤➤➤➤➤➤➤➤➤➤

HOW FIRST LADIES ENTERTAIN
THEIR FRIENDS

First Ladies tend to entertain their friends at lunch so that in the evening they can devote their attention to their husbands, just as any other wife would. But the First Ladies' luncheons are done with almost as much pomp and ceremony as the President's.

Pretend you are there. It is April 5, 1971, and First Lady Pat Nixon is entertaining the wives of the U.S. Senators. In fact, there will be 112 women present because a few wives of former U.S. Senators who live in the Washington area attend. Roger Williams, the noted American pianist, is scheduled to perform in the East Room following the luncheon.

Guests arrive at the diplomatic entrance about fifteen minutes early for the 1 P.M. luncheon and are escorted up the stairs and to the Blue Room by a White House military aide. At the Blue Room, they are greeted by Mrs. Nixon before they go in to luncheon in the State Dining Room. The round tables are covered with white organdy tablecloths over yellow, and the centerpieces are low bowls of yellow, white, and gold spring flowers.

Beside the ladies' placecards are small memento gifts from the First Lady: normally a crystallite paperweight about three by four inches enclosing a colored engraving of the White House *circa* 1845. For smaller lunches Pat Nixon signs each one by hand.

MRS. NIXON'S ANNUAL SENATE WIVES LUNCHEON

April 5, 1971

Cold Cream of Avocado Soup   Corn Sticks

Sugar Cured Virginia Ham
Cheese Soufflé
Tiny Peas
Bibb Lettuce Salad

263

Glace aux Fraises   Petits Four

The wine is: Wente Brothers Sauvignon Blanc

At dessert, the ladies are serenaded by the United States Army Strolling Strings.

Coffee is served in the Red, Blue, and Green Parlors, and then the ladies drift into the East Room, where the gold chairs are now set up as in a theater for Roger Williams' recital.

Now let's consider a smaller luncheon for a group of ladies, Pat Nixon's first formal luncheon at which she presided alone. Though, it must be recorded that President Nixon did put in a surprise appearance to say hello to everybody:

MRS. NIXON'S FORMAL LUNCHEON
FOR THE LADIES OF THE PRESS AND CABINET WIVES

Monday, February 17, 1969

Celery Consommé

Chicken and Mushroom Crêpes
Asparagus

Pinot Chardonnay
Hearts of Palm and Tomatoes Vinaigrette

Fresh Fruits au Kirsch
Demitasse

CELERY CONSOMMÉ

2 stalks and tops celery   Cooked julienne slices of celery
1 quart beef consommé

Add celery stalks and tops to beef consommé. Bring to boil, and keep hot over boiling water for 45 minutes, but do not let boil. Strain. Just before serving, add a little cooked julienne celery. Serves 6 to 8.

CHICKEN AND MUSHROOM CRÊPES

For filling:
2 cups cooked chicken meat,
  chopped
3/4 cup heavy cream
3/4 cup Basic White Sauce (see
  Index)
3/4 cup sliced mushrooms,
  sautéed in butter

Salt and pepper to taste
For crêpes:
2 eggs
2 egg yolks
2/3 cup flour
1/2 teaspoon salt
1-1/2 cups milk
Butter

Simmer chopped chicken in cream until liquid is reduced by half. Add the sauce and mushrooms. Add salt and pepper.

To make crêpes: Beat eggs and yolks together, and add flour and salt. Add milk, and stir mixture until smooth. Let batter stand for 1 hour before using.

To cook crêpes, melt butter in hot pan to coat it thinly. Pour in layer of crêpe batter. Turn over to brown the other side.

Spread crêpes with chicken and mushroom mixture. Roll them, and serve hot. Makes 12 crêpes, to serve 6.

How different First Ladies' parties today are from those of earliest administrations. Presidents Washington and Adams and their First Ladies did not shake hands with guests. They smiled, nodded, or bowed instead, following the royal manner of the European monarchs.

It was Thomas Jefferson who first instituted the democratic handshake. But the First Ladies did not immediately follow suit, for handshaking was considered a masculine custom. Ladies curtsied, then sat politely sipping rose petal tea.

Yes, how different those parties were from today's, when, for example, First Lady Lady Bird Johnson did not hesitate to invite her friends among the Cabinet ladies and Washington's female press corps to a big, noisy outdoor barbecue at the LBJ Ranch in Texas. Jetting there, of course.

Early in the century Helen Taft tried holding what she called a "garden party" on the lawn of the White House. For Lady Bird, the heavens smiled. For poor Helen, the party got rained out.

In the early days of the White House, First Ladies' parties for their friends were called "dove parties." Dolley Madison normally gave one a week for the wives of the Cabinet and other influential persons around town.

Some have thought Dolley a bit harebrained with her snuff sniffing and her feathered turbans, but she knew how to smile at the right people. Indeed some historians say that her husband owed his second term to Dolley's successful efforts to get Henry Clay to support him.

Pat Nixon is also considered a great political asset to her husband. She has gained a reputation for stamina and good nature. She has a special word for every guest and a friendly handshake. But it wasn't always thus. Some First Ladies seated themselves as on a throne and could not be approached by ordinary citizens attending White House receptions or levees, as they were called.

And some First Ladies were like tigers when crossed. Mary Todd Lincoln got so angry when the government refused to pay for the entertainment of a French prince that she sold government property—manure—to pay for it. It was meant for fertilizing the White House lawn.

Early First Ladies served a nonalcoholic punch when they entertained their friends. This is one that Elizabeth Monroe served at her gatherings:

MRS. MONROE'S FRUIT PUNCH

2 cups grape juice	Sugar to taste
2 cups orange juice	1 quart water
Juice of 10 limes	Mint sprigs
1 cup chopped mint	

Mix fruit juices and mint, and stand on ice 1 hour. Sweeten with sugar to taste. Mix with water, and pour into glasses which have been half filled with cracked ice. Add a sprig of mint to each glass. Serve immediately. Serves 12 to 15.

Also early in White House history a popular dessert was a "Fool." This was made with sweetened berries or fruit, cake crumbs, and whipped cream. The fruit is heated, mashed, and put through a sieve to remove seeds. Then it is combined with enough cake crumbs to absorb the juices, placed in individual glasses, and topped with whipped cream.

Early First Ladies actually served Rose Petal Tea to their friends at their socials. It's easy to make just as the servants might have served it for Abigail Adams or Dolley Madison.

ROSE PETAL TEA

Dry a quantity of rose petals. Then use them as you would tea, pouring boiling water over two teaspoons of petals in a cup and sweeten to taste.

Some First Ladies were quite studious. Lucretia Garfield resembled Jacqueline Kennedy in that she spent a great deal of time delving into the history of the White House and making plans to redecorate it by bringing back things from past administrations. And, of course, as everyone knows, within his first year tragedy struck and Garfield was assassinated.

Unlike Jacqueline Kennedy, however, First Lady Lucretia was left a poor woman with children to educate. There were no pensions for Presidential widows in those days, and money was solicited from the general public to see her through the rest of her life.

Only one First Lady that I have ever heard about worked for her husband—or worked for anyone. That was Mrs. James Polk, who acted as personal or confidential secretary to her husband, even in the White House.

The ladies of the White House, I think, divide themselves into three classes—those who hate to entertain and refuse to do it, those who hate it and overcompensate, and those who love to entertain.

I think the best example of the first category was the wife of Zachary Taylor, who decorated her living quarters of the White House to look like the home she had left behind in Louisiana and refused to leave these rooms to take part in the White House festivities. Her daughter, Betty, became the White House hostess by default, leaving Margaret Taylor content to smoke her pipe and weave rugs. She had predicted that her husband's election to office in 1848 would be the death of him, and it was. Ironically, it was probably food poisoning that did it. He had been invited to a Fourth of July celebration at the Washington Monument and partook heartily of the refreshments. Later he became violently ill and died several days later. Everyone blamed it on sour cherries and cold milk.

Mrs. Franklin Roosevelt belonged in the second class. Having grown up so shy that dancing was an ordeal, she threw herself wholeheartedly into the social world to help her husband, whose physical condition limited his social activity. No other First Lady in the history of the White House kept such a pace.

In the Roosevelt administration, guests came and went at will and stayed as long as they liked, and the kitchen was always in an uproar because the staff were never sure how many would stay for dinner. There was also an attempt to please guests by catering to their idiosyncrasies, to the extent that the guests themselves were delivering the orders to the White House staff.

Mrs. Eisenhower belonged in the third category. She loved people and loved to entertain, but believed in keeping a firm hand on all that happened under her roof. I think her knowledge of planning and organizing came from her years as a traveling military man's wife. She *had* to learn to set up housekeeping any place, any time, under any conditions —and to entertain graciously under the most adverse circumstances.

Mrs. Kennedy, too, seemed to enjoy acting as hostess at the world's most important table. She entertained with equal ease at small or large parties. She was a creative hostess and an innovator, who didn't do something in a particular manner just because it had been done that way a thousand times before.

For example, she set a precedent by having her first large luncheon in the East Room, bringing dining tables into a room which had not seen dining tables before. The luncheon was for the Women's National Press Club and the date was April 11, 1961. Her decorations were unique—huge ice sculptures of fish and swans; spun sugar baskets, holding lilies of the valley; and large Wedgwood jardinieres with cherry blossoms.

The food was set on a long buffet table, and the opulent array of dishes was reminiscent of the days of Jefferson: seafood Newburg with rice, baked ham, roast turkey, tongue, vegetable salad, pâté de foie gras with truffles en gelée, watermelon basket with melon balls, strawberries and grapes, galantines of turkey and ham, cold poached salmon with egg sauce, Hungarian goulash with noodles, finger rolls, petits fours, demitasse, salted almonds and mints, a choice of red or white wine. The china used was from the Wilson, Franklin D. Roosevelt, and Truman administrations.

Martha Washington, of course, never lived at the White House because the nation's capital was Philadelphia in the time of her husband's administration. So I think it safe to say that Dolley Madison is the best-remembered hostess of the White House. Mrs. Washington, incidentally, had to watch the clock. Her husband was known as a very punctual eater—always starting his dinner at the moment of 4:05. You could set your watch by it!

The history books picture a sweet and demure "Dolley" with a depth about the thickness of a sheet of paper, but the real Dolley was a hearty, hale character who used snuff and didn't hesitate to give her opinion.

In the manner of the day, the early First Ladies kept a carriage ready at all times and made as many as twenty social calls a day around Washington as well as kept a magnificent table for Washington officials, who always knew they would find pheasants and country hams, spoon bread, gingerbread, and cranberry tarts awaiting them.

For the ladies of official Washington, Mrs. Madison held a series of teas that were very gay and garrulous. The food was more fattening than delicate, but people were not calorie counting in those days. Dolley's tarts and cakes were copied by all the other ladies, just as later First Ladies' recipes have been eagerly sought after.

Dolley Madison knew how to entertain. She believed in having one servant or "man" to serve each guest at the table. The women who came to her parties whispered that she colored her cheeks and were properly shocked at the table when she passed her lacquered box of snuff to the men around her so they could have a dip. She actually presided at the head of the table and let her husband, James, whom everyone called "Little Jemmy" behind his back, sit in a lesser position along the side.

No wonder the exuberant and strong-voiced Dolley felt so in charge. "Jemmy" had been so shy around her that he had had to seek the help of Martha Washington to propose.

Even drop-in visitors at the White House were treated to Dolley's hospitality. It was her tradition to serve two things—a bouillon laced with sherry and her own famous Dolley Madison Layer Cake. Indeed it long continued to be the tradition at the White House to serve the same hot bouillon to guests who had come in from the winter's cold. Let's see how Dolley made it:

DOLLEY MADISON'S HOSPITABLE BOUILLON

4 pounds beef	3 small white onions
1 veal knuckle	1 bunch parsley
3 small carrots	6 quarts water
2 turnips	Sherry
1 pod hot pepper	

Place all the ingredients except the sherry in a large pot, and simmer for 6 hours. Cool and strain. Dolley liked to let her bouillon stand overnight before skimming off the fat. She would store the bouillon in a cool place and heat a portion of it as needed. Just before the hot bouillon was served, a little sherry was added. Serves 20.

DOLLEY MADISON'S LAYER CAKE

3/4 cup butter   3 cups flour
2-1/2 cups sugar   3/4 cup cornstarch
1 cup milk   8 egg whites, stiffly beaten
2-1/2 teaspoons vanilla

Cream butter and sugar. Add milk and vanilla. Sift flour, stir in cornstarch, and combine the dry ingredients with the liquid mixture. Now gently fold in the egg whites, and pour into four greased cake tins. Bake at 350° for 45 minutes, or until done.

DOLLEY MADISON'S CARAMEL ICING FOR LAYER CAKE

3-1/2 cups light brown sugar   4 tablespoons butter
1 cup heavy cream   1/2 teaspoon vanilla

Heat sugar, cream, and butter in a double boiler about 15 to 20 minutes. Add the vanilla, and decorate the cake.

Here is another Dolley Madison special to serve when you have company:

DOLLEY MADISON'S NUT CAKE

1/2 cup butter   2 cups flour
1 cup sugar   2 teaspoons baking powder
1 cup milk   1-1/2 cups chopped nuts
1/2 teaspoon vanilla   4 egg whites, stiffly beaten

Cream the butter and sugar. Add the milk and vanilla. Sift together the flour and baking powder, and combine the two mixtures. Add the nuts, and fold in the egg whites gently. Bake in a loaf pan for 50 minutes at 350°.

Dolley Madison had made such a smashing success that her successor, Elizabeth Monroe, was labeled a "snob" for refusing to make calls as Dolley had done and for leading a quiet life in the White House.

One dessert that you don't hear about today, but that was often served in the White House in the early days, was Trifle. It was made according to an English recipe:

OLD-FASHIONED TRIFLE

Sponge cake	Raspberry or blackberry jam
Sweet white wine	Whipped cream
Boiled custard	Sugar

Slice the cake, and line the bottom of a deep serving dish with the slices. Pour the wine over them. Fill the dish with custard. Spread a layer of jam on top of the custard and then top it with whipped cream, which has been sweetened with sugar.

It is surprising how many Presidents had to rely on women other than their wives to be their hostesses. The wife of Andrew Jackson's nephew, Emily Donelson, served as his hostess, when his wife, Rachel, died soon after his election, and just before she was to have moved to Washington. President Andrew Johnson's daughter, Martha Patterson, served as his First Lady because the President's wife was in poor health. The sister of President Chester Arthur served as his hostess because his wife did not live to see him become President. Under Van Buren, the hostess was a daughter-in-law and under the bachelor Buchanan, a vivacious niece —Harriet Lane Johnston—gave the pre-Civil War White House one of the liveliest eras it has ever had.

Mrs. Wilson's life in the White House was far from gay and social. During the grim war years, which began a year after her marriage, she spent her days as a volunteer of the Red Cross in menial work and her evenings answering the hundreds of letters she received from the mothers and wives of servicemen asking for help.

"Lemonade Lucy" Hayes banned alcoholic beverages from the White House—even for cooking. However, she did permit rum-flavored punch to be served just once, causing a furor in society, which thought Lucy had gone soft on "spirits." That was when a state dinner was given for visiting Russian diplomats. This one little culinary taboo has made her better remembered than many other First Ladies, and that in itself is a culinary oddity.

In modern White House history, Mrs. Hoover is said to have set the most elaborate table, for family meals as well as formal entertainment.

It pleased me, too, to know that Mrs. Hoover had a food passion which, if anything, surpassed Mrs. Eisenhower's liking for mint. Mrs. Hoover's weakness was orange and particularly orange juice. She drank it morning, noon, and night.

Eleanor Roosevelt's liking for scrambled eggs, I believe, belongs in the same category.

Another easy-to-fix recipe, which Mrs. Roosevelt often served to close friends, was Kedgeree:

ELEANOR ROOSEVELT'S KEDGEREE

1 cup boiled rice	White pepper to taste
1 cup flaked boiled whitefish	1 teaspoon grated onion
1/4 cup milk	3 hard-cooked eggs, chopped
1/2 teaspoon salt	Butter

Combine the rice and fish. Add the milk, salt, pepper, onion, and eggs. Place in a shallow baking dish, and dot with butter. Place in hot oven and brown the top. Serves 2 or 3.

Mrs. Eisenhower's friends could be sure of being served *her* favorite dessert:

MAMIE'S FROSTED MINT DELIGHT

1 package unflavored gelatin	1/2 pint heavy cream, whipped
1/2 cup cold water	2 teaspoons powdered sugar
1 16-ounce can crushed	Additional whipped cream
pineapple	Fresh mint leaves
1/3 cup apple-mint jelly	A few drops of pure mint extract

Soften the gelatin in the cold water. Then heat half a cup of syrup from the crushed pineapple, and add to the dissolved gelatin. Next, melt the apple-mint jelly, and combine it with the gelatin mixture, adding the drained pineapple and mint extract at the same time.

Place the mixture in the refrigerator until it starts to thicken. Then fold the whipped cream, which has been sweetened with the sugar, into the pineapple mixture. Pour into a mold, and let stand overnight in the refrigerator. When you unmold your dessert, preparatory to serving, decorate it with additional whipped cream and mint leaves. Serves 6 to 8.

Mrs. Eisenhower saw to it that Frosted Mint Delight was frequently on the menu for formal affairs at which her husband presided, as well as those luncheons at which she presided.

One of the musts of every season is the White House Luncheon for the Cabinet ladies. Here you will notice that mint is used to flavor cantaloupe balls.

MRS. EISENHOWER'S CABINET LADIES' LUNCHEON

Tuesday, May 17, 1955

Cantaloupe Balls
in Mint Lime Rickey

Braised Sweetbreads
Parsleyed New Potatoes
Rosé Wine   June Peas
Currant Jelly
Rolls

Orange and Roquefort Salad Bowl
French Dressing
Cheese Straws

Frosted Strawberry Mousse
Cookies

Assorted Nuts   Coffee   Candies

CANTALOUPE BALLS IN MINT LIME RICKEY

Cantaloupe
1/2 cup sugar
1/2 cup water
2 drops pure mint extract

3 tablespoons chopped mint leaves
Juice of 2 limes
Whole fresh mint leaves

Make cantaloupe balls using a melon ball cutter. Make a syrup of the sugar and water, boiling 10 minutes, then adding the mint extract and chopped mint leaves.

After you have cooled the liquid, add the lime juice. Strain and pour over the melon balls, and keep in the refrigerator for at least 1 hour before serving. Garnish with whole mint leaves in the individual glasses.

BRAISED SWEETBREADS

3 pairs sweetbreads
2 quarts boiling water
1/4 cup vinegar
1 onion, finely chopped
3/4 cup butter

Flour
Salt and pepper to taste
1 cup chicken consommé
1 pound mushrooms, sliced
Chopped parsley

Trim off any fat that clings to the sweetbreads; then place in boiling water to which you have added the vinegar. Cook for 20 minutes.

Remove from water; drain. Remove any membrane.

Brown onion in butter. Roll your sweetbreads in flour to which you have added salt and pepper, and brown in the pan with the onion and butter. After they are brown on all sides add consommé, and cover your pan. After they have simmered for about 5 minutes, add mushrooms. Simmer for an additional 40 minutes, turning the sweetbreads occasionally. If necessary, add more consommé. Serve as they are with the mushroom sauce over them. Sprinkle parsley over the top. Serves 6.

FROSTED STRAWBERRY MOUSSE

1 quart fresh or 2 packages
    frozen strawberries
1 cup sugar (if fresh berries are
    used)
1 teaspoon finely grated lemon
    rind

2 cups heavy cream, whipped
Additional whipped cream
A few whole strawberries

If you use fresh strawberries, add the sugar. Crush the berries in either case, and pass through a strainer which permits the seeds to pass through. Add lemon rind. Fold the whipped cream into the berries with a wooden spoon and pour into a mold. Keep in the freezer until firm. Unmold, decorate with additional whipped cream through your pastry tube, and place whole strawberries on top of the cream. Serves 6.

Another annual function for the First Lady is the Senate Ladies' Luncheon, which comes every April. Ten tables were necessary during the Eisenhower terms, and Mrs. Eisenhower would move from table to table chatting with all the ladies. Here are two such luncheons:

MRS. EISENHOWER'S SENATE LADIES' LUNCHEON

Tuesday, April 26, 1955

Hot Tomato Juice
Club Crackers

Chicken Tetrazzini
Buttered Carrots Julienne
New Peas
French Rolls
Butter

Bibb Lettuce in Salad
Green Goddess Dressing
Cheese Straws

Tartlet of Pears
Assorted Nuts   Coffee   Candies

See Index for the Chicken Tetrazzini recipe.
The Tartlet of Pears is the same one I made the first week in the White House (see Index).

Two years later I served the same group the following menu:

MRS. EISENHOWER'S SENATE LADIES' LUNCHEON

Tuesday, April 9, 1957

Cream Pepper Pot
Melba Toast
Celery Hearts   Queen and Ripe Olives

Salmon Mousse
Shrimp Sauce
Spinach and Rice Mold
Feather Rolls

Bibb Lettuce and Cress Salad

Rysavy French Dressing
Cheese Crescents

Peach Upside Down Cake
Brandy Sauce
Assorted Nuts   Candies
Coffee

SALMON MOUSSE

Court Bouillon (see Index)	Flour
3 pounds fresh or frozen salmon	1 slice stuffed olive
Salt and pepper to taste	Thin lemon wedges
7 egg whites	Radish roses
1/4 cup dry white wine	Parsley
1 quart heavy cream	

Start with a court bouillon, using only half the amount of the recipe. Add the salmon to your court bouillon. After the salmon is in the pot, do not let your liquid return to a full boil, but merely simmer very gently for 20 minutes.

Remove the salmon from the stock; cool; bone and grind the salmon meat twice through a grinder. Retain the stock for Shrimp Sauce (below).

Put your ground salmon in the electric mixer. Add salt and pepper and egg whites, one at a time, while running the mixer at high speed. Add wine just before taking it out of the mixer. Put the salmon in the refrigerator to cool.

Now whip the cream, and fold it into the cold salmon mixture with a wooden spoon.

Generously grease a large fish mold, and sprinkle with flour. Place a slice of stuffed olive where the eye is indicated in the fish mold, and carefully place the salmon mixture around it so that you do not disturb it. Fill the mold almost to the top, but allow for a tiny bit of rising. Put the form in a pan of boiling water, and place in a 375° oven about 45 minutes.

Serve hot as soon as you take it out of the oven. Unmold, of course, and place on a serving dish, decorating with lemon wedges all around the fish and placing a bouquet of radish roses on a bed of parsley at one end of the platter. Serves 8 to 10.

SHRIMP SAUCE FOR SALMON MOUSSE

1 pound unpeeled shrimp	3 tablespoons flour
Fish stock (from the Salmon	1 cup milk
Mousse)	Salt and white pepper, if
4 tablespoons butter	necessary

Cook shrimp for about 20 minutes in the fish stock which you made with your salmon. Remove the shrimp and peel, slicing half the shrimp and setting it aside and chopping the rest.

Make a cream sauce, starting with a *roux* of the butter and flour, to which you stir in, slowly, the milk and 1 cup of fish stock from the salmon. Cook until thickened. Now add the chopped shrimp and salt and pepper, and run through the blender until it is fine and smooth. Remove from the blender, and add the sliced shrimp, warming again in a double boiler, and you are ready to serve. The sauce accompanies the Salmon Mousse to the table in a separate dish.

Mrs. Eisenhower liked this Salmon Mousse recipe very much and it is one of the recipes I was asked to leave behind for future use at the White House.

Mrs. Kennedy combined the guest list for the wives of the members of the Cabinet and the Congress with that of the Congresswomen and served this interesting menu:

MRS. KENNEDY'S LUNCHEON
FOR CONGRESSWOMEN AND WIVES OF THE
MEMBERS OF THE CABINET AND THE CONGRESS

May 23, 1961

Demoiselles de l'Océan en Bellevue

Suprême of Capon Demidoff
Potatoes Parisienne
Green Beans Amandine

Pineapple Sherbet
Petits Fours

Demitasse

SUPRÊME OF CAPON DEMIDOFF

5-pound capon, cut into pieces
Salt and pepper to taste
Flour
Butter
1/2 cup carrots, sliced
1/3 cup turnips, sliced

1/2 cup small onions, sliced
3 stalks celery, sliced
1 cup mushrooms, sliced
2-1/2 ounces truffles, sliced
1/2 cup Madeira wine

Season the pieces of capon with salt and pepper. Roll in flour, and brown in butter. Add the following vegetables, all previously sautéed a few minutes together in butter: carrots, turnips, onions, celery and mushrooms. Cover and cook. When the capon is cooked, add the truffles. Arrange the capon pieces on a platter, and cover with vegetables. To the sauce remaining in the pan add the Madeira, heat and pour over the capon, and serve. Serves 6.

POTATOES PARISIENNE

Potatoes   Chopped parsley
Meat juice

With a ball vegetable cutter scoop out pieces of potato about the size of a hazelnut. Cook in a pan and cover. When they are done, roll them in any kind of meat juice; sprinkle parsley over them and serve.

The First Lady must preside at many teas as well as luncheons. Since there are so many more wives of Representatives than there are wives of Senators, it was necessary to hold a tea for them rather than a sit-down luncheon. About 450 legislators' wives attend the tea, and here were the quantities prepared for them:

TEA
FOR THE WIVES OF REPRESENTATIVES

Thursday, April 19, 1957

8 pounds brownies
5 pounds pecan balls
5 pounds coconut drops
4 chocolate square cakes (9 inches)
4 coconut cakes (9 inches)
4 orange cakes (9 inches)
4 Lady Baltimore cakes (9 inches)
Petits fours—600
Bread—8 white Pullman
  —8 whole wheat

Sandwiches—1,000
3 fowl
4 8-ounce cream cheeses
6 bunches watercress
5 pounds chocolates
2 pounds bonbons
2 pounds assorted mints
4 quarts coffee ice cream
4 3-pint lemon bricks
4 raspberry bricks
2 gallons lemon juice

A tea for 450 ladies is an affair requiring a great deal of planning and organizing. Some things had to come from the caterers. Sandwiches came from the pantry. My ovens went full blast until the cakes were done. Fondants and frostings were mixed by the gallon.

Pecan Balls are a nice pastry for a tea. Here is how I make mine:

PECAN BALLS

1-1/4 cups butter
1-1/3 cups granulated sugar
1 cup chopped pecans
2 tablespoons water

1 teaspoon cinnamon
2 cups flour
Powdered sugar

Combine the butter, granulated sugar, pecans, water, cinnamon, and, finally the flour. Beat in the electric beater for 3 minutes at medium speed. With floured fingers make little balls about the size of a small plum, and put on a greased baking pan. Bake at 325° for 30 minutes, or until done. When they are not yet cool, roll carefully in powdered sugar, being careful not to break them. Makes 75 balls.

COCONUT DROPS

4 egg whites
1-1/4 cups sugar
1-1/4 cups shredded coconut

1 teaspoon finely grated lemon
   rind
1 tablespoon flour

Beat the egg whites with the sugar until very stiff. Add coconut and lemon rind. Place in the top of a double boiler. Heat the mixture over boiling water, stirring with a wooden spoon, until it is hot to the touch of the fingertip. Take off from the double boiler, and continue stirring while you slowly sprinkle in the flour. When it has cooled completely, place the mixture in your pastry tube, and make little drops, using a large round opening because of the coconut. If you do not have a pastry tube, drop the little puffs off the end of your spoon with a knife onto the greased baking sheet which has also been lightly floured. Bake at 375° for 8 minutes, or until golden brown. Makes about 50 drops.

Besides entertaining the ladies, the First Lady must assist when the President entertains mixed company—although she is, I must admit, a junior partner at such times because the President traditionally is first and even precedes his wife into the Reception Hall. These receptions, which are given all through the social season for such groups as the diplomatic and even for the press corps, take a lot out of the strongest woman. At least one President's wife, Mrs. Fillmore, would rest a whole day in bed before each such affair.

It is strange to realize that the White House used a fireplace for cooking till Fillmore took office, when the kitchen proudly acquired that new-fangled luxury item—a cookstove. I liked to wander into the Broadcasting Room (now the office of the curator of the White House, Clem Conger), converted from the old kitchen, where the tremendous arc of the fireplace still stands—and dream, and dream, and dream.

But to get back to the current First Lady, Pat Nixon enjoys parties big and small and can stand for hours in a receiving line without wilting. Mrs. Truman, in comparison, dreaded large groups and long receiving lines, preferring small parties where everyone knew everyone.

Sarah Polk disapproved of affairs at which everybody appeared to be having a good time. At her official receptions, which she felt duty-bound to hold every week, no refreshments were served. And at the Polk inaugural ball, all dancing stopped when the President and his wife arrived, and no one dared dance until they had gone.

I wish I could have been around when Buchanan was President. His beautiful niece, Harriet Lane, was his hostess and used to ride around Washington on a white horse, making her calls.

In the Harding days one knew it was time to go home when Mrs. Harding had the Marine Band play "The End of a Perfect Day."

All our First Ladies have had trouble with souvenir hunters, and years ago the White House gave up using small spoons which were identifiable as coming from the White House. They made a perfect souvenir. All White House aides are trained to be on the lookout for souvenir hunters and are not at all shy about going up to the guest who has put something in his pocket and saying, "May I help you with that . . ." spoon or cup or ashtray.

Lou Hoover served tea every afternoon at four o'clock whether there was company or not—and nine times out of ten there was. Lillian Rogers Parks, who went to work for Mrs. Hoover as a girl, gave me the recipe for one snack that Mrs. Hoover and her friends never tired of:

MRS. HOOVER'S LACE WAFERS

1/2 cup molasses	1 scant cup flour
1/2 cup butter	1/2 teaspoon ginger
3/4 cup sugar	

Heat molasses to the boiling point and add butter, stirring constantly until butter melts. Add sifted dry ingredients, and continue stirring until all are blended.

Remove from heat, and drop from a wooden spoon in small amounts about 2 inches apart onto the back of a greased inverted sheet cake pan or cookie tray. Bake in a slow oven about 10 minutes.

Cool on pan a couple of minutes before removing with pancake turner. While slightly warm, roll around the handle of a wooden spoon to form a cone shape. Makes 50 to 60.

Only one First Lady is recorded as having been so sad to leave the White House that she broke down and cried—Edith Roosevelt. She loved the White House and everything about it. So did Teddy Roosevelt, who told his sons once, "I do not think two people have ever gotten more enjoyment out of the White House than your mother and I. We love the house itself, without and within. We love the gardens, the fountain, the lawn and each tree."

History records that when TR came in and found his wife packing to leave the White House and all in tears, he broke down and cried too.

Now for a fun recipe and to come full circle in First Ladies.

One of my prize possessions is a facsimile copy of the recipe for Martha Washington's Great Cake, as it was written out for her by her granddaughter, Martha Custis. It is datemarked Mount Vernon. I enjoy the quaint spelling as much as the recipe, although I have yet to save up enough eggs to try it. But I am sure some brave reader will.

Mount Vernon

To make a great Cake

Take 40 eggs and divide the whites from the yolks and beat them to a froth then work four pounds of butter to a cream and put the whites of eggs to it a spoon full at a time till it is well worked then put four pounds of sugar finely powdered to it in the same manner then put in the youlks of eggs and 5 pounds of flower and 5 pounds of fruit. 2 hours will bake it add to it half an ounce of mace and nutmeg half a pint of wine and some frensh brandy.

This was wrote by Martha Custis.
for her Grandmama

15

➤➤➤➤➤➤❮❮❮❮❮❮

CHRISTMAS WITH THE PRESIDENTS

It is Christmas at the White House. Imagine yourself arriving there ready to join the President for Christmas Dinner. You drive up the North Drive to the portico looking at all the exterior decorations and remembering that to the early Presidents Christmas decorations were unknown. In fact, Benjamin Harrison was the first President to put so much as one little Christmas tree in the White House.

That was in 1889, and President Harrison put that first White House Christmas tree in the Oval Room on the second floor. Family and friends trooped upstairs to marvel at this White House innovation.

But now each of the eight windows on the first floor flanking the front door is centered with a large candlelit wreath made of yew and fir with red berries and pine cones. The yews lining the front drive sparkle with tiny white lights as do the two eighteen-foot trees which stand on either side of the door. The chains of the hanging lantern are roped with lycopodium, and the lantern itself is decorated with holly and clusters of holly berries.

Now we enter the portico and pass into the White House where the White House Christmas tree, a nineteen-foot coniferous fir, stands in the center of the Great Hall. The tree comes from a different state each year, and it is covered with great balls, each bearing the name of a different state. It is delivered to the White House early in the month so tourists can enjoy it as they leave the White House.

Garlands of lycopodium with heavy clusters of holly berries decorate the six columns and the four torcheres in the Great Hall. More garlands of lycopodium outline the mirror and rope the Grand Staircase. The niches in the cross hall are filled with five-foot red poinsettias with smaller white poinsettias massed at their bases. The four crystal chandeliers in the hall are decorated with multicolored Christmas balls.

In the State Dining Room the mantel is outlined with masses of lycopodium, variegated English holly, and mistletoe. The Lincoln portrait there is garlanded with lycopodium. Christmas greens are entwined in the wall sconces and the chandelier.

283

Mantles and doorways in the Blue and Red Rooms are also massed with Christmas greens.

We've heard about the eighteenth-century Italian creche set up in the East Room, so we head for there. Two sixteen-foot trees stand at either side of the creche lighted and decorated with white and gold Christmas balls. A mixture of fir, balsam, and white and gold Christmas balls decorate the four mantles in the East Room. The doorways into the Green Room and into the Cross Hall are roped with lycopodium.

Upstairs President and Mrs. Nixon have still another family tree—a little ten-foot spruce—standing in the West Hall in the family quarters, decorated with the favorite family ornaments they have collected throughout the years, little Christmas balls from all over the world.

Before we consider what the Nixons serve at their Christmas table, let's look at the Christmas menu that accompanied that first Christmas Tree at the White House:

PRESIDENT BENJAMIN HARRISON'S CHRISTMAS DINNER

Christmas, 1889

Blue Point Oysters on the Half Shell

Consommé à la Royale

Chicken in Patty Shell

Stuffed Turkey
Duchess Potatoes   Braised Celery
Cranberry Jelly

Terrapin à la Maryland (Turtle)

Lettuce Salad with French Dressing

Mince Pie   American Plum Pudding   Tutti-Frutti Ice Cream
Ladyfingers   Macaroons
Fruits

Coffee

That was a seven-course dinner—quite a difference from the simple three-course Christmas dinner of President Eisenhower almost a century later, or that of the Nixons' now:

PRESIDENT RICHARD M. NIXON'S
FAMILY CHRISTMAS DINNER, 1970

December 25, 1970

Fruit Cup

Roast Turkey
Giblet Gravy   Chestnut and Apple Stuffing
Relish Tray   Cranberry Sauce
Mashed Potatoes
Acorn Squash with Maple Syrup

Blueberry Muffins
Mince Pie

Coffee

NIXONS' CHESTNUT AND APPLE STUFFING FOR TURKEY

This should fill a 10- or 12-pound bird. Stuff turkey, cover with aluminum foil, and bake at 350° for 3 hours or until done. When the bird is done, take off the foil, baste with butter, raise temperature to 450°, and brown to a golden color. Serves 10 to 12.

2 slices bacon, chopped
1 tablespoon butter
1 cup chopped onions
1 cup chopped celery
1/2 cup seedless raisins
4 cups chopped, pared, cored
    apples
6 cups fresh white bread cubes

4 cups boiled, coarsely chopped
    chestnuts
1 tablespoon salt
1 tablespoon chopped parsley
1 tablespoon poultry seasoning
2 eggs
1 cup warm milk
1 10- to 12-pound turkey

In large skillet, render the bacon, add butter, and sauté the onions and celery about 5 minutes, or until tender.

Pour into a large bowl, and with a plastic spatula, lightly mix in the remaining ingredients. Add milk and eggs last, and mix until well combined.

PAT NIXON'S MINCEMEAT PIE

To make Piecrust:
2 cups sifted flour
1 teaspoon salt
2/3 cup shortening
About 1/2 cup ice water

To make Filling:
3 cups (28 ounces) mincemeat
1/8 cup brandy
1/8 cup rum
1/2 cup applesauce
1 egg, beaten

Mix flour and salt together. Add shortening, and mix lightly; then add ice water. Divide into two parts. Use one part for bottom crust and one part for upper crust for a 9-inch pie pan.

Combine all filling ingredients except egg, and mix well. Fill 9-inch piecrust, and cover with upper crust. Brush with egg, and bake in a 450° oven for 10 minutes. Reduce heat to 350° and bake until golden brown 30 to 40 minutes. Serve warm.

Now let's see what other Presidents served at Christmas. Here is a staggering Christmas menu of the James K. Polks, who were in the White House from 1845 to 1849:

CHRISTMAS DINNER OF PRESIDENT JAMES K. POLK FAMILY

Oyster Soup

Roast Turkey

Baked Ham

Spiced Round of Beef
Salsify   Caramelized Sweet Potatoes
Celery   Rice   Cranberry Sauce

Grapefruit Salad   Plum Pudding
Fruit Cake   Charlotte Russe   Wine Jelly

Wine   Coffee

The array of desserts reminds me of the Kennedys' Thanksgiving feasts, which featured a multitude of pies, cakes, and ice creams.

Like President Nixon, FDR liked chestnut stuffing for his Christmas turkey. Here is the feast the Roosevelts enjoyed on their first Christmas as a Presidential family:

PRESIDENT FRANKLIN D. ROOSEVELT'S CHRISTMAS FAMILY DINNER

December 25, 1933

Clam Cocktail

Clear Soup   Beaten Biscuit
Relish Tray

Filet of Fish   Sauce Maréchale   Cucumbers
Hot Rolls

Roast Turkey   Chestnut Dressing
Deerfoot Sausage   Cranberry Jelly
Candied Sweet Potatoes   Creamed Onions   Green Beans
Cheese Straws

Plum Pudding with Hard Sauce
Ice Cream   Cakes   Cookies

Coffee   Candy

Eleanor Roosevelt liked duck on her birthday while Franklin D. Roosevelt liked it at Easter or New Year's—especially roasted with a potato dressing and served with applesauce on the side. Here is his recipe for duckling:

FDR'S ROAST DUCK WITH POTATO DRESSING

1 onion, coarsely chopped
4 tablespoons butter
3/4 cup dry bread crumbs
1 cup mashed potatoes

1 egg
1-1/2 teaspoons salt
1/2 teaspoon pepper
1 4- to 5-pound duckling

Sauté the onion in the butter until it starts to brown. Add bread crumbs, and sauté another minute. Then add potatoes, egg, and seasonings. Stir together until well blended; then stuff the duckling. Roast in 350° oven approximately 2 hours. Serve with a side dish of applesauce. Serves 4.

Christmas is a gay time at the White House. From the windows you can see the Christmas trees in the yard and on the Mall, glistening with brightly colored bulbs. Inside there are Christmas trees in every nook and cranny. The Eisenhowers had twelve trees at least. The Johnsons had two twenty-foot trees, one of them a cookie tree—some edible, some not.

For little Caroline Kennedy there was an eighteen-foot tree with gingerbread men, candy canes, dolls, and toys of every description.

I don't know how many presents a First Family gets, but they would certainly make a mountain. There are game birds and turkeys and hams and Yuletime plum puddings. There are the fruits from Florida, seafood from South Carolina, and delicacies from friends known and unknown in all fifty states.

Thomas Jefferson once received a thousand-pound cheese which was delivered by horse and wagon clear from Pennsylvania. President Eisenhower received cheeses, too, and on one occasion every member of the staff got a two-pound block of it. FDR received a fifty-pound cherry pie.

President and Mrs. Nixon are continuing the tradition begun by the Lyndon Johnsons of having portraits of Presidents that hang in the White House copied as gifts for friends and staff.

It seems that every President has had his favorite stuffing for his Christmas turkey. FDR liked chestnut stuffing. President Eisenhower liked oyster stuffing.

Let me give you the menus of two Christmas dinners I served at the White House.

PRESIDENT EISENHOWER'S FAMILY CHRISTMAS DINNER

Tuesday, December 25, 1956

Cream of Almond Soup

Celery Hearts   Assorted Olives

Roast Turkey
Oyster Stuffing

Cranberry Sauce   Giblet Gravy
Sweet Potatoes in Orange Shell
with Marshmallow Topping
Thyme Peas
Clover Leaf Rolls

Christmas Ice Cream

Fruitcake

Christmas Candies   Nuts

That dinner was for eight at 7 P.M. But the year before, Christmas dinner was for eighteen. You will notice certain similarities in the menu. For example, the salad course in each is left out to leave more room for turkey.

PRESIDENT EISENHOWER'S FAMILY CHRISTMAS DINNER

Sunday, December 25, 1955

Stone Crab Bisque
Toasted Sea Biscuits

Hearts of Celery   Assorted Olives

Roast Turkey with Dressing
Sausage Garnishings
Cranberry Sauce   Giblet Gravy
Mashed Sweet Potatoes in Orange Shell
Fresh Spinach Goldenrod
Rolls

Santa Claus Ice Creams
Fruitcake
Flaming Plum Pudding
Hard Sauce
Christmas Candies   Mixed Nuts

MAMIE'S CREAM OF ALMOND SOUP

1/4 pound butter
1 rounded tablespoon flour
3 cans chicken consommé
1 cup grated white peeled
  unroasted almonds

1/2 cup heavy cream
Whipped cream
Slivers of blanched almonds

Melt the butter in a frying pan, and add the flour to make a *roux*. Cook the *roux* with a little consommé until it loses the flour flavor. Then add consommé and the grated almonds, and cook for 10 minutes. Just before taking off the soup, add the cream very gradually, stirring constantly.

Cream the soup in the blender, and serve, topped with whipped cream over which blanched almonds have been tossed. Serves 6 to 8.

PRESIDENT EISENHOWER'S STONE CRAB BISQUE

1-1/2 cups fresh or canned crab
  meat
If you use fresh crab meat:
1 cup cut-up carrots
1 cup cut-up celery
1/2 cup onion
1 teaspoon thyme
1 bay leaf
Fish seasoning to taste

3 tablespoons butter
3 tablespoons flour
4-1/2 cups chicken consommé
  or crab stock
2-1/2 cups heavy cream
1/3 cup dry bread crumbs
Chopped parsley
Croutons, fried in butter

If you cannot find stone crabs on the market, use regular crab meat.

Using fresh stone crab, cook enough to make 1-1/2 cups crab meat. If you use canned crab meat, substitute chicken consommé for the crab stock which you can make by cooking stone crabs in salted water to which you have added carrots, celery, onion, thyme, bay leaf, and fish seasoning, which you can buy at the store. Cook 25 minutes for fresh crabs, 10 minutes for canned.

Now make a *roux* of butter and flour, adding the consommé or crab stock. Next add the cream, just before taking off the heat. Then pass the bisque through the blender, adding half of the crab meat only. Strain to make sure that there are no bits of shell before you put the liquid in the blender. When the bisque is creamy, take it off the blender, add the bread crumbs, and the remaining crab meat, and serve with a sprinkling of parsley and the croutons which have been fried in butter to golden brown. Serves 8.

If you like to experiment, try the Crab Bisque, which Mrs. Washington made for her illustrious husband. It was one of Franklin Roosevelt's favorite soups.

MARTHA WASHINGTON'S CRAB BISQUE

Enough crabs to make 1/2
   pound crab meat
1 tablespoon butter
1-1/2 tablespoons flour
3 hard-cooked eggs, mashed
Rind of 1 lemon, grated

Salt and pepper to taste
2-1/2 cups milk
1/2 cup heavy cream
1/2 cup sherry
Dash of Worcestershire sauce

Boil enough crabs in salted water to make 1/2 pound crab meat. Combine the butter, flour, eggs, lemon rind, salt, and pepper. Put the milk in a saucepan, and bring to a boil. Pour it slowly into the egg mixture.

Now combine the crab meat with the milk mixture, and boil gently for 5 minutes. Add the cream, and take off the stove before it comes to a full boil.

Add sherry and a dash of Worcestershire sauce. Serves 4 or 5.

PRESIDENT EISENHOWER'S HOLIDAY ROAST TURKEY

1 15- to 18-pound turkey
Giblets
6 cups water
1 medium onion, sliced
3 stalks celery
2 carrots
1 clove garlic
1-1/2 teaspoons salt
1-1/2 loaves stale bread
2 cups chopped celery
2 cups chopped onions
1 teaspoon salt

Pepper to taste
3/4 cup butter
2 quarts whole oysters
1 cup precooked or sautéed
   mushrooms
Cream, if needed
2 teaspoons salt
Pepper to taste
3 additional teaspoons salt
1/2 additional teaspoon pepper
Additional butter
Chicken consommé, if needed

Since most people do not get 40-pound turkeys for their Christmas and Thanksgiving feasts, I will scale down the recipe for a 15- or 18-pound turkey.

Clean the turkey, take out the insides, and cook the neck and all the giblets except the liver in the water (to which you have added the sliced onion, celery stalks, carrots, garlic, and salt.) Save the stock for stuffing.

Grind stale bread coarsely. Then add to it the same amount of bulk as the bread of the following ingredients: chopped celery, chopped onions, 1 teaspoon salt, and pepper to taste. I do not use sage or bay leaves, which I think spoil the flavor of a turkey stuffing.

The onion and celery are gently softened by sautéeing in the 3/4 cup butter before they are added to the bread.

Take the meat from the neck and gizzard, chop it fine, and combine this with the oysters, which have been parboiled in their own juice until the edges curl; the mushrooms; and finally, the liver of the turkey, which has been fine-chopped raw. Add this to the bread mixture, and season if necessary. Now add stock to make a dry stuffing, but if there is not enough liquid, add cream, which goes well with the oysters. Normally I add 1/2 cup cream to my stuffing.

Rub the 2 teaspoons salt and a bit of pepper inside the turkey, and stuff the turkey, sewing it shut. Then rub the outside with the 3 teaspoons salt, 1/2 teaspoon pepper, and additional butter. Tie the feet and wings. Cover the bird with aluminum foil, and bake at 375° for 3 hours or longer if necessary. Baste occasionally with chicken consommé or remaining stock, wrapping the foil so that it is easy to open the breast section.

When the bird is done, take off the foil, baste again, raise the temperature to 450°, and brown. Serves 16 to 18.

GRAVY FOR HOLIDAY TURKEY

Remaining consommé and stock   1/2 cup cooked finely sliced
2 teaspoons flour   mushrooms
1 can chicken consommé

Make the gravy from the remaining consommé and stock at the bottom of the roaster, first skimming off the grease. Add the flour, sprinkling into the roaster while stirring constantly. Add the chicken consommé, and continue to stir, cooking another 5 minutes. Strain and add water if gravy is too thick, and finally, stir in the mushrooms.

FRESH SPINACH GOLDENROD

Cook your spinach, making sure to take it off the heat before it loses any of its green color. Chop coarsely. Season with salt and pepper to taste, and top with chopped hard-cooked eggs for which you have separated your yolks and your whites. Two eggs are sufficient to serve 6. Place the yellow in the center, and make a circle a few inches wider around it with the white.

FLAMING PLUM PUDDING

1 plum pudding	1/2 cup butter
1/2 cup brandy	Additional 2 tablespoons brandy
1 cup sugar	

Heat the pudding in its box in boiling water. Put the pudding in a serving dish, and pour brandy over the top. Ignite the brandy, and carry flaming to the table.

To make a hard sauce, cream the sugar, butter, and additional brandy. Serve with the plum pudding. Serves 6.

A treasured gift from the White House at Christmastime, during the Lyndon Johnson administration, was a little package of Deer Meat Sausage made from deer from the LBJ Ranch in Texas. With it would be this note:

GREETINGS FROM THE DEER COUNTRY OF TEXAS

We hope your holiday season will be more delectable because of our hunting season. In Texas, from November 15, on, the hills are alive with the sound of hunters. Here is the result, killed this year by our trusty rifles on the LBJ Ranch.

Should you just happen to have the ingredients on hand, try our favorite recipe for—

DEER MEAT SAUSAGE

One-half deer
One-half hog
25 ounces of salt
20 ounces of black pepper

8 ounces of red pepper
2 ounces of sage

Mix together for 200 pounds of sausage.
Now, for how to prepare this delicacy:

BAKED DEER MEAT SAUSAGE

Place uncut sausages in a 400° oven, in an open pan with a small amount of water. Cook 10 minutes on one side; then turn and repeat on the other side. Slice in inch-long pieces and serve.

Lyndon B. Johnson always tried to spend Christmas at the LBJ Ranch in Texas surrounded by family and friends. Here is one of his Christmas menus as served there:

PRESIDENT LYNDON B. JOHNSON'S FAMILY CHRISTMAS DINNER MENU

Christmas Day, 1965

Ambrosia

Roast Turkey
Corn Bread Stuffing
Cranberry Salad with Homemade Mayonnaise
Green Beans Amandine
Asparagus

Fruitcake
Eggnog

Coffee

THE JOHNSON HOLIDAY CRANBERRY SALAD

2 cups cranberries   1/2 cup chopped celery
1-1/4 cups cold water   1/2 cup chopped nuts
1 cup sugar   1/2 teaspoon salt
1 envelope unflavored gelatin

Cook cranberries in 1 cup of the water for 20 minutes. Stir in sugar, and cook 5 minutes longer. Soften gelatin in remaining cold water. Add to hot cranberries, and stir until dissolved. Cool, and when mixture begins to thicken, add celery, nuts, and salt. Turn into mold that has been rinsed in cold water. Chill until firm. Serves 6 to 8.

The Johnsons served the salad with Lady Bird's Homemade Mayonnaise:

LADY BIRD'S HOMEMADE MAYONNAISE

1 egg yolk	1/4 teaspoon paprika
2 tablespoons vinegar	Dash of cayenne pepper
1 cup vegetable oil	1/2 teaspoon dry mustard
1 teaspoon salt	

Put egg yolk into small bowl, and beat thoroughly. Add 1 tablespoon of the vinegar, and beat again. Beat in oil gradually, adding a teaspoon at a time until 1/4 cup is used; then add 1 to 2 tablespoons at a time. As mixture thickens, add salt, paprika, cayenne, mustard, and remaining vinegar. If oil is added too rapidly, mayonnaise will curdle. To remedy this, beat a second egg yolk into curdled mixture at once, and continue as above. Keep mayonnaise in a moderately cold place. Excess heat or freezing will cause oil to separate and come to the top. If this happens, skim oil off. Serve mayonnaise with all types of salads. Makes about 1-1/4 cups.

The Johnsons' Corn Bread Stuffing is made according to a recipe Lady Bird used since the early days of her marriage.

JOHNSON FAMILY'S CORN BREAD STUFFING

4 slices white bread, toasted	3 large onions, chopped
Medium-size pan of corn bread	1/4 cup butter
Stock from turkey	Salt, pepper, and sage to taste
6 eggs	1 10- to 12-pound turkey
1 stalk celery, chopped	

Mix together bread and corn bread that has been crumbled with stock from turkey. Be sure to use enough stock so mixture will not be stiff. Add eggs and remaining ingredients. Bake slowly for 1 hour. Serves 10 to 12.

In delving into the cookery of the first Presidents, I found an account dating back to George Washington's administration of the Father of Our Country's Christmas Eve dinner in 1795.

It was described in a letter from Theophilus Bradbury to his daughter, Mrs. Hooper, written while the occasion was still fresh in his mind, December 26, 1795. The letter tells how there were about twenty in the party, including several Congressmen and the Vice President.

As Bradbury tells it, "We took our leave at six, more than an hour after the candles were introduced. No lady but Mrs. Washington dined with us. We were waited on by four or five men servants dressed in livery."

The best part of the letter is the description of how the table was set around a six-foot-long decoration rimmed with silver and having in its center a plaster of paris pedestal with male and female figures on it. The menu, which he calls "an elegant variety," makes the Nixon Christmas dinner appear most humble:

GEORGE WASHINGTON'S CHRISTMAS EVE DINNER, 1795

Roast Beef   Roast Turkey

Veal

Duck   Baked Ham

Oranges, Apples, Nuts   Almonds, Figs, Raisins

Puddings and Jellies

Wines and Punch

Undoubtedly the usual vegetables were served, but were not mentioned by Mr. Bradbury.

You might be interested to try George Washington's turkey stuffing made without giblets since Washington preferred the giblets used only in the gravy:

PRESIDENT WASHINGTON'S TURKEY STUFFING

7 cups dry bread crumbs	6 stalks celery, chopped
2-1/2 teaspoons salt	1 medium onion, chopped
3/4 teaspoon pepper	1/4 pound butter, melted
1 teaspoon baking powder	3/4 cup boiling water
1/2 teaspoon thyme	1 10- to 12-pound turkey
1/2 teaspoon sage	

Combine bread crumbs, salt, pepper, baking powder, thyme, and sage. Add celery and onion. Stir in the butter and water. Your stuffing is ready for the turkey. Serves 10 to 12.

In early times easily stored root vegetables were featured in the holiday season. George Washington, for example, liked potatoes, especially combined with mutton:

GEORGE WASHINGTON'S STOVED POTATOES WITH MUTTON CHOPS

10 medium potatoes	Salt
4 pounds mutton chops	3 cups cut-up onions
2 cups heavy cream	3 tablespoons butter
Black pepper	

Peel and slice the potatoes; slice mutton chops. In a large casserole put a layer of potatoes dotted with cream, then a layer of mutton covered with a generous amount of pepper, a little salt, and onions. Add another layer of potatoes and so on until the dish is full, ending with top layer of potatoes. Dot with butter. Bake slowly in moderate oven (325°-350°) for 1-1/2 to 2 hours. Serves 8 to 10.

This dish was supposed to have been served Washington for Christmas dinner in 1776:

GEORGE WASHINGTON'S SWEET POTATO PUDDING

1 pound butter	1/2 pint heavy cream
2 pounds sweet potatoes, mashed	1 teaspoon nutmeg
1 pound sugar	1/2 cup brandy
2 eggs	

Add butter to potatoes while hot. Beat sugar and eggs; add cool potatoes, nutmeg, cream, and brandy. Bake in buttered baking dish in hot oven for about 45 minutes.

One of Martha Washington's holiday puddings is fun to make in today's kitchens:

MARTHA WASHINGTON'S PLUM PUDDING

2-1/2 pounds prunes
1-1/2 pounds seedless raisins
3/4 cup brandy
2 teaspoons cinnamon
1/2 teaspoon ground cloves
1 teaspoon allspice
2 teaspoons mace
1-1/2 teaspoons nutmeg

2 pounds beef suet
1/2 cup grated orange peel
1/4 cup grated lemon peel
1 pound citron, chopped
1 cup flour
7 eggs, beaten
2 cups sugar

Two days before you want to make your pudding, cook the prunes and raisins. Let them steep for 2 days in the water in which they were cooked, first adding the brandy, cinnamon, cloves, allspice, mace, and nutmeg. Keep refrigerated.

The day you bake drain the liquid off. Combine the beef suet, orange peel, lemon peel, and citron with the flour, eggs and sugar. Steam in a buttered loaf pan at low heat for 6 hours, covering tightly.

I have also enjoyed making Martha Washington's Holiday Fruitcake. You might too:

MARTHA WASHINGTON'S HOLIDAY FRUITCAKE

4 cups flour
1 pound butter
2-1/2 cups sugar
2 eggs, beaten
3 pounds currants
2 pounds raisins
1-1/4 pounds citron, chopped
1 pound hickory nuts

1 cup water
1/4 cup brandy
1 tablespoon ground cloves
2 tablespoons powdered
   cinnamon
3 teaspoons mace
3 teaspoons nutmeg

Combine the flour with the butter, which has been blended with the sugar and eggs. In a separate bowl combine the currants and raisins with the citron, nuts, water, and brandy.

Before mixing the two sets of ingredients together, sprinkle the cloves, cinnamon, mace, and nutmeg over the fruit. Bake in four well-greased large loaf baking tins, in a slow (325°) oven for 2 to 3 hours. Serves 60 to 80.

Now compare that with Dolley Madison's dark fruitcake:

DOLLEY MADISON'S FRUITCAKE

2 cups butter
3 cups dark brown sugar
1/2 cup dark molasses
2 teaspoons cream of tartar
13 eggs, separated
4 cups flour
1 teaspoon allspice
2 teaspoons cinnamon

2 teaspoons grated nutmeg
1 teaspoon baking soda
3 to 4 cups seedless raisins
3 to 4 cups currants
1-1/2 cups citron
2-1/2 cups blanched almonds,
    finely minced

Cream butter, sugar, molasses, and cream of tartar. Beat egg yolks well, and add to butter-sugar mixture. Beat egg whites until stiff. Sift flour with spices and baking soda, and add to batter alternately with egg whites. Dredge fruit in flour; then add fruit and nuts to batter.

Line 4 loaf pans with greased waxed paper, and bake in slow (250°) oven for 5 hours. Serves 50 to 60.

Now for one of the treats Jefferson enjoyed at Christmastime:

JEFFERSON'S FRUIT PUDDING

2-1/2 cups flour
1 teaspoon allspice
1 teaspoon ground cloves
1 teaspoon salt
1 cup seedless raisins
1-1/2 cups currants

1 cup chopped suet
1 cup sour milk
1 teaspoon soda, dissolved in 1
    tablespoon hot water
1/2 cup molasses

Blend flour with allspice, cloves, and salt; then mix together with the remaining ingredients. Turn into mold, and cover tightly. Set pan down in boiling water, and steam 3 hours. Serves 8 to 10.

Another holiday treat I like especially is a fig pudding that Benjamin Harrison enjoyed some eighty years ago and which I made once at the White House before I realized we would be deluged with puddings and fruitcakes each Christmas.

HARRISON'S FIG PUDDING

1 teaspoon baking soda	1 cup suet
2 tablespoons hot water	2 cups coarsely chopped figs
3 eggs, well beaten	1/2 teaspoon cinnamon
3 cups flour	1/2 teaspoon nutmeg
3/4 cup milk	1 cup dark molasses

Dissolve the boiling soda in the hot water. Make a batter of the eggs, flour, and milk. In a separate mixing bowl combine the suet with the figs, cinnamon, nutmeg, dark molasses, and the dissolved soda. Add the batter to the fig mixture, mix thoroughly, and pour into a well-buttered mold. Steam for 5 hours, covered tightly, and serve with hard sauce. Serves 8 to 10.

Christmas is just not Christmas without some homemade candy in the White House as any place else. Mamie Eisenhower always made fudge at the holidays. The President himself christened it Million-Dollar Fudge before they were married:

MRS. EISENHOWER'S MILLION-DOLLAR FUDGE

1 3-1/2-ounce can evaporated milk	1 12-ounce package of sweet chocolate, chopped
4-1/4 cups sugar	1 8-ounce jar marshmallow whip
2 tablespoons butter	2-1/2 cups chopped walnuts
1/4 teaspoon salt	
1 12-ounce package semisweet chocolate, chopped	

Mix the milk, sugar, butter, and salt in a saucepan, and bring to a boil. Stir continuously for 7 minutes. Then pour the boiling mixture over the remaining ingredients, which you have ready in a mixing bowl. Beat until the fudge is creamy, and pour into a buttered pan. Cool, and cut into squares. Makes about 5 pounds candy.

President Johnson liked to nibble homemade peanut brittle at Christmas:

LADY BIRD JOHNSON'S PEANUT BRITTLE

1-1/2 cups sugar
1/2 cup water
1/2 cup light corn syrup
1-1/2 cups raw or parched
   peanuts

1 heaping tablespoon butter
1/2 teaspoon salt
1/2 teaspoon baking soda

Put sugar, water, and syrup in a large skillet, and cook until a bit of the mixture forms a hard ball when dropped in cold water. Add peanuts. Cook until mixture is a rich golden brown, stirring all the time. Add butter, salt, and baking soda. Stir and pour immediately into a buttered pan. As soon as it cools a bit, pull and stretch to make as thin as possible. When cold, break into irregular pieces. Makes about 1-1/4 pounds candy.

The Lyndon Johnsons always had Old-Fashioned Double Divinity around the house:

LADY BIRD'S OLD-FASHIONED DOUBLE DIVINITY

2 cups sugar
Dash of salt
2/3 cup water

1/2 cup light corn syrup
2 egg whites, slightly beaten
1 teaspoon vanilla

Combine 1/2 cup of the sugar, salt, and 1/3 cup of the water, and cook until a small amount of syrup forms a soft ball in cold water. In another saucepan cook the remaining sugar and water and the corn syrup until it forms a hard ball in cold water. Cool the first syrup slightly, and add it slowly to egg whites, beating constantly for about 1 to 2 minutes, or until the mixture loses its gloss. Add the second syrup in same way. Add vanilla, and turn into a greased pan. Cut into squares when cold. Makes about 40 pieces.

One of the treats the Nixons enjoy at Christmas is California Date Bread:

PAT NIXON'S CALIFORNIA DATE BREAD

1/2 cup chopped walnuts	3/4 cup boiling water
1 7-1/2-ounce package dates,	2 eggs
chopped	1 teaspoon pure vanilla extract
1-1/2 teaspoons baking soda	1 cup sugar
1/2 teaspoon salt	1-1/2 cups sifted all-purpose flour
1/2 cup butter	

Combine the walnuts, dates, baking soda, salt, butter, and boiling water; let stand 20 minutes.

Heat oven to 350°. Butter a 9-by-5-by-3-inch loaf pan. With a fork beat the eggs; then beat in the vanilla extract, sugar, and flour. Mix in date mixture until just blended. Turn into pan. Bake 1 hour 5 minutes, or until done. Cool in pan 10 minutes; remove from pan, and finish cooling on rack. Makes 1 loaf.

As a special treat at Christmas I made nut bread for Mrs. Eisenhower's breakfast. This makes a lovely holiday season breakfast novelty. You might like to try it this year:

WHITE HOUSE NUT BREAD

2 egg yolks	2 teaspoons baking powder
1/2 teaspoon finely grated lemon	1 teaspoon salt
rind	2/3 cup coarsely chopped
1 cup milk	English walnuts
2/3 cup sugar	1/3 cup chopped pecans
2 cups flour	

Combine the egg yolks, lemon rind, milk, and sugar and add the flour, baking powder, and salt.

Beat in the electric mixer until well blended; then add the walnuts and pecans, and let beat an additional 3 minutes. Pour the batter into a well-greased loaf tin, and let it rest for 25 minutes. Then bake in a moderate oven (350°) for 50 minutes, or until a toothpick comes out clean. You will notice there is no shortening in this recipe. It is a nice, dry nut bread and the nuts have enough oil so that they provide the shortening.

How about trying Mrs. Nixon's Christmas cookies this year cut in the shape of Christmas trees and Santa Clauses? If they are to be tied to your tree, make little holes near the top of each cookie as soon as they come out of the oven, while they are still soft.

PAT NIXON'S CHRISTMAS TREE COOKIES

4 cups sifted flour
2/3 teaspoon baking soda
1/4 teaspoon each cinnamon,
    allspice, ginger, and mace
8 ounces honey

2 tablespoons dark corn syrup
1/2 cup sugar
1 egg
Colored sugar or melted
    chocolate to decorate

Preheat oven to 350°. Combine flour, baking soda, and spices. Blend honey, syrup, sugar and egg. Combine the dry ingredients with the honey mixture, and roll dough to 1/4-inch thickness. Cut into desired shapes with cookie cutters. Brush with water, and sprinkle with colored sugar; or after baking, dip in melted chocolate. Bake 10 to 12 minutes, or until firm. Makes 50 to 60.

While the wives are trying their White House recipes, perhaps their husbands would like to experiment with a spiced toddy which Thomas Jefferson found pleasant during the holiday season:

JEFFERSON'S SPICED HOT TODDY

2 quarts water
1-1/2 quarts brandy
1 cup rum
1 cup sugar
8 baked apples

Bouquet garni consisting of:
1 teaspoon whole cloves
1/2 teaspoon nutmeg
1/2 teaspoon whole allspice

Heat the water, and add the brandy, rum, sugar and bouquet garni. Let the bag of spices simmer for 15 to 20 minutes, and remove. Then pour the hot toddy into four scalded quart jars, in each of which you have placed 2 baked apples.

The toddy is ready to drink within several hours and can be reheated as needed just before serving. The ladies may prefer a little more sugar in their toddy, and this can be added in heating their portions. Makes about 4 quarts.

You will find more interesting drinks suitable for holidays in Chapter 13, "At Home with the Washingtons, Lincolns, and Other First Families Through History." But for now here is one more Jefferson special:

JEFFERSON'S HOT SPICED CIDER

10 whole cloves   1 quart sweet cider
10 small pieces stick cinnamon   2 tablespoons sugar
10 whole allspice   1/4 teaspoon salt

Put the spices in a cheesecloth bag. Add to the cider along with the sugar and salt. Boil for 1 minute. Let stand a few hours. Remove spice bag, heat, and serve.

16

━➤➤➤-➤➤➤-◀◀◀-◀◀◀

BIRTHDAYS, WEDDINGS, RECEPTIONS, AND OTHER SPECIAL OCCASIONS AT THE WHITE HOUSE

At the White House, when a function demands the presence of more guests than can be accommodated at a sit-down dinner, the President holds a reception. Any hostess wishing to entertain many guests at one time would do well to study the menu for one of the Nixon receptions and serve the same canapés or to try some of LBJ's Mexican-type Noche Specials or his Jailhouse Chili Dip.

Or, if you want to be really different, you can try to reconstruct the spread that was served when one of your old-time favorite Presidents was inaugurated.

Of course, there are also the White House wedding receptions. Perhaps you'd like to serve what was eaten at Lynda Bird Johnson's wedding reception.

Or taste Tricia Nixon's wedding cake.

It is interesting to see what has been served at wedding receptions for Presidential children through the years. When John Roosevelt, the son of Franklin D., married Anne Lindsay Clark in 1938, the menu included not only ham, turkey, and chicken, but also fifteen huge Kennebec River salmon and two lambs sliced for sandwiches. Besides champagne—500 bottles—there were gallons of "temperance punch" to please those who felt repeal had been a mistake.

White House weddings invariably set a whole nation afire with excitement. Everyone wants to know what was served and how to prepare the same things. I have Lynda Bird Johnson's wedding reception menu from December, 1967. It was almost as opulent as in the days of Madison and Jefferson:

LYNDA BIRD JOHNSON'S WEDDING RECEPTION

December, 1967

Lobster Barquettes
Crab Meat Bouchées
Smoked Salmon with Capers
Cold Shrimp with Dressing
Stuffed Mushrooms
Molded Chicken Liver Pâté
Quiche Lorraine
Miniature Shish Kebab
Assorted Raw Vegetables, Watercress and Roquefort Dip
Country Ham with Biscuits
Assorted Cheeses, Finger Sandwiches
Miniature Eclairs
Chocolate Roulades
Cream Puffs
Strawberry, Apricot, and Blueberry Tartlettes
Petit Fours

LADY BIRD JOHNSON'S
QUICHE LORRAINE

Pastry for two 9-inch pies
13 slices bacon, chopped
9 eggs
2 pints heavy cream
1/4 pound grated Gruyère
  cheese

1/4 pound grated Parmesan
  cheese
Salt and pepper to taste

Line pie pans with pastry. Fry chopped bacon until crisp, and drain. Beat eggs and cream together thoroughly, and strain. Add the bacon, grated cheeses, and seasoning. Pour mixture into pie shells. Bake for 45 minutes in 350° oven. Quiche should be firm but not brown; do not overcook.

When cool, cut in diamond shapes to serve. May be reheated, if desired. Makes about 60 small pieces.

MINIATURE SHISH KEBAB

2 pounds filet of beef, cut into bite-size pieces
4 green peppers, cut into 3/4-inch squares
4 large onions, quartered and separated into layers

1 pound mushroom caps
1 cup soy sauce
1/3 to 1/2 cup Worcestershire sauce
4 cloves garlic, crushed
1/2 cup oil

Arrange beef, peppers, onions, and mushroom caps alternately on small skewers or heavy toothpicks.

Blend soy sauce, Worcestershire sauce, garlic, and oil thoroughly. Place kebabs in a flat dish, and pour marinade sauce over. Marinate at least 24 hours, turning once. May be left 3 or 4 days or even frozen in the sauce if suitable.

To cook, drain kebabs, and broil until brown, turning once. Makes about 50.

LOBSTER BARQUETTES

2 tablespoons finely diced shallot or scallion
3 tablespoons butter
2 cups lobster meat, diced
1/3 to 1/2 cup cream sauce

25 oval pastry shells (barquettes)
1-1/2 cups whipped cream
1 cup hollandaise sauce
1/8 teaspoon cayenne pepper
Grated Parmesan cheese

Sauté shallot or scallion in butter until just tender. Add lobster meat and cream sauce, mixing very carefully. Fill each pastry shell three-fourths full.

Next fold whipped cream into hollandaise sauce, seasoning with cayenne pepper. Spread on top of lobster mixture, and sprinkle with cheese. Broil only until sauce is bubbly and faintly browned. Serve immediately. Makes 25.

WATERCRESS AND ROQUEFORT DIP

1/2 pound Roquefort cheese
4 ounces cream cheese
1 cup heavy cream

Drop of Tabasco
1 cup watercress, finely chopped

Cream Roquefort and cream cheese until soft and creamy. Blend in cream until mixture is fluffy but firm enough to be dipped. Mix Tabasco in well, and fold in watercress.

Pour into bowl to use in center of a large platter, and surround with pieces of raw vegetables, such as cauliflower, pepper strips, carrots, celery, or any others desired. Serves 15 to 20.

CHOCOLATE ROULADE

6 eggs, separated
1/2 cup sifted powdered sugar
1/8 teaspoon salt
5 tablespoons cocoa, sifted with
    2 tablespoons flour

1/2 teaspoon cream of tartar
1 teaspoon vanilla

Beat egg yolks until thick. Add sugar, slowly, sprinkling in while beating, until smooth. Add vanilla, salt, and cocoa-flour mixture.

Beat egg whites with cream of tartar until just stiff, and carefully fold into batter.

Line an 8-by-12-inch pan with greased paper, and spread batter evenly over this. Bake about 15 minutes in a 325° oven.

Cool in pan for 5 minutes; then turn out onto clean towel sprinkled with powdered sugar. Remove crusty edges, roll up in towel, and cool on rack. When cool, fill with Chocolate Cream Pastry Filling. Serves 8 to 10.

CHOCOLATE CREAM PASTRY FILLING

1/2 cup granulated sugar
5 egg yolks
5 tablespoons flour
1-1/2 cups milk

2 ounces baking chocolate,
    grated
1 teaspoon vanilla
Powdered sugar

Cream granulated sugar and egg yolks until fluffy light. Add flour.

Scald milk, adding chocolate and stirring until melted. Add the milk and chocolate to the egg mixture gradually, stirring continually, cooking until sauce thickens. Add vanilla; strain; then allow to cool.

When thoroughly cool, spread cake with filling, and roll into a log. Sprinkle with powdered sugar, and serve.

When Luci Johnson married Pat Nugent and had her reception at the White House, this was the cake recipe:

LUCI JOHNSON'S WEDDING CAKE

1/2 cup white seedless raisins	3/4 cup sugar
Apple juice	5 unbeaten egg whites
1-3/4 cups cake flour, sifted	3/4 cup chopped candied
1 teaspoon double-action baking	pineapple
powder	1 cup chopped pecans
1/4 teaspoon salt	1/2 teaspoon almond extract
1/2 cup butter	1/2 teaspoon vanilla extract

Cover raisins with apple juice, and let soak in refrigerator 2 or 3 days. Drain and spread on towel to dry.

Sift flour once and measure. Add baking powder and salt, and sift together three times.

Cream the butter thoroughly; add sugar gradually, creaming together until light and fluffy. One at a time, beating thoroughly after each, add the egg whites.

Add soaked raisins and candied pineapple, pecans, and flavoring, mixing well. Add flour, a little at a time, beating after each addition.

Blend until smooth; pour into two 9-inch layer pans, which have been greased, lined with heavy paper, and greased again. Bake until done, about 1 hour 15 minutes, in a slow oven (300°), or until toothpick comes out clean.

SEVEN-MINUTE ICING

1-1/2 cups sugar	1/4 teaspoon cream of tartar
5 tablespoons cold water	2 egg whites
1/4 teaspoon salt	1 teaspoon lemon extract

Mix together all ingredients except lemon extract in top of double boiler.

Beat constantly, while cooking over rapidly boiling water, about 7 minutes, or until stiff peaks are formed.

Remove from stove. Add lemon extract, and beat about another minute. Cool slightly before icing cake.

But there has been more romance in the White House than one normally thinks.

President Cleveland at forty-nine years of age, in spite of a very marked age difference, fell in love with and married his ward, Frances Folsom, when she was twenty-two. The wedding took place in the White House, and Frances, the daughter of the President's old law partner, became the youngest First Lady ever to grace the White House.

The White House luncheon menu read:

GROVER CLEVELAND'S WEDDING LUNCH

June 4, 1886

Château d'yquem

Moët et Chandon

Chicken Consommé

Soft-Shell Crabs
Sweetbreads in Shells
Snipes on Toast

Garden Salad

Cake and Ice Cream

That night there was an informal wedding reception supper in the family dining room of the White House. The most memorable thing about it was that a model of a ship fashioned out of roses was used as a centerpiece for the table.

WEDDING SUPPER OF
GROVER AND FRANCES FOLSOM CLEVELAND

Terrapin Soup

Spring Chicken   Cold Meats

Salads

Fish   Pâté de Foie Gras

Ice Cream   Bonbons

Fruits

Champagne for Toasts

The nation waited with bated breath to see what kind of hostess a twenty-two-year-old girl would make. She was magnificent. The crowds at the White House were so great that three receptions a week were held for the public. Sometimes 3,000 came in one afternoon, and every so often the line had to be stopped for a few minutes so that the First Lady could rest from the ordeal.

Her husband lost the election of 1888, and when she came back to the White House in 1893, she was the mother of a year-and-a-half-old daughter. Nothing was the same; a fickle public forgot how they had flocked to her, and now they were full of criticism of her every move—how she reared her child, how on occasion she failed to accompany her husband and therefore was remiss in her duties.

But she was young enough to disregard the criticism, have a couple more children—one of whom was the first President's child to be born in the White House—and live her private life as she chose.

President Wilson found love over the luncheon table at the White House. I'd give a pretty penny to know what the menu was. But when he married Edith Bolling Galt on December 18, 1915, here is what he had at the wedding luncheon served at her home not too far from the White House:

WOODROW WILSON'S WEDDING LUNCHEON

December 18, 1915

Oysters

Capon   Virginia Ham
Salad
Cheese Straws

Pineapple Ice
Cake
Fruit Punch   Coffee
Nuts   Chocolates

It is interesting to see White House wedding menus of the past. When

President Grant's daughter, Nellie, married an Englishman named Algernon Sartoris on May 21, 1874, this was the wedding breakfast:

NELLIE GRANT'S WEDDING BREAKFAST

May 21, 1874

Soft Crabs on Toast

Chicken Croquettes with Fresh Peas
Aspic of Beef Tongue
Broiled Spring Chicken

Strawberries with Cream
Wedding Cake Iced with Doves, Roses, and Wedding Bells
Ice Creams and Ices
Fancy Cakes

Punch   Coffee   Chocolate

But the most unusual feature of the Grant wedding was not the menu. It was that the bridegroom, Algernon, carried a bouquet.

Julie Nixon and her fiancé, David Eisenhower, decided to avoid the limelight as much as possible and married while her father was still President-elect.

JULIE NIXON'S WEDDING CAKE

1 cup sugar	1 teaspoon vanilla extract
1 cup butter	2 cups flour, sifted
6 eggs	1/4 teaspoon salt
1/2 lemon rind, grated	

Beat the sugar and butter until foamy; gradually add eggs, one at a time. Add lemon rind and vanilla. Gradually fold in flour to which salt has been added.

Pour into two greased layer cake pans and bake in a moderate (325°) oven for about 30 to 40 minutes, or until toothpick comes out clean.

Julie Nixon's wedding cake was constructed in six tiers with a set of columns between the fifth and sixth tiers. The cake had a lemon filling and was covered with almond paste and fondant icing.

What does a White House wedding invitation look like? Well, that to Tricia Nixon's wedding looked the same as any other except that at the top of the ecru white engraved invitation was a gold embossed Presidential coat of arms. The invitation read:

The President and Mrs. Nixon
request the honor of your presence
at the marriage of their daughter
Patricia
to
Mr. Edward Finch Cox
on Saturday, the twelfth of June
one thousand nine hundred and seventy-one
at four o'clock in the afternoon
The White House

Even at the White House, a bride tries to conform to all the traditional good-luck charms of "something old, something new, something borrowed, something blue." For Tricia Nixon the *something old* was the diamond and sapphire engagement ring that had belonged to Eddie Cox's grandmother, and the *something new*, her wedding gown. The *something borrowed* was a pair of diamond and pearl drop earrings belonging to her sister, and the *something blue* was the label sewn into her gown.

Now for a recipe you will certainly want to try, although on a smaller scale: Tricia Nixon's wedding cake. It is one of Pat Nixon's own recipes for what Chef Haller described as a white pound cake.

It was made in the White House kitchens. It was beautiful.

TRICIA NIXON'S WEDDING CAKE

1 pound sugar
1 pound butter at room
  temperature
1/2 pound cake flour
Grated rinds of 2 lemons
Pinch of salt

11 unbeaten egg whites
Additional 1 pound cake flour
2-1/2 teaspoons baking powder
7 egg whites
Additional 1 cup sugar

Preheat oven to 325°. Use 12-by-2-inch round paper-lined cake pan.

Cream together in blender the 2-1/4 cups sugar, butter, 2-1/8 cups cake flour, lemon rind, and salt.

Add slowly 11 egg whites.

Sift together additional cake flour and baking powder. Add to creamed mixture slowly until smooth.

Beat together 7 egg whites and additional sugar, adding sugar slowly to egg whites before egg whites are completely stiff. Fold egg whites into flour mixture.

Pour batter into pans, and bake for about 1 hour.

A tempest swept the nation when a New York *Times* home economist tried the recipe as released before the wedding and announced it would not work. Later some of us talked to Chef Haller about this and he said that the advance release had erred in specifying a baking time of only 45 minutes, which was not long enough for the cake to bake properly.

Now we must get on with the recipe for the frosting for the wedding cake. Of course there are things you cannot do, such as decorate your wedding cake replica with lovebirds made from blown sugar. But you can make the Royal Frosting which was used to decorate the cake.

TRICIA'S ROYAL FROSTING

1 cup apricot pulp	1-1/2 cups powdered sugar,
1 cup almond paste, creamed	sifted
with 1 tablespoon corn	1/2 teaspoon cream of tartar
syrup	Additional powdered sugar,
3 egg whites	sifted

First cover the surface of the cake with a very thin layer of apricot followed by a very thin layer of almond paste.

Put egg whites in a large bowl, add 2 tablespoons of the sugar, and beat 3 minutes, using a perforated wooden spoon. Repeat until 1-1/2 cups sugar are used.

Add cream of tartar gradually as mixture thickens. Continue adding sugar by spoonfuls, beating until frosting is stiff enough to spread. Spread cake thinly with frosting. When this has hardened, put on a thicker layer, having mixture somewhat stiffer than the first coating.

You may want to compare Tricia Nixon's wedding buffet food with that served at the White House wedding reception of Lynda Bird Johnson, earlier in the chapter:

TRICIA NIXON'S WEDDING RECEPTION

Ke-bobs
Brioche à la Reine
Crêpes Fondue Gruyère
Fried Shrimps in Coconut
Capon Canapés
Smoked Salmon Canapés
Alaska King Crab
Rolled Ham
Rolled Roast Beef
Tartlettes of Roquefort Cheese
Oueufs Farcies
(Stuffed Eggs)
Roulade Bar-le-Duc
Napolitains
(small napoleons)
Barrichons
Almond Slices
Paris Brest Puffs
Eclairs
Heart-Shaped Petits Fours Glacées

Now here are Chef Henri Haller's recipes for a few of the reception delicacies:

FRIED SHRIMPS IN COCONUT

2 pounds (44 to 50) raw shrimp	1/4 teaspoon white pepper
2 fresh coconuts	1 teaspoon Worcestershire sauce
4 eggs	1 cup flour
1 teaspoon salt	1/2 pound clarified butter

Peel and clean shrimps, and marinate in coconut milk. Put the white of the coconut through the shredder machine.

Break the eggs into a mixing bowl. Add salt, pepper, and Worcestershire sauce. Beat well—about 1 minute.

Drain shrimps. Roll in flour, and put into egg mixture. Remove from egg mixture, and roll in shredded coconut. Using an iron skillet, fry the shrimp in the clarified butter on both sides until golden brown, about 6 minutes' cooking time. Remove shrimps from skillet, and place on paper towel for 1 minute. Serve immediately. Serve Sauce Piquante (below) separately. Serves 6.

SAUCE PIQUANTE

3 tablespoons chopped chutney
1 teaspoon Worcestershire sauce
3 drops Tabasco
Juice of 1/2 lemon

1 cup mayonnaise
1 teaspoon chopped chives
Pinch of salt

Chop chutney very fine, and put into stainless-steel bowl. Add Worcestershire sauce, Tabasco, lemon juice, and mayonnaise. Mix well. Add chives, and a pinch of salt, if desired. Serves 6.

KE-BOBS

1/4 cup soy sauce
Juice of 1 lemon
5 teaspoons corn oil
4 teaspoons Worcestershire sauce
1 teaspoon Dijon mustard
4 or 5 drops Tabasco
3 pounds tenderloin of beef, cut
   into 1/2- to 3/4-inch
   squares

2 onions, sliced
4 green peppers, cut into 1/2-
   inch squares
1 8-ounce can button mushrooms,
   quartered

Make a marinade of the liquid and paste ingredients, and bring almost to a boil. Place the meat and vegetable bits on small individual wooden skewers, alternating ingredients of beef, onion, and green pepper beginning and ending each skewer with mushroom.

Snip off the wooden end or tip of the skewer which shows. Brush ke-bobs with the hot marinade, and let cool in refrigerator overnight, ready for broiling, in shallow baking dish.

Just before needed, brush again with marinade, pop under broiler, and broil for 3 to 5 minutes on each side, or until meat is browned. Makes 24.

CRÊPES FONDUE GRUYÈRE

Five 8-inch very thin French pancakes or crêpes will make about 30 1-inch pieces of crêpes, cut diagonally, after filling and rolling.

1 cup very thick Béchamel Sauce	1 teaspoon chopped parsley
(see Index)	1-1/2 cups finely diced Swiss
2 egg yolks	Gruyère cheese
1 teaspoon Worcestershire sauce	Flour
Pinch of nutmeg	1 egg, beaten
Salt to taste	Bread crumbs
Pinch of white pepper	

Make the béchamel sauce. Remove from heat. Add egg yolks one at a time. Add Worcestershire sauce, nutmeg, salt, white pepper, and parsley. Cool. When cold, fold in diced Gruyère cheese. Divide cheese mixture on the five pancakes. Roll each pancake, and cut diagonally—1 inch wide.

Roll fondue pieces first in flour, then egg, then bread crumbs. Fry in French fryer at 375° until golden brown. Serve immediately.

The Nixons have given many white tie receptions. In fact, the menus at these times are almost uniformly the same.

Let us consider the evening of February 8, 1971, the date of the traditional White House formal reception for the diplomatic corps.

As the diplomatic guests arrived through the diplomatic entrance on the south side of the White House, a harp and violin played in the Diplomatic Reception Room. Then all during the reception, the United States Marine Corps Orchestra played in the North Lobby, just inside the front door of the White House.

Now for the menu for the beautifully set-up buffet:

RECEPTION
TO HONOR THE DIPLOMATIC CORPS

Monday, February 8, 1971

Beef Brochettes
Chicken Livers with Bacon
Small Brioche à la Reine
Cheese Tartelettes

Caviar Bouchées
Smoked Salmon Rosettes
Anchovy Canapés
Beef Rolls
Ham and Asparagus Rolls
Pâté de Foie Bouchées
Roquefort Cheese Canapés
Deviled Eggs
Shrimp and Crab Fingers on Ice
Orange Juice   Champagne

And here is how to have a White House party of your own:

BEEF BROCHETTES

Fillet of beef   Trace of garlic powder
Salt and pepper to taste

Cut beef into 1-inch square cubes, and salt and pepper generously. Add garlic powder. Spear on metal skewers. Arrange skewers in upright position on rack in dripping pan. Bake in hot oven (425°) for about 5 minutes. Remove from skewer. Insert toothpicks, and serve.

CHICKEN LIVERS WITH BACON

Chicken livers   Salt to taste
Thin bacon slices

Clean and cut raw livers into bite-size pieces. Wrap a slice of bacon around each piece. Fasten with toothpick. Put in broiler over dripping pan, and bake in hot oven (425°) until bacon is crisp, turning once. Salt before serving.

CHEESE TARTELETTES

1 package piecrust mix   1/4 pound Swiss cheese, finely
3 eggs   grated
1/4 cup sour cream   1/4 teaspoon celery or poppy
1/8 teaspoon pepper   seeds
1/2 teaspoon grated onion

Prepare piecrust mix as label directs. Roll out into 18-by-12-inch rectangle, trim edges and cut into twenty-four 3-inch squares. Press each square into a muffin pan cup to form a small tart shell. With an egg beater thoroughly beat eggs with sour cream; then stir in pepper, onion, Swiss cheese, and celery or poppy seeds. Into each tart shell pour about 2 teaspoons of cheese mixture, and refrigerate. About 30 minutes before serving, preheat oven to 425°, and bake about 5 minutes. Reduce heat to 325° and bake about 12 minutes longer, or until golden brown. Serve warm. Makes 24.

CAVIAR BOUCHÉES

Puff Paste balls (see Index)   Caviar
Sour cream

Fill Puff Paste balls with sour cream mixed with caviar in equal proportions.

ANCHOVY CANAPÉS

1/2 cup anchovies   1/4 pound sweet butter

Combine anchovies and butter, and blend together in blender until you have a smooth paste. Chill and make canapés, forcing mixture through a pastry bag with a star tube.

BEEF ROLLS

Dried beef   Prepared mustard or horseradish
Cream cheese

Cut beef into even pieces. Spread with cream cheese, highly seasoned with mustard or horseradish. Roll tightly, and refrigerate. Cut into bite-size pieces, and serve on toothpicks.

HAM AND ASPARAGUS ROLLS

Thinly sliced ham   Cooked asparagus spears
Cream cheese

Roll ham slices, which have been spread with cream cheese, around asparagus spears. Decorate tops with more cream cheese, forced through the pastry tube in interesting shapes.

PÂTÉ DE FOIE BOUCHÉES

Puff Paste balls (see Index)	1 small onion, finely minced
Chopped liver	Dash of basil
Bit of butter	1 tablespoon cognac
1/2 clove garlic, finely minced	Salt and pepper to taste

Fill Puff Paste balls with smoothly blended mixture of all the ingredients.

ROQUEFORT CHEESE CANAPÉS

Stale bread	Roquefort cheese
Butter	Grated onion (optional)

Cut bread 1/4 inch thick. Remove crust, and cut in desired shapes—oblongs, rounds, triangles, etc. Toast and butter each piece on one side. Meanwhile, beat with electric mixer equal amounts of butter and Roquefort cheese until fluffy; add onion, if desired. Spread on canapé, or decorate the canapé with this mixture through a pastry bag with a star tube.

DEVILED EGGS

Hard-cooked eggs	Mustard
Melted butter or mayonnaise	Cayenne pepper
Salt and pepper to taste	Anchovy paste
Lemon juice	Capers

Cut eggs in halves. Remove yolks; put whites aside. Mash yolks with fork; moisten with butter or mayonnaise. Season to taste with all remaining ingredients except capers. Refill whites with the mixture through pastry tube, and decorate with capers.

SAUCE FOR SHRIMP AND CRAB FINGERS ON ICE

1 cup catsup
1/2 cup chili sauce
1/4 teaspoon Tabasco
1 tablespoon horseradish
1-1/2 teaspoons prepared
mustard

1-1/2 teaspoons Worcestershire
sauce
Juice of 1 lemon
1-1/2 tablespoons chopped
parsley

Combine and mix thoroughly all ingredients. Makes about 1-1/2 cups.

When a First Lady is named "Pat" and was born on the eve of St. Patrick's day, as Thelma "Pat" Nixon was, you may be sure that much is made of St. Patrick's Day at the White House. Especially when the Prime Minister of Ireland and his wife happen to be state guests.

So that's how it happened that the President declared "An Irish Evening" at the White House on March 16, 1971. The 300 guests, in addition to the Prime Minister and his wife, included the Irish ambassador to the United States and the United States ambassador to Ireland.

Following an Irish-oriented entertainment, President and Mrs. Nixon received their guests in the Blue Room. There was a buffet in the State Dining Room, and cabaret tables were set up in the Cross Hall, next to the Entrance Hall.

RECEPTION
TO HONOR THE PRIME MINISTER OF IRELAND
THE HONORABLE JOHN LYNCH AND MRS. LYNCH

Tuesday, March 16, 1971

Beef Ke-bobs
Chicken Liver with Bacon
Cheese Tartelettes
Ham and Asparagus Rolls
Beef Rolls
Stuffed Eggs
Breast of Capon Canapés
Salmon Canapés
Roquefort Cheese Canapés
Irish Coffee   Champagne
Pat Nixon's Birthday Cake

You have already seen how most of these things on the menu were made for the diplomatic reception, but there is one we can do now:

BREAST OF CAPON CANAPÉS

Bread slices   Thin slices capon breasts
Butter   Thinly sliced pickles
Mustard

Trim the crusts from several slices bread, cut into desired shapes, and toast lightly. Spread with butter and mustard, and cover with thin slices of capon breasts. Decorate with pickles.

The Beef Ke-bobs on the Irish reception menu are the same as the Beef Brochettes for the diplomatic reception.

PAT NIXON'S BIRTHDAY CAKE
(Lady Baltimore Cake)

1 cup butter at room temperature   1 cup milk
3 cups sugar, sifted   1/4 teaspoon almond extract
4 teaspoons baking powder   1 teaspoon vanilla extract
1/2 teaspoon salt   Additional 1/8 teaspoon salt
3-1/2 cups cake flour   8 egg whites

Blend butter and sugar gradually, and beat until light and creamy. Add baking powder and 1/2 teaspoon salt to cake flour, and sift twice. In three parts, add the flour mixture to the butter mixture. Gradually add milk with almond extract and vanilla. Add 1/8 teaspoon salt to egg whites; beat egg whites until stiff; fold lightly into cake batter.
Bake cake in two greased 9-inch cake pans in a 350° oven for about 40 minutes. Remove cake from pan, and cool.

PAT NIXON'S WHITE ICING

2 cups sugar   1/8 teaspoon cream of tartar
1 cup water   1/8 teaspoon salt
2 egg whites   1 teaspoon vanilla extract

Boil sugar and water until a bit of the syrup forms a soft ball when dropped into cold water. Beat egg whites, cream of tartar, and salt until frothy, adding syrup in a thin stream, beating constantly. Add vanilla. Ice cake immediately.

Birthdays at the White House were big family occasions for the Eisenhowers. The President's birthday was October 14 and Mamie's November 14. The first year I was at the White House Mrs. Eisenhower held her party at Gettysburg, but I sent the cake, which was carefully boxed and hand-carried all the way.

The trouble was worth it because several days later I got a wonderful thank-you note from Mrs. Eisenhower.

The birthday cake which so pleased Mrs. Eisenhower was one which I had learned in Prague many years ago when I was studying pastry. It is called Czechoslovakian Birthday Cake.

CZECHOSLOVAKIAN BIRTHDAY CAKE
(November 14, 1955—Mrs. Eisenhower's Birthday)

12 eggs
Rind of 1 orange, finely grated
1-2/3 cups sugar
3 cups flour

1/2 pound butter, melted
6 tablespoons Cointreau or other good liqueur

Break the eggs in a metal mixing bowl, and add the orange rind and the sugar. Set the metal mixing bowl on top of boiling water, and beat with a wire beater until it is a little warmer than lukewarm.

Then put the bowl under the electric mixer, and beat until fluffy and cold. It will double in volume.

Now fold in the flour very slowly, using a wooden spoon, and pour the warm butter slowly into the batter in a ribbon or string. Be sure that you only fold in the flour and do not beat or you will cause the cake to fall.

Pour the batter into three 12-inch pans, bake at 350° for 30 minutes, or until the cake springs back into shape when touched.

Let the cakes cool, but before they are completely cooled, take them out of pans and place upside down on a rack.

Sprinkle 2 tablespoons Cointreau or other good liqueur on each layer, so that it will soak into the cake.

FILLING

1/2 pound sweet butter	3 tablespoons some liqueur used
1-1/2 pounds powdered sugar	for cake
1 teaspoon vanilla extract	

Combine the butter with the sugar, vanilla, and liqueur. When the cake is cold, put this filling between the layers, building the layers as high as you can.

FROSTING FOR MRS. EISENHOWER'S BIRTHDAY CAKE

I used the fondant recipe which I had used at the Garretts' residence. That's the one that, in a roundabout way, helped me get to the White House in the first place. You will find the recipe in the Index. For this cake, I doubled the recipe.

To decorate the cake still further, I made Cream Royale, which is 4 cups powdered sugar, 4 egg whites, and 4 teaspoons lemon juice mixed until stiff. Put it into a pastry tube, and using various tips, draw scallops and other patterns around the edges—even on the curved sides of the cake (which you can do by tilting the cake slightly).

On President Eisenhower's birthday in 1957 I trimmed his birthday cake with the Presidential seal, which I molded from almond paste and tinted with vegetable coloring.

That birthday cake made the front pages of many newspapers around the country in a photograph of the President, the First Lady, and all the rest of the family, including little David, examining it.

I used the First Lady's Devil's Food Cake recipe.

PRESIDENT EISENHOWER'S BIRTHDAY CAKE
(October 14, 1956—President's Birthday)

5 cups flour	2 cups sour milk
2 teaspoons baking soda	6 egg yolks, beaten
2 rounded teaspoons baking powder	2 teaspoons vanilla extract
	1-1/3 cups cocoa powder
1/2 teaspoon salt	1 cup boiling water
1 cup butter	6 egg whites, stiffly beaten
4 cups sugar	

Combine the flour, baking soda, baking powder, and salt. Then cream the butter, sugar, sour milk, egg yolks, vanilla, and cocoa dissolved in boiling water. Add the dry ingredients to the liquid ingredients; then fold in the egg whites. Pour into four 9-inch cake tins, and bake in a 375° oven for 25 minutes, or until a toothpick comes out dry.

Turn out of the pans while still warm, and cool upside down on racks.

WHITE FROSTING FOR PRESIDENT'S CAKE

4 egg whites, unbeaten	2 teaspoons vanilla extract
4 teaspoons light corn syrup	3 cups sugar
10 tablespoons cold water	Dash of salt

In the top of a double boiler cook the egg whites, corn syrup, cold water, vanilla, sugar, and salt until the sugar has dissolved. Beat with an egg beater until the frosting is stiff enough to stand up in peaks. By hand it takes more than 10 minutes, but a portable electric beater cuts the time to 5 minutes. Just as soon as the frosting is thick enough to spread, spread it on the cake with a spatula.

One word of caution—be sure to wipe away any sugar granules that collect on the sides of your double boiler to keep the frosting from crystallizing.

But you might say that birthdays aren't what they used to be around the White House. I think the birthday dinner to end all Presidential birthday dinners was that of President Grant, which seemed almost endless: two soups; chicken; fish; vegetables; salad; an "extra course," before the main course—filet of beef and artichokes; breast of chicken; more vegetables; sweetbreads served with spaghetti and sauce; a sherbet to cool the palate; roast squab; salad; and six desserts, not counting the birthday cake.

It is small wonder, in view of the lavish tastes Grant acquired, that he became so impoverished after his Presidency.

Now let's see what the Kennedys served at a reception—the one honoring the Justices of the Supreme Court and their wives. When I was at the White House, the Justices were entertained at a formal dinner, but the Kennedys eliminated many of the traditional formal dinners and substituted less formal affairs.

The judicial reception took place on October 10, 1961, and the floral decorations rivaled the delicacies spread out on a long table in the dining room. In the Red Room the flowers were white—tuberoses and chrysanthemums. In the East Room they were orange, yellow, and white—daisies and chrysanthemums. In the corridors, blue and white flowers—delphiniums, carnations, lilies, and spider chrysanthemums—filled the air with fragrance.

The food—both hot and cold—tempted the guests' appetites: Pâté de Foie Gras in Aspic of Wine Jelly; platters of sliced, rare beef; hot seafood hors d'oeuvres in puff paste; quiche Lorraine; celery, cauliflower buds and carrot strips with a sour cream and chive dip; whole roast turkeys; cheese and crackers and small cookies.

PÂTÉ DE FOIE GRAS IN ASPIC OF WINE JELLY

See Index for recipe.

HOT SEAFOOD
HORS D'OEUVRES IN PUFF PASTE

30 small Puff Paste turnovers (see Index)	1/4 teaspoon white pepper
3 tablespoons butter	1/3 teaspoon paprika
1-1/2 tablespoons flour	Few drops Tabasco
1 cup heavy cream	2 tablespoons sherry
1 cup fish stock or chicken consommé	3/4 pound shrimp, diced
	1 small lobster, diced
3/4 teaspoon salt	1/2 pound crab meat
	Chopped parsley

Bake the puff paste turnovers, and keep them in a warm place. Then make a *roux* of the butter and flour. Add the cream, fish stock or consommé, salt, pepper, paprika, and Tabasco, and cook gently until it thickens. Then add the sherry; fold in the shrimps, lobster, and crab meat. Keep hot in a double boiler. Empty the center of each turnover, and fill with the seafood mixture. Sprinkle with parsley, and serve very hot.

JACKIE KENNEDY'S QUICHE LORRAINE

1 cup flour
1/4 cup butter
1/4 cup lard
Pinch of salt
2-1/2 tablespoons ice water
10 strips lean smoked bacon
1/2 cup grated Swiss cheese

2 tablespoons minced onion
Additional 1 tablespoon butter
1 cup light cream
3 large eggs
Additional pinch of salt
Pepper to taste

Make a piecrust of the flour, 1/4 cup butter, lard, first pinch of salt, and ice water. Let it stand 1 hour in the refrigerator. Then roll it out in a circle, and put it in your pie pan.

Fry the bacon, drain off the fat, crush the bacon, and cover the piecrust with it. Sprinkle the Swiss cheese over the bacon. Also sprinkle the onion, which you have sautéed in the additional butter, over the cheese and bacon.

Beat the cream in a bowl with the eggs, and add the second pinch of salt and pepper; pour this mixture over the bacon, cheese, and onion, and place the quiche in the oven. Bake about 30 minutes at 400°. The top should be golden brown. Serve warm. Serves 6.

President Johnson liked canapés with a bite to them—"When I bite them, they should bite me back," he would say. One of his favorites was this:

LBJ'S NOCHE SPECIALS

Tortillas
Deep hot fat

Grated Cheddar cheese
Jalapeno peppers

Cut tortillas into quarters, and fry in deep hot fat until brown and crisp on both sides. Drain, and put about 1 teaspoon cheese and 1 slice of pepper on each quarter. Place in hot oven until cheese begins to melt. Serve at once.

LBJ's favorite chili dips are in the chapter "At Home with the Johnsons." You might want to try them at your next party, to make it a *hot* time in the old town, Johnson style.

One new holiday celebrated in the White House in recent years is UN Day. Here is the interesting menu selected by Mrs. Kennedy for that day:

MRS. KENNEDY'S
MENU FOR UNITED NATIONS DAY

October 24, 1961

UNITED STATES	Boula-Boula Soup
INDIA	Minced Lamb Curry with Rice
EUROPE	Salade Mimosa
FRANCE	Charlotte de Pommes

MRS. KENNEDY'S BOULA-BOULA SOUP

2 cups fresh green peas	2 cups canned green turtle soup
Salt and pepper to taste	1 cup sherry
1 tablespoon butter	1/2 cup heavy cream, whipped

Cook the peas in boiling water until tender. Puree them in the blender. Reheat and add salt, pepper, and butter. Combine with the turtle soup and sherry, and heat, but do not boil. Pour into serving soup cups; put unsweetened whipped cream on each cup; place for a moment under the broiler to brown the cream topping, and serve immediately. Serves 6.

MRS. KENNEDY'S MINCED LAMB CURRY

3 pounds boned lamb shoulder	1 cup light cream
3 tablespoons salad oil	2 tablespoons flaked coconut
1 medium onion, chopped	2 tablespoons minced dill pickle
4 cloves garlic, minced	2 tablespoons minced
4 teaspoons curry powder	watermelon pickle
1/2 teaspoon powdered	1 teaspoon monosodium
coriander	glutamate
1 teaspoon paprika	Dash of cayenne pepper
2 tablespoons tomato paste	Salt to taste
2 tablespoons finely crushed	
blanched almonds	

Remove all the excess skin and fat from the lamb, and cut it into small, thin slices. Cover with boiling water, and set aside. Heat the oil in a large heavy skillet, and add onion and garlic. Cook over low heat, stirring often, until the onion is soft but not brown. Stir in the curry powder, coriander, paprika, tomato paste, and almonds. Then stir in the cream, and bring to a boil. Add coconut, pickles, monosodium glutamate, and cayenne, and stir to blend well. Remove the lamb slices from the water, and add to the mixture in the skillet. Bring to a boil. Then lower the heat, and simmer 45 minutes to 1 hour, or until lamb is well done. Add salt, if necessary. Serves 8. Serve with rice and the usual curry accompaniments.

JACQUELINE'S CHARLOTTE DE POMMES

Thin-sliced white bread
1/2 cup butter, melted
6 or 8 large cooking apples
Additional 2 tablespoons butter

2 or more tablespoons sugar
1 teaspoon lemon juice
1 cup heavy cream, whipped

Remove the crusts from the slices of bread, and dip the slices into the melted butter. Now use them to line a charlotte mold or a small deep casserole. Peel, core, and quarter the apples, and sauté them in the additional butter until soft. Add the sugar and lemon juice. Fill the bread-lined mold with the apples, and place the mold on a baking sheet. Bake at 350° until the top is brown—about 45 minutes. Cool. Unmold and top with whipped cream. Serves 6 or 8.

For comparison, Mamie Eisenhower served the following menu the previous year.

MRS. EISENHOWER'S UN DAY DINNER MENU, 1960

Pea Soup
(Netherlands)

Croutons

Hearts of Celery   Ripe Olives

Fish Soufflé
(Belgium)

Danish Tomatoes   Veal Paprika
                                   (Austria)

Savory Creamed Potatoes   String Beans
(Ecuador)   (Uruguay)

Rye Bread   Mixed Salad
(Sweden)   (Indonesia)

Queen of Puddings
(New Zealand)

Coffee
(Brazil)

MAMIE'S AUSTRIAN VEAL PAPRIKA

1/4 cup flour   1/2 cup vegetable oil
1 teaspoon salt   1 teaspoon paprika
1/2 teaspoon pepper   3 medium tomatoes
1-1/2 pounds boneless veal, cut   1/2 cup hot water
   into bite-size pieces   1/2 cup sour cream
1/3 cup chopped onion

Mix flour with salt and pepper. Cut veal into 1-inch cubes, and dredge with flour mixture. Sauté onion and veal cubes in oil, sprinkling with the paprika and cooking until meat is well browned. Stir often to prevent meat from sticking.

Cut tomatoes into small pieces, mix with hot water, and press through sieve. Add the strained mixture to browned meat, cover, and simmer 1-1/2 hours, or until meat is tender. Add sour cream, and simmer very gently for 15 more minutes. If desired, more paprika may be added for flavor. Serves 4.

Let us now consider what food was served at the inaugurals of Presidents of days gone by.

For President Buchanan's inauguration, a special building was put up at a then gigantic cost of $15,000. Guests danced, dined and wined. The wine alone was said to have cost $3,000.

PRESIDENT JAMES BUCHANAN'S INAUGURAL BALL
RECEPTION

March 4, 1857

Oysters

Saddle of Mutton
Saddle of Venison
Sliced Beef Tongue
Sliced Ham
Chicken Salad
Biscuits and Rolls

Ice Creams
Cake

Wine

Late-nineteenth-century inaugural balls were the occasion for Roman feasts with tables spread in an opulence of foods buffet style. The Benjamin Harrison inaugural feast of March 4, 1889, held in the old Pension Office Building, shows us what they were like:

PRESIDENT BENJAMIN HARRISON'S
INAUGURAL BALL RECEPTION

March 4, 1889

Bouillon

Steamed Oysters
Chicken Croquettes
Sweetbreads
Terrapin
Bluepoints in Ice
Assorted Roll Sandwiches
Chicken Salad
Lobster Salad

Baked Ham
Cold Tongue
Boned Turkey   Quail

Pâté de Foie Gras
Terrine of Game

Ice Cream   Orange Ice
Candy   Assorted Cakes

And here is what was served at the James Garfield inaugural ball of
March 4, 1881. This one, incidentally, was held at the Smithsonian and the
U.S. Marine Band was conducted by the great John Philip Sousa.

PRESIDENT GARFIELD'S INAUGURAL RECEPTION

March 4, 1881

Pickled Oysters

Chicken Salad
Roast Turkey   Roast Hams   Roast Beef
Spiced Tongue

Fruits and Relishes
Breads   Jelly   Rolls

Ice Cream   Ices
Assorted Cakes

Tea   Lemonade   Coffee

As soon as a new President enters office, he knows that his battle of the
"bulge," as well as the *budget,* has begun.

One of the first things I learned at the White House is that Presidential
families are grateful for the days when there is no company and they can
cut their calories drastically.

Nixon became fond of a 415-calorie luncheon. LBJ had a 410-calorie dinner, and Eisenhower, who was extremely conscious of his diet, systematically managed to keep his daily intake to 1,500 to 1,800 calories.

It is a constant temptation around the White House to overeat, and eating is not the least of the occupational hazards of the Presidents.

Index